Southwest Asia

Latinidad

Transnational Cultures in the United States

This series publishes books that deepen and expand our understanding of Latina/o populations, especially in the context of their transnational relationships within the Americas. Focusing on borders and boundary-crossings, broadly conceived, the series is committed to publishing scholarship in history, film and media, literary and cultural studies, public policy, economics, sociology, and anthropology. Inspired by interdisciplinary approaches, methods, and theories developed out of the study of transborder lives, cultures, and experiences, these titles enrich our understanding of transnational dynamics.

Matt Garcia, Series Editor, Arizona State University, School of Historical, Philosophical, and Religious Studies; and Director of Comparative Border Studies

For a list of titles in the series, see the last page of this book.

Southwest Asia

THE TRANSPACIFIC GEOGRAPHIES OF CHICANA/O LITERATURE

Jayson Gonzales Sae-Saue

RUTGERS UNIVERSITY PRESS
New Brunswick, New Jersey, and London

Library of Congress Cataloging-in-Publication Data
Names: Sae-Saue, Jayson Ty Gonzales, author.
Title: Southwest Asia : the transpacific geographies of Chicana/o literature/
Jayson Gonzales Sae-Saue.
Description: New Brunswick, New Jersey : Rutgers University Press, [2016] | Series:
Latinidad: transnational cultures in the United States | Includes bibliographical
references and index.
Identifiers: LCCN 2015035673| ISBN 9780813577173 (hardcover : alk. paper) | ISBN
9780813577166 (pbk. : alk. paper) | ISBN 9780813577180 (e-book (epub)) | ISBN
9780813577197 (e-book (web pdf))
Subjects: LCSH: American literature—Mexican American authors—History and criticism. |
Mexican Americans—Asia. | Internationalism in literature.
Classification: LCC PS153.M4 S235 2016 | DDC 810.9/86872—dc23
LC record available at http://lccn.loc.gov/2015035673

A British Cataloging-in-Publication record for this book is available from the British
Library.

Excerpts from *Korean Love Songs from Klail City Death Trip* by Rolando Hinojosa reprinted
courtesy of the author.

Copyright © 2016 by Jayson Ty Gonzales Sae-Saue
All rights reserved
No part of this book may be reproduced or utilized in any form or by any means, electronic
or mechanical, or by any information storage and retrieval system, without written
permission from the publisher. Please contact Rutgers University Press, 106 Somerset Street,
New Brunswick, NJ 08901. The only exception to this prohibition is "fair use" as defined by
U.S. copyright law.

Visit our website: http://rutgerspress.rutgers.edu

Manufactured in the United States of America

For my family—from all over the globe

CONTENTS

Acknowledgments   ix

Introduction: The Promise and Problem of Interracial Politics for Chicana/o Culture   1

1. Racial Equivalence and the Transpacific Geographies of Chicana/o Nationalism in *Vietnam Campesino, The Revolt of the Cockroach People,* and *Pilgrims in Aztlán*   23

2. Forging and Forgetting Transpacific Identities in Américo Paredes's "Ichiro Kikuchi" and Rolando Hinojosa's *Korean Love Songs*   45

3. Conquest and Desire: Interracial Sex in Daniel Cano's *Shifting Loyalties* and Alfredo Véa's *Gods Go Begging*   65

4. Through Mexico and into Asia: A Search for Cultural Origins in Rudolfo Anaya's *A Chicano in China*   91

5. Chinese Immigration, Mixed-Race Families, and China-cana Feminisms in Virginia Grise's *Rasgos asiáticos*   111

Coda: Chicana/o Studies Then and Now: Paradigms of Past and Future Critique   127

Notes   139

Bibliography   157

Index   171

ACKNOWLEDGMENTS

In many ways, it feels awkward to list only my name as the author of this book. I do not pretend that it is a culmination of my solitary efforts and thinking. Instead, this book is the reward of having had wonderful intellectual allies interested in the questions I brought to this project years ago, and the encouragement of dear friends who have supported me unconditionally. I am indebted to all of you who have helped me along the way.

First, I thank Anna Brickhouse and John-Michael Rivera for guiding me during my earliest years of literary study. I thank David Palumbo-Liu for his patience over the years as I negotiated (often incoherently) the sets of questions that I bring to bear in the following pages. I also thank Ramón Saldívar, who since day one expressed faith and a deep interest in this project. I cannot overstate how much of a privilege it has been to work with such a committed scholar.

Thank you, Jennifer Vargas, for the incalculable hours of stimulating conversation on books and on life in general. You have always been and always will be a great friend and intellectual collaborator. I thank Lupe Carillo for her humor, intellect, and humility. Thanks to Elda María Roman, Ju-Yon Kim, and Nirvana Tanoukhi. Nigel Hatton, I thank you for your boundless energy and joy. I was lucky to have you when we entered graduate school together at Stanford University. I am just as fortunate to have you as colleague and friend years later.

I have been equally privileged to be surrounded by a community of supportive colleagues at Southern Methodist University. Thank you to Angela Ards, Greg Brownderville, Cara Diaconoff, Darryl Dickson-Carr, Thomas DiPiero, Ezra Greenspan, Michael Holohan, Ross Murfin, Jasper Neel, Beth Newman, Timothy Rosendale, Martha Satz, Rajani Sudan, and Bonnie Wheeler. Collectively, you have created a space that is intellectually productive. Also, it is fair to say that without the support and spirit of collegiality you have fostered in our department, this book would not have been written.

I am especially grateful for, and humbled by, the many hours Steven Weisenburger, Nina Schwartz, Dennis Foster, Dan Moss, Richard

Bozworth, Irina Dumitrescu, Tim Cassidy, Tim Albrecht, and Willard Spiegelman invested in reading early drafts of this book. Each has offered invaluable suggestions on how to improve it and how to get it published. I would also like to thank Lisa Siraganian for taking a heavy pen to various iterations of this book during its early and latter stages. Moreover, I thank Lisa for her boundless encouragement. Indeed, I am fortunate to have landed at SMU. I do not write this lightly, but it has been made clear to me that an academic does not stay sane, much less productive, without smart, supportive, and caring colleagues.

I am also pleased to acknowledge my graduate students whose queries and comments have helped me clarify my arguments over the years, especially Kelly Evans, Anna Hilton, Summer Kokic, Seth McKelvey, Lauren Miskin, Anna Nelson, Christopher Stampone, and Meghan Tinning. I am also happy to be able to thank Benjamin Johnson, Andrew Graybill, Neil Foley, John Chavez, and Jaime Javier Rodriguez for sharing a deep regard for southwestern history and culture over the years. Thank you, Luis Fraga, for your keen interest in this work, despite the vast disciplinary differences of our respective fields. Thank you, Antonio Salazar, Esteban Villa, and Malaquías Montoya, not only for the rights to reproduce your art in this book, but also for the important contributions you have each made to Chicana/o communities during the last five decades. Thank you, Evelyn Hu-Dehart, for your pioneering interest in cross-racial matters at the US-Mexico border, and for your attention to my own take on transpacific issues. Thank you, José Aranda Jr., Pricilla Ybarra, Krista Komer, and Christine Bold for helping to open up venues in which to share my work. And thank you to the special collections staff of the California Ethnic and Multicultural Archive at the University of California, Santa Barbara, and the staff at the Nettie Benson Latin American Collection at the University of Texas.

I am exceptionally grateful for Matt Garcia's incredible interest and unyielding faith in the significance of this book. I could never imagine that what started as a casual campus conversation about Chicana/o culture on a humid Arizona afternoon would develop into my having had the pleasure to publish this book with Rutgers University Press. I am also especially thankful for Leslie Mitchner's sharp attentiveness and scrupulous care, both of which have made it a pleasure to publish this book. I am equally grateful for Gary Von Euer's and Jessi Aaron's keen eyes during the editing process. I would also like to give special thanks to Claudia Sadowski-Smith and Maria Herrera-Sobek. Each of you has been a model of commitment to our field and its evolution. Along the way, each of you has posed important questions and made invaluable suggestions that have helped me conceptualize this project.

Portions of this work originally appeared in shorter and earlier versions of my essay "Aztlán's Asians: Forging and Forgetting Cross-Racial Relations in the Chicana/o Literary Imagination," published in *American Literature* 85:3 (2013): 563–589. I am grateful for permission of the publisher, Duke University Press, to reprint this material.

I want to thank my late Nana, Emma Eres, for showing me as a child that national borders cannot contain Mexican cultural ideas or their values. Listening to the corridos on the radio in your van and hearing you share southwestern folklore taught me at an early age how culture organizes daily life and the spaces we travel through. I want to thank my mother, Corrina Gonzales, for her unbelievable determination to continue to raise my sister and me after our father left when we were still but small children. Mom, I appreciate that you gave me the know-how to survive in an unjust world, one that we all have learned can be very cruel. Moreover, I am grateful for your being a model of endurance and for instilling in me the work ethnic necessary to write this book. I also thank my sister, Tawnee. You are the utmost model of strength. Your courage and your compassion inspire me.

I want to dedicate this book to Lukas Sebastian and Tobias Alexander, mis dos hijos. Every day, both of you, despite the headaches and worries, give me tremendous joy. There is nothing that gives me more satisfaction than sharing with you in your discoveries of the world and watching you grow and develop. I hope this book will be part of your discovery and growth one day. And to Jessica Sundin. You have taught me by your example how powerful one's determination can be. There is no way that I could have written this book without your support, your patience, and your faith. I admire the intensity with which you work, the compassion with which you help strangers, and the patience with which you lead and treat others. I thank you with all my energy for your commitment to share your life with me, even during those moments when the research and writing threatened to bury me. Nobody has taught me about patience and dedication like you.

Southwest Asia

Introduction

The Promise and Problem of Interracial Politics for Chicana/o Culture

> But still I wonder ... I must ask myself what the shouts
> of solidarity mean.
> —Oscar Zeta Acosta, *The Revolt of the Cockroach People*

In the final pages of José Antonio Villarreal's novel *Pocho* (1959), protagonist Richard Rubio walks out of the narrative, leaving unresolved the problems of patriarchy and cultural dislocation that shape the text.[1] Embedded in US social structures of racial difference and divorced from values that once organized life in Mexico, Richard is unable to imagine his bicultural future by the novel's end. Indeed, the narrative's open form postpones indefinitely Richard's cultural transformations, reminding readers that the processes of this Chicano's political emergence will require his looking back to the formative figures of the past, all of whom will influence his identity in the future.

Perhaps this is why the penultimate paragraph of this classic Chicana/o novel details Richard's reflections "of all the beautiful people he had known" (187). In this instance, he recalls one last time his immigrant father, Juan Rubio, whose tragic demise reveals to his American-born son the limitations of Mexican ideals in the United States. Richard proceeds to name other influential figures of his childhood: his mother, a Portuguese poet who challenges his ideologies of human sexuality; a middle-class school girl who motivates him to explore his aesthetic judgments; and "Rooster," the leader of a Pachuco gang who demonstrates acts of political militancy against the Anglo social order. Since these figures will shape his cultural and political sensibilities as he matures, it is predictable that Richard should recall them as the narrative concludes. Less expected, however, is that during this crucial moment of self-reflection Richard also commits to memory Thomas Nakano, a Japanese American neighbor about to be sent to a US internment camp.

Despite Thomas's relative invisibility in the narrative, the entry of this Japanese American into Richard's consciousness on the eve of his political emergence gestures provocatively to the underexamined relations between Mexican Americans, Asia, and Asian Americans in early Chicana/o culture. If Juan Rubio symbolizes for his son the destruction of traditional cultural values, then Thomas represents how Richard's emergent political consciousness must negotiate war between the United States and Japan, including the oppression of Japanese Americans.[2] Villarreal writes:

> [Richard and his closest friends] had been so engrossed in the day that *they did not notice that Thomas Nakano had joined them until he spoke.* "I just came to say goodbye, you guys," he said. The boys looked at him shamefacedly. Since the war had begun, they had avoided him tactlessly. He knew their discomfort, and it embarrassed him. "I got nothing to do with the war fellas," he said. "I'm an American just like you guys. I just come to say goodbye, 'cause we gotta go away to a relocation center in a few days, an' I don't know if I'll get to see you guys before I leave."
>
> They all said goodbye, *and somehow the fact that Thomas was to be removed from their lives made it easier to be friends with him* again for a few minutes. . . .
>
> "In a way I'm glad we're going away, 'cause things are getting kinda rough for Japanese people around here. . . .
>
> "These [Anglo] guys jumped me and kicked the piss out of me. I didn't even get to hit even one of them at least, 'cause I wasn't expecting them to beat me up, being I knew them from school and a couple of guys from my old scout troop. They hurt my feelings more than anything else. . . ."
>
> "Jesus Christ!" Richard exclaimed in disgust. This was it! *Now he was getting out!* (181–184, my emphasis)

Here, Richard demonstrates an acute awareness of how local issues of discrimination cut across a spectrum of racial differences, yet he remains uncomfortable with his discovery and his subsequent political actions. In one of the few instances in which he acts as an agent for social change, Richard engages Anglo bigotry directly on behalf of an Asian American boy whose impending removal from their California neighborhood both disturbs and *gladdens* him. Speaking to this historic moment of internment, George Lipsitz reminds us that many Mexican Americans felt more vulnerable to racist attacks after Japanese American relocation, while the hiring of Mexican American labor to replace internees brought temporary prosperity to many working families like Richard's.[3] In this vein, this proto-Chicano text expresses an ambivalent form of affirmative action against racial intolerance when Richard "gets out" and organizes a group of Mexican Americans to take violent revenge on the Anglo gang responsible for assaulting his Asian American neighbor. Afterward, Richard thought how "it was all wrong. What he had done was as wrong as what they had done to Thomas. It had been like a small battle in a big war, and that war was also wrong" (184–185).

Richard's relationship with Thomas reveals how this important Chicana/o novel anchors an emergent political consciousness—one about to "get out"—in the context of a pivotal trauma of Asian and Asian American history (Japanese American internment). To be sure, Richard's interethnic encounter signals a key moment in his political awakening that exceeds Anglo-Mexican relations, for in this instance his oppositional sensibilities materialize directly from an engagement with *Asian American* oppression. Richard recognizes in this moment that his dilemmas of identity formation are implicated not only within racial tensions between Anglos and Mexican Americans, but also within global conflicts between US Anglos, Asians, and Asian Americans—"like a small battle in a big war."

Politically influential and implicated in armed conflicts in the Pacific Rim, the Asian American figure in Villarreal's novel makes visible what cannot be seen by Chicana/o literary critiques bounded by Anglo-Mexican antagonisms at the US-Mexico border, or contemporary paradigms of hemispheric cultural critique. The textual marginality of this character who lacks representational weight in a narrative that acknowledges having "forgotten Thomas was even there" (178), seemingly justifies the lack of attention critics have invested in the broad racial constellations and transpacific geographies of early Chicana/o culture. Yet as this book will show, what has escaped the critical eye by inhabiting the margins of Chicana/o writings often generates the core political values of many important texts. Indeed, *Pocho* represents just one of numerous texts that illustrate how Asia and Asians inspire this culture's oppositional rhetoric.

Tracing the marginalized presence of Asia and Asians in Chicana/o writings, this book spotlights how these places and figures have repeatedly provoked political awakenings in Chicana/o culture over the last six decades, including during the formative years of its literary renaissance. One of its central arguments is that the pattern of marginalization of Asia and Asians in the Chicana/o literary imagination symbolizes the historical tensions of a political culture committed to articulating local community concerns on the one hand, and its consistent engagements with transpacific and interracial issues on the other. It will demonstrate how the oppositional values of Chicana/o texts committed to expressing local social dilemmas regularly emerge from an interest in exploring and imagining the racial dynamics of Pacific Rim politics. To be sure, the consistent yet marginal presence of Asian spaces and bodies in this community's literary imagination signals not their triviality, but rather their troubling and provocative significance in Chicana/o cultural politics.

In a historical context, Laura Pulido has explored the significance of this dynamic between local and internationalist politics in Chicana/o communities. She notes that generations of Mexican American activists have "struggled with the tensions inherent in building an [interracial], antiracist and anticapitalist movement."[4] Her work on the interethnic elements of Chicana/o activism during the 1960s and 1970s, for example, reveals that the Third World Left's interracial and internationalist political ideologies were often mired down in narrow nationalist principles that focused on "questions of identity, [local] community empowerment, antiracism, and [nationalist] culture."[5]

George Mariscal notes a similar tension between Chicana/o cultural nationalist ideologies and global political thinking during the Vietnam War era. Mariscal has shown that narrow cultural nationalisms in particular often functioned as the operating ideology for many Chicana/o political organizations, despite their having formed oppositional political attitudes within interracial and international purviews. Recognizing that the collective identities Chicana/os forged at the local level could not be separated from transnational and interracial political concerns, Mariscal concludes that within Chicana/o activism an ethnicity-based politics emerged as a "necessary precondition" for mobilizing Chicana/o communities.[6] As a result, a contradictory impulse developed alongside the emergence of local and narrow political sensibilities: Chicana/o nationalism, Mariscal notes, "functioned as an organizing tool that could point either to sectarian forms of regressive 'nationalism' or toward coalition building.... Chicana/o internationalism [and interracial thinking], then, existed in a complementary and at times conflictive relationship with narrow nationalisms throughout the Viet Nam War period."[7] The collective identities that Chicana/os forged at local levels were not unrelated to the transnational and interracial politics that inspired them, yet they appeared to be so as a result of an ethnicity-based politics that developed as a condition for political mobilization.

When read against the interracial political attitude the Chicano protagonist in Villarreal's novel expresses toward his Japanese American counterpart, the political positions that Pulido and Mariscal highlight begin to gesture to the ways cross-racial and transnational ambivalence in Chicana/o culture, exceed any particular Asian group and transcend any singular episode of US intervention in the Pacific. To this point, this book reveals how Chicana/o writings consistently express political ambivalence concerning interracial and transnational thinking, across both a range of particular Asian groups and during distinct episodes of US aggressions in the Pacific. Further, it spotlights how this ambivalent attitude regenerates itself across regional and historical differences that constitute the various Chicana/o experiences that give shape to Chicana/o culture.

One of the main findings of this book is that the contradictions between nationalist and transnational political thinking—including the tensions between ethno-nationalist and interracial politics that scholars such as Pulido and Mariscal reveal—assume a distinct aesthetic form in Chicana/o writings *before, during, and after* the 1970s. To be sure, Asian political crises—ranging from Japanese internment in the United States to the US imperial war in Vietnam—consistently inspire oppositional political attitudes in Chicana/o communities across the US Southwest. Yet these cross-racial political interests, this book shows, have largely remained marginalized in Chicana/o political writings, and mostly symbolic for Chicana/o social protest. Except for a few instances in this community's labor history, Chicana/os, Asians, and Asian Americans are rarely seen as demonstrating meaningful and sustained cooperation in any single activist struggle.[8] My position is that the consistent appearance of Asia and Asians in Chicana/o literature speaks to a prolonged interest in political crises across the Pacific Rim, and that their marginalization speaks symbolically to how Chicana/o communities perceived the risks of casting their political focus across ethnic differences, and across the globe.

From this vantage point, the regular yet peripheral appearances of Asia and Asians in Chicana/o writings not only highlight a pattern of ethnicity-based forms of political emergence, but also gesture toward extra-literary matters of transnational inspiration across distinct Pacific Rim crises that are hardly recognizable within any given text's representative architecture. For example, famed Chicana/o poet Alurista rarely inserts Asia and Asians into the innovative semantic systems he developed during the 1970s in order to articulate his ethno-cultural themes, including his notions of Aztlán as the spiritual homeland of Chicana/os.[9] Nonetheless, Alurista has spoken in unambiguous terms about the significance of Asia in his work, and in Chicana/o poetic production more generally. For example, during his participation in a high-profile panel at the 1983 annual meeting of the Latin American Studies Association, Alurista presented a talk entitled, "Ideology and Aesthetics in the Meaning of Chicana/o Poetics, 1965–1975."[10] On this occasion, Alurista makes clear how interracial and international contexts generate the ethno-cultural poetics in his work and in the poetry of some of the major writers of his generation: Rodolfo "Corky" Gonzales, José Montoya, Abelardo Delgado, and Sergio Elizondo. Reflecting on a decade of Chicana/o poetic production, Alurista concludes that "the American War in Viet Nam, a paradigmatic example of America's transnational militarism, *establishes the conditions* for Chicana/o literary production and its *processes* of poetic signification."[11] According to the unofficial poet laureate of Aztlán, the American War in Vietnam conditions the *very possibilities* for Chicana/o poetic invention between 1965 and 1975. This undermines interpretative practices that view the literary work of this era exclusively through a nationalist lens, or even through a hemispheric vantage point of Latin American internationalism.

To be fair, skeptics may charge that Alurista overstates the case of Vietnam's centrality in Chicana/o aesthetic production. His affirmations regarding its significance in the works of the Chicana/o poets for whom he speaks are certainly speculation. For example, it is far more likely that for José Montoya—a veteran of the Korean War—this conflict, and *not* the American War in Vietnam, "establishes the conditions" for personal literary innovation. One needs only to recall how Montoya's seminal work "El Louie" (1969) tracks a Chicano's social demise after his return from the Korean peninsula.[12] This poem highlights poignantly the shortcomings of US democracy as suffered by Chicano soldiers and their communities.[13]

Still, Alurista's claims regarding the influence of Vietnam on Chicana/o poetics highlight an underexamined dynamic concerning circumpacific political thinking and the influence of Asian political spaces on Chicana/o culture. At the very least, his declarations about the American War in Vietnam speak powerfully to a contradiction hardly acknowledged in Chicana/o ethno-national poetics: his literary constructions of "Aztlán" read both as a potent nationalist symbol *and* as an imaginary transnational political space whose poetic invention is born from Asian inspiration. To bring this point to bear, Alurista concludes his 1983 talk by conceptualizing Aztlán as a political territory that references a particular history of Anglo-American imperial expansion and as a cultural geography without racial or national frontiers, declaring that the Chicana/o "word, sign, metaphor, and glyph refuse . . . to be servile to others. We are Aztlán without borders."[14]

Identifying US military aggressions in Southeast Asia as a precondition for Chicana/o processes of poetic signification—which themselves bear only faint traces of Asia or its constituents—Alurista speaks to a glaring paradox in Chicana/o cultural practices: the vehement objection to US imperial violence against Asians, and the simultaneous subordination of the Asian presence in this community's literary imagination. Like Richard in Villarreal's *Pocho*, Asians and Asia remain peripheral elements in

Chicana/o narratives across the last half of the twentieth century, despite their having played a constitutive role in the oppositional politics in the imaginations of many Chicana/o writers. This dialectic between the narrow ethnic values at the core of much of Chicana/o literature, and the repeated delimitation of Asians and Asia within the poetic structures of this community's cultural products, shapes much of this study.

Of course, it is difficult to address this narrative configuration between ethno-cultural centrality and Asian marginality in the context of a monolithic Chicana/o political culture. Chicana/o literature—like the Chicana/o Movement itself—is diffuse, often divided by regional, gendered, and classed issues that make it difficult to speak of a unified or fully coherent cultural practice. To this point, Ignacio García argues that "the Chicano Movement was not so much a singular social process as much as a coalescing of numerous philosophical, [cultural], and historical currents within the community that came together at a particular time and place."[15] Certainly, the multiple ideologies of the Chicana/o Movement make it tricky to characterize as constituting any single political or poetic agenda, either across institutions or between its major cultural figures, many of whom I examine here and who claim their origins across the US Southwest. However, I submit that this lack of coherence is not unrelated to the contradictory forces at play in Chicano/o political and cultural practices, which oftentimes oscillate between narrow ethno-nationalist thinking and its consistent international and interracial considerations, particularly with respect to Asia and Asians. To bring this point to bear, I briefly analyze the polemical yet widely popular Chicano writer Oscar Zeta Acosta.

Acosta's *The Autobiography of a Brown Buffalo* (1972) and its sequel, *The Revolt of the Cockroach People* (1973), both fictionalize moments of interracial and transnational Chicana/o political efforts. The latter text in particular, which imagines the Chicana/o Movement in California, depicts several instances of interracial solidarity during large-scale protests of the American War in Vietnam. In one memorable scene, Buffalo Brown (the protagonist and the author's alter ego) joins an ethnically diverse lineup of speakers at the University of California, Los Angeles. Their goal is to rally against US encroachments into Cambodia by raising awareness about the escalation of the Vietnam War. The narrative describes the events at the rally, including the speeches given by activists Angela Davis and Rudolfo Corky Gonzales. Acosta writes:

> Corky Gonzales is to be on the program. And so is Angela Davis, the black professor who only recently was kicked off campus by Governor Reagan's Board of Regents. I [Brown], too, have been invited to speak. The crowd rumbles with anticipation. . . .

> A tall kid with a bushy beard comes to the mike. "Ladies and gentlemen ... our first speaker is Angela Davis."
> Roar Roar Roar. Stomp, clap, stomp, clap. Power to the people!
> The lithe slow figure of the black beauty comes to the stage. She is the heroine of the day. She has told the world that she is a member of the Lamumba Club, a communist and an intellectual. The students and professors love her.
> "We are here to protest the slaughter of the students at Kent State.... We are here to join hands to fight against the warmongers.... We are here to tell Richard Nixon that he can't continue to bomb and kill the poor yellow brothers and sisters in Vietnam, in Cambodia ... or [to shoot students at] Kent State!
> "Now, what we've got to understand, what we've got to see, is that the war in Vietnam, just like the war at Kent State, both are products of the *system* in this country." (176)

The inclusion of a black activist voice in this highly influential Chicana/o novel exemplifies, like Thomas in *Pocho*, how the peripheral position of a minority character classifies a spectrum of ethnic difference in this culture's oppositional imagination. And like *Pocho*, the narrative here resists exploring the material relations between Chicana/os and other minority groups, including the individual qualities of their lives. Indeed, *Pocho* never explores Thomas's interiority to the degree of providing an image of his singular consciousness, nor does it explore the historical complexity of Japanese internment. In this instance, Angela Davis—a figure whose political ideas match the intensity of Acosta's—is similarly introduced exclusively through her overdetermined exteriority, and through a flattened brand of oppositional values. She walks into the novel highlighted as "the lithe slow figure" and walks out having expressed only a *generic* revolutionary sentiment that never surveys the historical contours of Black Nationalism, or the complexities of the ongoing war killing "yellow brothers and sisters in Vietnam, in Cambodia." If Thomas in *Pocho* represents an implied experience of Asian American discrimination in relation to Chicana/o injustice, then Angela Davis's one-dimensional representation in *Revolt* also serves as an allegory for the *ideas* of black oppression and of the growing colonial war in Southeast Asia.

The flatness of this African American character, and of the "yellow brothers and sisters" in Asia whom the novel never dedicates narrative energy in rounding out, generates important questions regarding their role in the narrative's political rhetoric. *Revolt* makes clear that its narrative must pay attention to the oppression of other minority groups and to the war in Vietnam because they are implicated in Chicana/o political development. The figure of Angela Davis serves this function almost exclusively when she expresses, "Now, what we've got to understand, what we've got to see, is that the war in Vietnam, just like the war at Kent State, both are products of the *system* in this country." The narrative makes it clear that this "system" is one that oppresses whites, blacks, Asians, Asian Americans, *and* Chicana/os.

Still, the narrative's representation of Angela Davis as what E. M. Forster has popularly conceptualized as a "flat character," and the text's transitory reference to "yellow brothers and sisters in Vietnam," challenge the novel's focus on Chicana/o political concerns that constitute its thematic core.[16] Casting a dilated gaze between distinct racial populations and peeking into Southeast Asian politics, this foundational Chicana/o novel, like *Pocho*, inevitably runs the risk of having its story of Mexican American self-determination destabilized by non-Chicana/o figures and Asian territories. Indeed, Angela Davis's prompt disappearance from *Revolt*, and the novel's complete erasure of the "yellow brothers and sisters" in Asia, open up the narrative space to voice local Chicana/o concerns once Corky Gonzales and Buffalo Brown take to the stage. The narrative itself thus functions as a double for the physical stage at the protest rally, with each ethnic figure vying for space in order to voice its community's respective political needs. This point is brought to bear once Corky Gonzales speaks. He says:

And thank you, Angela. We are with you in your fight against Reagan, sister. . . .

Now I am as angered as you over the deaths of four students. . . . But where is Kent State? . . . Let me tell you something. We teach our people . . . to become involved in *local* issues. . . . We are just as much against the war as anyone. In fact, we have greater reasons for hating this war. Our people, the Chicanos, are being killed at twice our rate in the population. . . . Of course we are against the war. . . . But we've got to take care of business at home first. . . .

Now I'm told that you had a mini-riot on the campus yesterday. . . . They tell me that the Chicano students were holding a *Cinco de Mayo* celebration at Campbell Hall and that the pigs came in and busted some heads. Young boys and girls were clubbed down to the ground right here. . . .

So I would only add that you should get involved with the struggles in your own backyard . . . not just on the campus, but in the barrios, in the ghettos, wherever you find the forces of reaction working against the people. (177–178)

Here, the text represents radical poet and activist Corky Gonzales recalibrating the oppositional politics of the narrative away from the American

War in Vietnam (which constitutes the very premise of the protest rally). Instead, he directs his concerns toward local community issues in the barrios of Los Angeles. Having removed Angela Davis from the stage and "the yellow brothers and sisters" in Asia from its narrative interests, *Revolt* ultimately concludes this rally by prioritizing a political focus on "local struggles" and then aligning Corky's and Buffalo Brown's oppositional attentions. Ultimately, Corky's political message falls perfectly in line with the narrative's larger oppositional rhetoric, which is directed at Chicana/o issues of police brutality, educational discrimination, cultural eradication, and other afflictions plaguing the community. For this reason, Corky's brief appearance in the novel is very much unlike Davis's. The narrative does not circumscribe his interiority as he departs from the novel, so much as reinforce the local Chicana/o sensibilities that constitute the foundation of the text's political architecture. In other words, instead of representative flatness, Corky's appearance metonymically represents a central Chicana/o consciousness at the core of the text itself. This consciousness, unequivocally oppositional and resolutely committed to local (and oftentimes ethnic nationalist) political issues, is ultimately singularized in the figure of Buffalo Brown. For this reason, it is hardly surprising that Brown functions as an echo to Corky on matters of local injustice once he finally takes to the stage:

> I have come to join in protest against the war [in Vietnam]. I have come to meet with you to add my words of sorrow for the kids shot down at Kent State yesterday. . . . But more than that, I have just come to ask you to join in the support of local issues. Just like Corky said . . . you know . . . death is not uncommon to us. We Chicanos have been beat up, shot up, kicked around, spat on and . . . fuck, they've taken everything we've had. . . . Death at the hands of the pigs is nothing new to us. . . .
> *But still I wonder . . . I must ask myself what the shouts of solidarity mean.* (179, my emphasis)

Concluding Brown's speech by emphasizing local political action and delimiting interracial concerns, this text's aesthetic arrangement calls into question its own commitment to cross-racial and transnational politics. Before a largely white and middle-class audience, Brown expresses doubts regarding student solidarity once "the fires start up"; he publicly poses a query regarding the significance of the crowd's "shouts of solidarity." However, the narrative's lack of dedication to fleshing out its non-Chicana/o figures and to rounding out the social content of the American War in Vietnam—which is the very premise of the rally—call into question the novel's own commitment to solidarity and to protesting the war in Southeast Asia. Indeed, the lack of representative weight given to the individuated politics of non-Chicana/os and to Asia highlights how interracial and transnational dilemmas set the stage (literally) for mobilizing Chicana/o protest. Yet this text also demonstrates how the war in Asia simultaneously threatens to derail the narrative's political emphasis away from what Corky and Brown identify as more pressing issues in the community. In this regard, the politics of the narrative's arrangement—in which Chicana/os compete with other minorities for articulating their respective community concerns—recasts Brown's rhetorical query away from the rally's student population and toward the novel's own composition: What do these *representations* of transnational political thinking mean?

Acosta's aesthetic arrangement is one of many examples in Chicana/o literature that symbolizes the contradiction between interracial solidarity, transpacific thinking, and narrow ethnocentric narrative formations. Indeed, the text's representation of the student protests at UCLA shows how the conflict between local and circumpacific politics often emerges in the context of solidarity efforts, yet with various degrees of separatism. Unsurprisingly, this incongruity between political alignments and oppositional foci not only manifests itself in the narrative structures of Chicana/o writings, but also in the public speech-acts of its cultural brokers.

For example, whereas Acosta's novel symbolically imagines solidarity between minorities during an antiwar rally in 1970, the author made less-than-enthusiastic gestures toward bridging interethnic differences during that same year. On May 28, 1970, at an assembly sponsored by the Southern Christian Leadership Conference Community Coalition in Los Angeles, Acosta joined Reverend Jesse Jackson and a group of Asian students to condemn US policies in Vietnam as "fascist and imperialistic."[17] On this day, Jackson accused the US government of "racist and oppressive policies," ending his speech with a quote from the *Declaration of Independence* that calls for regime change, saying, "It is their right [the people's], it is their duty, to throw off such government and provide new guards for their future security."

According to the Federal Bureau of Investigation, which kept a file on Acosta during the 1970s, the novelist concurred with Jackson's sentiments regarding the repressive nature of the United States and the need for a new government. Yet Acosta differed significantly with his civil rights colleague on matters of interethnic unity. Unapologetically, Acosta damned the United States for being historically responsible for the oppressive conditions of Mexican Americans, but he ended his speech by driving a sharp wedge through the interracial coalition the rally appeared to showcase. According to the FBI, Acosta called for "unity among minority races" but stated that all racial groups, including Asians and blacks, "would have to accede to the territorial demands of the Mexican Americans" once Chicana/os realized the national formation of Aztlán. In other words, Acosta expressed support for interethnic coalitions, yet he concluded that all other racial minorities would remain subordinate—if not excluded from the Chicana/o nation-state entirely—after Chicana/os reclaimed their territorial rights.

This rally on the steps of the Los Angeles City Hall and the protest in Acosta's novel both demonstrate ambivalence toward Chicana/o efforts at interracial cooperation during the height of the Chicana/o Movement. Brian Behnken has shown that more opportunities for cooperation between Chicana/os and other racial groups existed during the Vietnam War era than in other periods of US history. However, Behnken concludes that in this period minorities often came to regard each other as competitors for political power and limited institutional resources.[18]

Yet access to resources was not always the primary impediment to solidarity. The spatial grounding of Acosta's and other Chicana/os' political appeals according to the political geography of Aztlán (US Southwest) oftentimes generated explicit denials of competing ethnic claims in the region. On the steps of Los Angeles City Hall, for example, Acosta's deployment of Aztlán as the Chicana/os' future nation-state undermined any logic of interethnic solidarity. Indeed, "Aztlán," when interpreted literally as a territorial signifier, is incongruous with the language and strategies of other US ethnic groups, including Asian Americans, African Americans, and Native Americans, for whom the US Southwest was never imagined to be a future Chicana/o state. In its nationalist modality, then, the Chicana/os' spatially grounded politics required that the community delimit its relationships with other aggrieved minority groups and demarcate ideological and territorial boundaries around competing civil rights claims, including those of indigenous groups living on reservation lands across the US Southwest.

As such, Acosta's remarks reveal how Aztlán sometimes functioned literally in Chicana/o political rhetoric, less as a means to foster real-world alliances and more as a strategy to establish claims of territorial origins. Indeed, Acosta's collaboration with Jesse Jackson, and his remarks on the need for Asians and blacks (as well as, presumably, all other minorities) to abandon the US Southwest, illustrate an instance in which Chicana/os relied on separatist appeals for redress, despite their having cooperated with other ethnic leaders in the community. Political pleas for access to limited resources—and more radical appeals for territorial sovereignty—all resulted in the subordination of cross-racial and transnational elements of Chicana/o political speech.

This give-and-take dynamic of jockeying for political power during the 1970s did not exist between Chicana/os and Vietnamese, however. Clearly, the latter were fighting a bloody yet politically successful war far from US borders, instead of jousting for limited resources and claims of indigeneity within them. For this reason, Chicana/o claims of solidarity with Vietnamese peasants would not only be inspirational or contextual—such as in Alurista's declaration that the US war against this population had established the conditions for Chicana/o poetic production. Instead, assertions of Chicana/o alliances with Vietnamese peasants—and more radical appeals for an "Aztlán without borders" that extends into Asia—could only be symbolic, as a result of the distinct sociospatial experiences of Chicana/os and Vietnamese living on *opposite* sides of the Pacific.

Given the lack of contact and rivalry, the Vietnamese revolutionary, itself coded with high symbolic value, provided Chicana/os with an ideal image for communicating the intensity of the Mexican American's political resistance without the threat of competition. This partly explains why Chicana/o culture so often makes gestures toward interracial solidarity with this Asian group, despite Chicana/os and Vietnamese revolutionaries having *never* done so throughout their political histories. To be sure, many Chicana/os imagined the political semblances between their struggles at home and those in Southeast Asia as similar battles for freedom and national sovereignty. In extreme instances, Chicana/o culture considered these struggles as not just similar, *but rather as the same fight* for freedom in and of itself.

As a result, Chicana/o culture oftentimes imagined local oppositional heroes in the image of Vietnamese freedom fighters who were determined to defeat, against all odds, violent US forces. For example, a 1973 issue of *Los Más Cabrones*, a popular Chicana/o art magazine of the era, included a full back-page portrait of Vietnamese revolutionary Ho Chi Minh to inspire local political resistance (see figure 1). Below the profile of the Vietnamese leader reads "Los Agresores Yanquis Fracasaron" (The Yankee Aggressors Failed), reminding local Spanish-speaking readers how dedication to revolutionary ideals can defeat powerful US institutions that oppress both Chicana/os *and* Asians. Clearly, the portrait of Ho Chi Minh serves to arouse Chicana/o revolutionary sentiments. Yet it also calibrates the community's struggles as both similar to and related to those of Asian peasants suffering US imperialist aggressions half a world away.

Malaquías Montoya's painting *Viet Nam Aztlán* (1973) offers another example of cultural efforts to imagine Chicana/o protestors in the image of Southeast Asian freedom fighters, unambiguously illustrating cultural efforts to conflate oppositional politics across the Pacific (see figure 2). This painting depicts a profile of a Viet Cong soldier that is slightly refracted behind a silhouette of an urban Chicano protestor. Above their heads reads "Doàn Kêt Chiên Thăńg/UNIDOS VENCERAN." Both translate

Fig. 1. "The Yankee Aggressors Failed!" Back page of Chicana/o street magazine, *Los Más Cabrones* 1:2 (February 1973).

loosely as "united they will overcome," signaling an idyllic desire for solidarity between Chicana/o and Vietnamese populations. Indeed, for many Chicana/o artists and political brokers of the era, the new image of a politically attuned Mexican American was nothing less than the romantic abstraction of itself as an Asian double, one fighting similar battles for democratic freedoms six thousand miles away—and with whom it would never form a direct political alliance.

Despite the consistent production of the Vietnamese as a political double, another image of identity emerged in Chicana/o culture during this period, and more popularly so: the Aztec Indian. During the 1970s, widespread formulations of Chicana/o identity imbued with indigenous cultural pride

Fig. 2. Malaquías Montoya, *Viet Nam Aztlán*, 1972. Offset lithograph, 26 x 19 1/8 in. Courtesy of Malaquías Montoya.

challenged the viability of regarding the Vietnamese peasant as a political twin. Furthermore, the overwhelming insistence on establishing a cultural continuum between contemporary Chicana/os and Mesoamericans of the precolonial era often curtailed efforts of imagining regional struggles as local inflections of the war in Southeast Asia. Mariscal brings this point to bear, noting that "with few exceptions, the journals, newspapers, and literary magazines published by the Chicano Movement in the late 1960s and early '70s [began to make] infrequent references to the war [in Vietnam].... In more radical publications, the occasional poem or public opinion survey was embedded among commentary on what were considered to be the more pressing issues of ethnic origins (e.g., Mexican and pre-Columbian culture)."[19]

Chicana/o culture's romantic constructions of its racial lineages often framed the discourses of Aztlán and US colonialism exclusively around the US Southwest according to a logic of neo-indigenismo, which not only idealized native roots, but also delimited the transpacific orientations of many Chicana/o writers and artists. To be sure, this paradigm shift gave strength to the nationalist values that reached their apex during the 1970s, romantically connecting Chicana/os to precolonial populations in order to stress ideas about territorial indigeneity and bring into focus local political matters instead of attending to transnational concerns, particularly in Asia. This issue is perhaps best encapsulated by the two most popular mantras of the Vietnam War era, "*La Guerra Está Aquí, en Aztlán*" (The War Is Here, in Aztlán) and "*Mi Raza Primero*" (My People First). The latter of these, according to Ernesto Chávez, became the unofficial slogan for the Chicana/o Movement generally,[20] and it helped inscribe its participants into a distinct ethnic group imagined to have directly descended from indigenous populations. The slogan "Mi Raza Primero" epitomizes a popular desire to shift Chicana/o political concerns away from extra-ethnic and transnational matters and toward local community issues (see figure 3). In this sense, its consistent cry at marches protesting the American War in Vietnam sharply intone a dilemma between divergent ideologies: one that prioritizes "my people first," in which the community self-fashions itself according to romantic fantasies of Mesoamerican genealogies, and another

Fig. 3. "Our Fight Is at Home"/"Mi Raza Primero." Antiwar march, Seattle, Washington, ca. 1971. Courtesy of Antonio Salazar/Chula Vista Foto.

that privileges third world concerns in Asia, in which the community self-fashions itself according to romantic abstractions of Asian revolutionaries.

The following chapters identify and then examine this ideological two-step between the "barrio" and Asia in the aesthetic architecture of key Chicana/o texts. The Chicana/o literary imagination has long cast a broad narrative gaze across an interracial political landscape, one that far exceeds Chicana/o communities and frequently peers into Asia well before the American War in Vietnam. Yet the lack of depth and detail these texts often afford non-Chicana/o figures and Asian spaces calls attention to the gap between their one-dimensional narrative depictions and their material historical referents, raising fundamental questions about the ways in which interracial and transnational matters impact the politics of representation in Chicana/o culture. What is the ideological function of Asia and Asians in the oppositional (and sometimes reactionary) cultural politics that important Chicana/o texts formulate? How do representations of the Pacific Rim contribute to the ways Chicana/o writings articulate social, cultural, and political issues in Mexican American communities? What does the dialectical configuration between Chicana/os and Asians in Chicana/o art yield for understanding the political emergence of Chicana/o cultural values, including their nationalist, gendered, and classed formations?

These questions form the core of this entire study. It justifies its particular focus on Chicana/o-Asian relations by demonstrating how Chicana/o communities configure self-perceptions outside the hemisphere and in relation to an Asian other against which the United States has pitted Mexican Americans during times of war throughout the twentieth century. This project becomes more urgent when we recall that a large number of important Chicano writers served in US military efforts across the Pacific, including World War II, the US occupation of Japan, the Korean War, and the American War in Vietnam. This book attends to writings by many Chicano veterans of these conflicts, including Américo Paredes (US Occupation of Japan), Rolando Hinojosa (Korean War), and Alfredo Véa and Daniel Cano (American War in Vietnam), as well as others. Indeed, the long history of Mexican American soldiering in US wars throughout the Pacific Rim (and the large Asian population in the US West) reveal why Asian characters appear so frequently in Chicana/o narratives, especially in male-authored texts. The political urgency to speak to local community issues and to comment on racial injustice in the US West without extra-ethnic and geopolitical distractions, I shall show, explains their consistent textual marginalization.

This is not to suggest that Chicana/o literature privileges Chicana/o-Asian relations as more progressive or significant than other forms of interracial contact. Nor does it suggest that Chicana/o-Asian encounters are representative of cross-racial dynamics in Chicana/o literature more generally. Instead, this study will show that Asia and Asians factor significantly into the ideological production of writings by many key Chicana/o authors, whose works often form the core of this community's literary canon. It is a dynamic that remains to be fully explored by literary scholars, despite a long genealogy of historians having already uncovered the importance of Asian wars in the political pasts of many Chicana/o communities. For example, Mario García, George Sánchez, David Gutiérrez, Lorena Oropeza, and Richard Griswold del Castillo, among others, have shown how World War II, the Korean War, and the American War in Vietnam each represent significant moments in Chicana/o political history.[21] These scholars have revealed how Mexican American participation in these conflicts has contributed significantly to the political and cultural becoming of many Chicana/o communities, marked by their involvement in labor movements, their rise into the middle class through access to the US GI Bill, and their insertion into a class of professional artists.

Only a handful of literary scholars, however, have examined at length the impact of these conflicts on Chicana/o literary themes, and even fewer have regarded the influence of Asia and Asians on—to use Alurista's phrasing—"its processes of poetic signification." There exists no book-length study on these literary matters; much important work remains to be done regarding the underexplored impact of Asia and Asians on the themes and aesthetic features of key Chicana/o texts before, during, and after the 1970s.[22] This book addresses this gap in the cultural and critical past of Chicana/o communities, and in doing so it establishes an alternative literary history anchored not only at the US-Mexico border, but also across the Pacific Rim.

Chapter 1 begins this study by asserting that key texts of the Chicana/o literary renaissance collapse Chicana/o and Asian identities and flatten geographical differences between the United States and Asia, thereby linking economic and social injustices in the West to US military aggressions in Vietnam. Examining Oscar Zeta Acosta's novel about the Chicana/o moratorium, *The Revolt of the Cockroach People* (1973), Luis Valdez's antiwar play, *Vietnam Campesino* (1971), and Miguel Méndez's experimental text, *Peregrinos en Aztlán* (1974), this opening chapter uncovers narrative forms of racial conflation that problematically imagine Chicana/os and Vietnamese as, in the words of Valdez, "the same people." This chapter also maps the narrative terrains of these texts, which layer US geographies over those of Asia. It identifies this spatial feature as a cultural strategy by which to calibrate US colonial violence in Vietnam as an image of local struggles for ethnic autonomy in the US West.

Because these texts instill cultural pride by maintaining that the US West and Southwest is Aztlán, the home of the Aztec Indians, they consider Chicana/os not as newcomers, but as peoples indigenous to the land. In its separatist modality, however, this conceptualization of territorial space delimits the potential for interracial solidarity across other racial spectrums, for Aztlán has often come to represent "the name of that place that will at some future point be the national home of a Chicano people reclaiming their territorial rights."[23] In this sense, chapter 1 shows that the transnational figurations of Aztlán in Acosta's, Valdez's, and Mendez's texts decouple this nationalist space away from the local, thus representing more than a future nation-state, or "the land taken by the United States in [the] nineteenth century."[24] Instead, this chapter shows that the poetic process of collapsing racial and spatial difference in these texts conceptualizes Aztlán as an expansive political territory that extends *across the Pacific Rim*, revealing how this key word of the Chicana/o cultural lexicon symbolizes not only a particular history of Anglo-American imperial expansion, but also a larger and more general history of US aggressions in Asia.

Having unpacked the narrative features that encapsulate the contradictions between nationalist and transpacific political ideas in Acosta's, Mendez's, and Valdez's texts, and having plotted them as part of a larger history of the tension between ethnocentric and transnational orientations in Chicana/o culture, I continue in chapter 2 with an examination of Américo Paredes's "Ichiro Kikuchi" (1948–1949) and Rolando Hinojosa's *Korean Love Songs* (1978). This chapter identifies these key exemplars of Chicana/o literature as cultural forms that construct oppositional identities in the image of Asians *before* the American War in Vietnam. In an era in which large numbers of Mexican American soldiers testify to having had imagined themselves as legitimate members of the US nation-state, these narratives reveal how early wars in Japan and Korea conditioned alternative forms of self-identification fashioned in the image of an Asian other. As Mexican Americans fitted in the uniform of US power that exerts itself relentlessly against Asians overseas, yet also as minorities who recognize their subjugation to that power at home, the protagonists of Paredes's and Hinojosa's texts express what Homi Bhabha calls in a different yet related context, the "jagged testimony" of the subaltern.[25] The interracial associations these texts establish cut against the grain of historiographies that equate Mexican American soldiering during the mid-twentieth century with self-perceptions of their having become "common members" of US society. Instead, Paredes's and Hinojosa's narratives, I show, challenge histories that write this community's inclusion in the US democratic project by calling attention to the imagined racial and political equivalences between Chicana/os and Asians fighting on opposite sides of the same wars.

Representations of Asia and Asians in these texts illustrate how transnational and interracial thinking drive the oppositional politics of Chicana/o culture before the American War in Vietnam. Yet Paredes's and Hinojosa's narratives also represent early instances of Chicana/o ambivalence about Asian encounters in this community's literary culture. While these texts communicate early instances of Chicana/o self-determination in a Pacific Rim context, how they marginalize their Asian characters in their respective stories symbolizes this culture's ideological conflicts between local and global priorities. As such, this chapter argues that the narrative deletions of Asians in Paredes's and Hinojosa's texts project a future political culture, one compelled to demarcate racial boundaries around its community interests as a "tactical decision in order to organize [its] constituencies."[26]

Chapter 3 proceeds to demonstrate within frameworks of gender and colonialism that Asian encounters in the Chicana/o literature do not always produce progressive political responses. Navigating the interstices of race, gender, and nationalism, this chapter examines the representations of interracial sex in Daniel Cano's *Shifting Loyalties* (1995) and Alfredo Véa's *Gods Go Begging* (1999). In doing so, it reveals how Chicana/o-Asian relations in these instances reproduce US imperial ideologies that Chicana/o culture has long opposed. This chapter identifies reactionary politics in the sexual encounters between Chicano men and Asian women in these works by regarding them in the context of Edward Said's concern that subaltern populations will eventually adopt the "orientalizing processes of domination" developed by colonial powers, despite their own experiences of subjugation.[27] Read against the explicit anti-imperialist politics that thematize Cano's and Véa's novels, this chapter argues that their depictions of interracial liaisons deconstruct their anti-hegemonic values, for the Chicano's conquest of the female Asian body stands metonymically for the US colonial actions that these texts seemingly stand to critique.

This chapter on interracial liaisons dovetails with chapter 4, which focuses on Chicana/o Orientalisms in Rudolfo Anaya's *A Chicano in China* (1986). This text contains the romantic features of imagined racial symmetries between Chicana/os and Asians that highlighted throughout the book. However, this narrative departs from a context of US-Asian conflict to explore theories of prehistoric migrations from Asia to the Americas.[28] In order to undercut the European roots of Chicana/o culture, Anaya's text constructs a myth of shared origins between Chicana/os and Chinese during the narrator's voyage across the Pacific Ocean. Situating Anaya's travelogue alongside the counter-colonial poetics of Mexican poet Octavio Paz, who regarded Asian influences on pre-Columbian culture in order to deemphasize Mexico's European past, I argue that Anaya's text attempts to affirm the Chicana/o's indigenous origins by participating in a cultural project developed south of the US-Mexico border, one which—according to Paz—verifies that "American man is of Asiatic origin."[29]

Insisting on discovering a precolonial seed of Chicana/o culture, Anaya's narrator travels from the Americas to China in search of common legends between Chicana/os and ancient Chinese, ones he believes will unearth a hidden kernel of Mesoamerican knowledge. En route, I argue, he internalizes constructions of the "Orient" not as other, but rather as a foundational self, insisting on theories of Asian origins for Amerindian populations and thereby quickly confirming assumptions of the Chicana/o's Asian heritage. To this point, this chapter shows that Anaya's text not only mirrors the efforts of Mexican writers who obsessed over theories of early Asian migrations to the Americas, but also that it resembles the efforts of Chicana/o nationalists of the 1970s who insisted on a cultural continuum between contemporary Mexican Americans and Mesoamericans of a precolonial era. It is here, this chapter reveals, where the contradictions of Chicana/o cultural ideologies on Asia come full circle: while cultural nationalists of the 1970s marginalized ideas of Chicana/o and Asian sameness in order to romanticize Chicana/o indigenous heritage, *A Chicano in China* insists on transpacific equivalences in order to fantasize about this *same* Native American lineage.

Chapter 5 reintroduces the impact of gender on Chicana/o-Asian relations by examining Virginia Grise's *Rasgos asiáticos* (*Asian Traits*, 2011). This play reminds us that Chicana/o-Asian encounters occur not just overseas, but also within the formative history of Chinese immigration to the US-Mexico borderlands. This chapter expands the underexamined history of Chinese immigration and persecution in northern Mexico at the turn of the twentieth century to assess the racial and gendered values of Grise's play. To be sure, this history forms the backdrop of Grise's drama about mixed-race marriages of the era, and it forms the material basis for how this drama articulates life as a lesbian Chinese-Chicana a century later.

To begin, this chapter argues that the play's geographical and temporal movements between the Americas and Asia function differently from earlier strategies of spatial flattening in 1970s Chicana/o culture. It shows how the play's intergenerational conversations between the US-Mexico border and Asia refuse to collapse distinct geographies into an undifferentiated political landscape of "sameness," thereby yielding ideological concepts very different from the romantic forms of interracial solidarity examined in chapters 1 and 2. Refusing to collapse racial and territorial distinctions for purposes of political convenience, *Rasgos* instead produces its ideologies of identity by negotiating the gaps of a community's fractured past, including the oft-forgotten history of Chinese migrants in the US-Mexico borderlands. These temporal gaps and historical ambiguities, this chapter shows, are marked by this drama's dominant formal features, all of which condition the possibilities of articulating its mixed-race feminist politics.

The play's irregular distribution of empty and dark spaces marks its transpacific and intergenerational movements; its linguistic combinations of Spanish, English, and Cantonese make audible the Chicana/o community's silence regarding its Asian heritage; and the heroine's fractured conversations on race and gender speak to the difficulties of voicing a mixed-race feminist politics in Chicana culture. The play's temporal gaps, its challenging linguistic interplays, and its historical ambiguities collectively communicate how the Chicana heroine cannot learn to *know* her Asian ancestry. Still, this drama's constant movement between various cultural trajectories articulates how she can nevertheless learn to *remember* her forgotten Asian heritage. As such, I argue that the play constructs its feminist ethics by imagining "China-cana" identities that are conscious of—yet struggling to come to terms with—the mixed-race genealogies of a culture that has historically marginalized its own "Asian traits."

This book's coda situates the interracial and transnational features of Chicana/o literature that I examine in chapters 1 through 5 within past and contemporary discussions on Chicana/o cultural studies. The interracial elements between Mexican Americans, Asians, and Asian Americans in Chicana/o literature over the last seven decades reveal that these groups are not as divorced as early critiques of borderlands culture insist, nor are they as removed as traditional paradigms of area or ethnic studies suggest. To be sure, the constitution of Chicana/o identity in this community's literary culture has never been a strictly local process. My modest hope is that this book brings this point to bear by excavating the significance of Chicana/o culture's underexamined—and oftentimes ignored—"rasgos asiáticos." These transpacific matters are not just concerns of our post-millennium era, or the consequences of our contemporary global age. Instead, as I shall demonstrate, they are cultural issues of our formative transnational pasts, and of our fascinating cross-racial imaginations.

1

Racial Equivalence and the Transpacific Geographies of Chicana/o Nationalism in *Vietnam Campesino, The Revolt of the Cockroach People*, and *Pilgrims in Aztlán*

When mapping the appearance of Asia and Asians in the Chicana/o literary archive, one notices that texts produced during the Vietnam War era imagine this space and racial group more than those written during any other period of Chicana/o cultural history. Indeed, the frequency with which Asia and Asians appear in Chicana/o texts during this era of literary output is largely a result of two interconnected issues. One, it corresponds to the Chicana/o renaissance, or what Juan Rodríguez terms *el florecimiento*,[1] the blossoming of Chicana/o culture inspired by an emergent literary spirit; and two, it reflects the consolidation of a Chicana/o political identity activated by widespread protests to US violence in Southeast Asia. The confluence of these developments—large-scale cultural production and nationwide opposition to the US war in French Indochina—helps explain the regularity with which Vietnam and Vietnamese figures make their way into important Chicana/o literary forms, including three key works of the 1970s: *Vietnam Campesino, The Revolt of the Cockroach People*, and *Peregrinos en Aztlán* (*Pilgrims in Aztlán*).

To be sure, these works do not simply contain "curious" images of racial and spatial diversity. Instead—as this chapter reveals—these important texts illustrate a prominent pattern in Chicana/o narratives that establish racial equivalences between Mexican Americans and Vietnamese freedom fighters, while also layering geographies of local social protests over the bloody terrains of Southeast Asia. This narrative strategy of racial and spatial flattening, which fails to make distinctions between peoples and places, yields an unmistakable ideological message of Chicana/o protest; it imagines how regional issues of injustice plaguing the Mexican American community are linked—if not equivalent—to matters of US imperial violence half a world away.

Yoking regional struggles for democratic freedoms to US military aggressions in Vietnam, this narrative pattern of racial and spatial conflation complicates standing literary histories that focus on the nationalist ideologies unmistakably coded into Chicana/o writings of this era. Indeed, the force of this narrative arrangement that imagines racial and spatial equivalences across the Pacific Rim has been largely lost on generations of critics who have instead assessed—and understandably so—how *Vietnam Campesino*, *Revolt*, and *Pilgrims* deploy nationalist ideas such as Aztlán for the purposes of framing Chicana/o cultural politics and for addressing pressing regional issues at home.[2] However, as this chapter shows, these three exemplars of Chicana/o literature not only code a rhetoric of Chicana/o nationalism, they also reveal how Asian elements of racial and spatial difference *produce* the primary values of their stark oppositional ideas. These key texts of the Chicana/o literary canon communicate how representations of social relations at the US-Mexico border take shape by imagining the relations between the United States and Vietnam. In other words, Asian racial and spatial difference in these works highlights a common yet underexamined textual strategy of the 1970s that flattens distinct populations and places in order to assert Chicana/o literature's core value of resistance to Anglo America, writ large.

Vietnam Campesino

Perhaps nowhere in the Chicana/o literary archive do Asia and Asians more powerfully assert local oppositional politics than in Luis Valdez's early dramas, which he termed "*actos*."[3] If the disproportionate character spaces of Asian Americans in *Pocho* symbolize a preliminary instance of cross-racial political thinking, then Valdez's *Vietnam Campesino* (1970) shows Asian politics literally taking center stage in Chicana/o cultural efforts to inscribe local community values.[4] Juxtaposing and overlapping Asian territories with geographies of the US-Mexico borderlands, *Vietnam Campesino* begins almost immediately by conceptualizing a transnational space from which to articulate a host of Chicana/o political concerns, including racial forms of labor exploitation and the unequal value of

Mexican American citizenship in US society. From the urban barrio to rural agricultural settings in which Mexican Americans endure horrendous labor conditions,[5] *Vietnam Campesino* demonstrates an acute engagement in regional issues afflicting the community. Yet it does so through a global critique that regards the local as a political inflection of a specific crisis in Asia. That is, this play considers local labor dilemmas in California and the crisis in Vietnam as interrelated symptoms of the same geopolitical illness: US Anglo power.

Unapologetically political and resolutely oppositional to US imperial hegemony, *Vietnam Campesino* thematically takes issue with the US military's intrusions into local labor strikes in Delano, California, and with the disproportionate number of Chicano deaths in Vietnam. The *Utah Chronicle* reports that during the California grape boycott of the late 1960s, which was spearheaded by Mexican American labor in the region, the US Defense Department increased its supply of grapes to the military by 350 percent.[6] Matt Garcia notes that Richard Nixon's increase in the Defense Department's purchase of grapes more than doubled to 16 million pounds in the first year of his presidency alone.[7] To compound the problems for Mexican American labor, Nixon not only increased the military supply of this fruit to US soldiers, but he also encouraged the South Vietnamese government to increase its grape imports by more than 2.8 million pounds in 1969, compared to only 350,000 pounds two years earlier.[8] The effect of this exponential rise in demand turned South Vietnam into the world's third-largest importer of grapes; it included considerable economic benefits for the US agricultural industry responsible for their export. As one might expect, Chicana/o labor viewed the substantial increase in the military's demands for grapes with intense cynicism, for it directly impacted this community's enduring strike on local growers.

In the course of this lasting labor struggle, a disproportionate number of Chicano men from California and the US West were dying in the jungles of Vietnam. Ralph Guzman writes that by 1969, soldiers with Spanish surnames from the US West and Southwest made up 20 percent of all combat and noncombat deaths. In that year, the Bureau of the Census reports that only 11 percent of the population in these regions had last names of Spanish origin. Furthermore, Guzman highlights that while a disproportionate number of Mexican Americans were dying in Vietnam, making up 20 percent of all casualties, people with Spanish surnames made up only 1 percent of the student population at the University of California at that time.[9]

Set against this amount of extreme racial bias, *Vietnam Campesino* reveals how conflicts in Asia inevitably shaped Chicana/o political identities on both global and interracial scales during the 1970s. To emphasize this point, the play manages its geographical and racial differences by denying distinctions between the classed politics of Mexican American migrant laborers and Vietnamese peasants fighting US imperialism in the Indochinese peninsula. In this sense, *Vietnam Campesino* does much more than link Chicana/os and Asians within global structures of US hegemony across distinct geopolitical spaces. It also formulates romantic political alliances by imagining California as Vietnam and then considering the Vietnamese peasant as an emblematic figure against which to conceptualize Chicana/o political identity proper.

The transnational and cross-racial links between California migrant labor and Asian farmworkers occur most forcefully in the play when Don Coyote, a Mexican American contractor hired to break a labor strike, assumes the identity of the South Vietnamese president, "Dan Ky Ho Ti." In this particular scene, Don Coyote/Dan Ky Ho Ti partitions the stage between several characters: "Army General Defense"; "Vietnamese Man"; "Vietnamese Woman"; and a Mexican American family consisting of "Padre," "Madre," and "Hijo." Showing how the force and farce of US efforts to install a puppet president in Southeast Asia affect the quotidian lives of Mexican American migrant laborers, Valdez writes:

> PRESIDENT: (*Shoots one of the Vietnamese, holds gun against his head and gives speech.*) We South Vietnamese are a peace-loving people, and we ask you Americans to keep sending your troops to South Vietnam for as long as we need them. Thank you. How was that, General? (*Hands back gun.*)
> GENERAL: Just fine, Mr. President. Here you are (*gives him a wad of bills.*) Go buy yourself a case of Cokes. . . . Get out of here! (*The South Vietnamese president exits. Campesinos have been watching intently.*)
> PADRE: (To his wife.) *Oye, vieja, esas gentes son iguales que nosotros* [Hey, those people are the same as us—my emphasis and translation].
> MADRE: ¿Verdad que sí? Y a ellos también les dicen comunistas. [Isn't it true? And they also call them communists—my translation].
> PADRE: Pero nomás son pobres campesinos [Yet, they are no more than poor farmworkers—translation mine]. (*To Vietnamese.*) ¡Oye Vietnam! (*Vietnamese turn toward campesinos. PADRE and MADRE give them the peace sign.*) (115)

The link between the Mexican American labor contractor and the Vietnamese president in this instance, according to Jorge Huerta, is "made very apparent by exaggerating the connection. The audience is forced to see the real-life counterparts and events in a new light, reassessing their faith in what the [US] government has been telling them."[10] Undoubtedly, the representation of the Mexican American labor contractor and the Vietnamese president by the same actor presses the audience to question the government's rationale for war. However, instead of merely calling into question the United States' dubious mission to curb the spread of communism, the bridging of Mexican American and Asian identities in this scene also demands that audience members process its lived experiences of exploitation relative to Vietnamese oppression, and to recognize the transnational reach of US power that abuses both groups.

Although Huerta rightly notes how *Vietnam Campesino* draws parallels between the racial dynamics of contract labor in California and the proxies of US power in Southeast Asia, what remains less examined is how this *acto* advocates forms of political self-determination by collapsing interracial differences between Chicana/os and Vietnamese peasants into being "the same." To be sure, *Vietnam Campesino* flattens interracial unions between these two groups not only by linking Chicana/o identities to the crisis in Vietnam, but also by equating Mexican American laborers and Vietnamese peasants ("Those people are the same as us"). In accord with Valdez's commitment to protest theater, *Vietnam Campesino* imagines an idyllic instance of interracial solidarity between Chicana/os and Asians intent on rallying against US Anglo hegemony. Yet in doing so, this *acto* depicts a singular Asian subject stripped of its historical particularity and articulated exclusively in relation to Mexican American experiences of class difference (see figure 4). In this sense, the image of a politically conscious Mexican American is nothing less than Chicana/o culture's projected abstraction of a Southeast Asian peasant, for the play produces an image of Chicana/o labor as an unmediated reflection of Vietnamese farmworkers, despite the significant historical and racial differences between these two groups. It is unsurprising, then, that Valdez duplicates this romantic form of racial and political symmetry in the sister-play of *Vietnam Campesino*, *Soldado Razo* (1971), in which the protagonist recognizes the faces of his immediate family on the bodies of slaughtered Vietnamese villagers.

Locating Chicana/o social identities beyond the US-Mexico border and figuring its political constitution relative to an Asian other, *Vietnam Campesino* reorganizes what Homi Bhabha calls, in a different yet related context, the "imaginative horizon of ideology."[11] This form of ideological expansion into Southeast Asian politics regularly motivated Valdez and other community leaders to collaborate with Vietnamese students during antiwar rallies, with the effect of linking larger war protests to Chicana/o labor issues and to other complaints emerging from Mexican American communities.[12] The play illustrates most forcefully this expanding scope of Chicana/o political ideology in its final scene, which once again collapses global and local political dilemmas to reveal once and for all that the war

Fig. 4. "Those people are the same as us." Performance of *Vietnam Campesino*, 1970. Courtesy of Luis Valdez and El Teatro Campesino.

in Vietnam is fundamentally an expression of the same power imbalances that structure everyday life for Chicana/os in California.

To conclude the play, Hijo, his family, and Vietnamese Man and Woman address the audience directly. In this *parabasis*—the break between the play's fictional world and reality—these figures communicate explicitly the farmworker's pressing political issues:

> HIJO: The war in Vietnam continues, asesinando familias inocentes de campesino. Los Chicana/os mueren en la guerra, y los rancheros se hacen ricos [The war in Vietnam continues, murdering innocent farmworker families. Chicana/os die in the war, and growers get rich], selling their scab products to the Pentagon. The fight is here, Raza! En Aztlán. [my translation].
> VIETNAMESE WOMAN: (*Rises.*) En Aztlán.
> MADRE: (*Rises.*) En Aztlán.
> VIETNAMESE MAN: (*Rises.*) En Aztlán.
> PADRE: (*Rises.*) En Aztlán. (They all raise their fists in the air, in silence.) (120–121)

Hijo's direct address to the audience in the play's coda underscores a link between US aggressions in Vietnam and the economic injustices Mexican

Americans experience "en Aztlán"—the Chicana/o spiritual homeland that corresponds geographically to the US Southwest. In this sense, this concluding scene of interracial solidarity deploys a key word of the Chicana/o cultural lexicon as a space of oppositional politics for both Chicana/os *and* Asians, pressing the audience to regard these identities "as the same" and to conceptualize Aztlán as a cultural and political geography that extends from precolonial spaces of the Americas to contemporary territories in Vietnam.

The stage for *Vietnam Campesino* consequently serves as a cognitive map that calibrates Chicana/o political and economic dilemmas as interracial and global matters.[13] Fredric Jameson asserts that cognitive mapping is a "pedagogical political culture that seeks to endow the individual subject [or community] with some new heightened sense of its place in the global system," allowing us to "grasp our positioning as individual and collective subjects and [therefore] regain a capacity to act and struggle which is at present neutralized by our spatial as well as our social confusion."[14] If, as Jameson argues, global capitalism produces a sense of spatial and cultural confusion, then *Vietnam Campesino* negotiates this disequilibrium by positioning Chicana/o and Vietnamese labor identities "as the same" and then "mapping" Chicana/o economic and political concerns directly onto Asia. Ultimately, California and Asia become impossible to differentiate, a point brought to bear during a critical moment in the play when Hijo cannot make a distinction between his parents' shack in California and a Vietnamese hut (arranged side by side) when the army orders him to burn down the latter.

For Chicana/os, the economic injustice *Vietnam Campesino* explores is certainly not specific to the 1970s. Nor are the play's interracial features. To be sure, the classed and interracial elements of the play remind us of historical episodes of transnational alliances in Chicana/o politics that date back to the early years of the twentieth century. For example, Japanese and Mexican agricultural workers in Oxnard, California, formed the Japanese Mexican Labor Association (JMLA) in 1903 to organize a strike against owners, banks, and merchants vested in the sugar beet industry that monopolized labor in that region.[15] El Congreso del Pueblo de Habla Española, founded in 1938 by Guatemalan-born Luisa Moreno, represents another major transnational effort at organization, this time by international leftists, according to Mario García, to form an interracial coalition for "securing basic rights for all Mexicans and all Spanish-speaking people in the United States."[16] Emma Tenayuca and Homer Brooks similarly endorsed class-based political unity across national and racial differences in their seminal essay, "The Mexican Question in the Southwest," published in *The Communist* in 1939. Interracial elements of Chicana/o politics also figure in Mexican American attempts to establish an independent republic in the US Southwest under the "Plan de San Diego" (1915), a manifesto that calls, as Juan Gómez-Quiñones reminds us, for a coalition of Mexican Americans, "the black," "the Indian," and "the Oriental" to fight for national autonomy.[17]

Interracial and international elements of early Chicana/o politics are likewise present in Valdez's early nonfiction. In an essay entitled "The Tale of the Raza" (1971), originally published in the New Left magazine *Ramparts*, Valdez recalls the victory of the United Farm Workers (UFW) in the Delano labor strike (1965–1970), which inspired his production of *Vietnam Campesino*. This labor strike, which was a collaboration between Filipino and Mexican American workers, included a strategic boycott campaign that crippled the growers' countermeasures to ease the labor crises in the region. The UFW's success in this instance followed on the heels of yet another popular manifesto in Chicana/o political history, one which Valdez himself drafted at the behest of César Chávez for the National Farm Workers Association and the UFW Organizing Committee. The "Plan de Delano" (1966) recognizes the repression of ethnic communities across the United States, calling for unity among all farmworkers, including "the Negroes and poor whites, the Puerto Ricans, Japanese, and Arabians, in short all of the races that comprise the oppressed minority groups in the United States."[18]

To be sure, the early politics of Mexican American revolutionaries and the New Left constitute an important prehistory to the interracial discourses found in *Vietnam Campesino*. However, this play's vision of an inclusive Chicana/o political community remained largely symbolic, for except in the notable cases of the JMLA and the Delano labor strike of 1965, Chicana/os and Asians rarely succeeded in forming significant and sustained political alliances. Indeed, the play's own erasure of the large Filipino contingent of the UFW Organizing Committee—including the more than one thousand Filipino members of the Agricultural Workers Organizing Committee, which originated the Delano labor strike that Valdez's play imagines—speaks to the ambivalence regarding Asian otherness in Chicana/o political culture. Dawn Bohulano Mabalon notes that this manner of delimiting the Filipinos who actively participated alongside their Mexican American counterparts in securing contracts with California grape growers reveals how this history "in popular culture, [is] seen as a Chicano movement, [and] not as the multiethnic alliance that it actually was."[19] Tellingly, *Vietnam Campesino* contributes to this historical forgetting, for it elides Asian difference and overlooks Filipino farmworkers in the very instance in which it expresses imaginary transnational affiliations in Vietnam, reflecting the tenuous identity politics that often drove Chicana/o protest culture of the 1970s.[20]

To be sure, this process of cultural forgetting and the romantic interracial ideologies found in *Vietnam Campesino* often conflicted with nationalist forces of the play's contemporary era, ones that largely marginalized interethnic and transnational political thinking for the purpose of articulating a distinct ethnic identity. George Mariscal reminds us that cultural nationalism became the primary tool for both imagining Chicana/o identity and for galvanizing its mobilization, despite communities having demonstrated intense transnational political sensibilities throughout the 1970s.[21] Juxtaposed to the Chicana/o-Asian relations in *Pocho, Vietnam Campesino,* and *Soldado Razo,* the rise of cultural nationalism generated new fantasies about the Chicana/os' pre-Cortesian origins in order to articulate ethnic pride and to legitimate its political struggles.

Chicana/o "Movement poetry" (1967–1974) in particular revealed that imaginary Chicana/o-Asian symmetries oftentimes proved incompatible with an emergent literary focus on establishing an indigenous heritage.[22] While the nationalist phase of the Movement did recognize ethnographic evidence of a "great journey" from Asia to the Americas during the Ice Age, it strove not to consolidate Asian and Chicana/o political identities, but to stress the latter's indigenous roots and its territorial rights in the region.[23] Regarding this overt romanticization of a pre-Cortesian past in Chicana/o literature, Francisco Lomelí notes that an entire generation of Chicana/o poets activated political sensibilities by explicitly incorporating "a neoclassical indigenous slant [and] by tapping into Amerindian values."[24] Mariscal underscores this point by noting that the most pressing issues of Chicana/o writings of the 1970s revolved around matters of pre-Columbian culture in order to address local community grievances by using nationalist political values.[25]

Placing an emphasis on pre-Cortesian values, nationalist elements of Chicana/o culture not only elided its racial differences, but also obscured its gendered differences. *Vietnam Campesino,* I have shown, coalesces Asian and Chicana/o identities irrespective of racial particularities. Yet it also disregards gender issues in order to imagine utopian and cohesive political alliances. Indeed, for many Chicana/os, gender and cross-racial matters became divisive issues that threatened the focus on nationalism as "the common denominator for uniting all Mexican Americans" and their efforts "to win political and economic control of [their] communities."[26] In response, women in the Chicana/o Movement organized the first national *Chicana* conference (Houston, Texas, 1971) to address specifically the perceived conflicts between feminist discourses and the nationalist ideals of Chicano politics.[27]

Although many Chicanas at the conference agreed to bracket their grievances for the purpose of expressing solidarity with their male counterparts, one recognizes how this double distraction of race and gender oftentimes informed the basic values of Chicana/o protest literature. For example, in her poem "La hora de todos" (1972), Portilla de la Luz links the American War in Vietnam to her own political struggles and to social justice efforts around the world. She writes: "Vietnam, Vietnam, your tragedy extends and escapes all distances and hours/. . . In your just and heroic struggle/ The destiny of my struggle is decided/Which is the struggle of being and of preserving the right to live/For all that is human and beautiful in life."[28] Yoking the American War in Vietnam to her community and to her own personal destiny, de la Luz forges a poetics of protest against US injustice in two separate hemispheres, showing how the war in Southeast Asia simultaneously generates local and global political sensibilities *across* normative male and female gendered differences.

Unfortunately, Chicana/o literature's larger emphasis on nationalist values not only obfuscated its gendered, interracial, and international features, it also established ethnic and regional boundaries for assessing Chicana/o culture for much of the twentieth century. According to George Sánchez, Chicana/o Studies' insistence on regional methodologies framed by an "Anglo/Mexican" binary stems from nationalist segments of the field, and from the political necessity to comment on racial oppression in a manner that directly engages the Anglo social authority.[29] Alvina Quintana adds that by "prioritizing self-determination," early Chicana/o Studies sought "to legitimate [its] immediate oppositional struggle" by stressing "ethnic autonomy" as it competed for "institutional recognition and support."[30] Claudia Sadowski-Smith agrees with Quintana, noting that various cultural nationalisms that US minorities forged in response to repression "fell back into ethnic absolutism [when] they became isolated from one another after their institutionalization in the US academy in the form of ethnic and race studies."[31] By the late 1970s, cultural critics overwhelmingly highlighted the ways in which Chicana/o literary products articulated ethnic and regional matters over cross-racial and transnational ones. Whereas both high-profile writers, like Luis Valdez, and less visible ones, like Portilla de la Luz, explored interracial and global concerns, the critical consensus of contemporary culture focused on indigenous tropes and ethnic nationalism as the standards for political critique, all to the exclusion of Chicana/o literature's multiracial and transnational orientations.

Despite the interracial and global political thinking evident in Chicana/o literary forms, what remains certain is that ethno-nationalism functioned as the operating ideology for many cultural and political critiques. As such, the underexamined global contours of Chicana/o culture solicit important questions about how the community's art conceptualizes transpacific spaces and how it imagines cross-racial proximities. To be sure, Chicana/o culture was politically attached to the antiwar movement for many writers, activists, and critics of the 1970s, but cultural brokers of the era often marginalized these transpacific orientations due to ways in which the community perceived its tenuous position in US society.[32] That is, Chicana/o nationalist formulations were inspired consistently by the community's recognition of itself in the suffering and valiant resistance of Vietnamese peasants, while regional economic and political realities conditioned an emphasis on narrow ethno-cultural values without extra-ethnic interference.

The Revolt of the Cockroach People

Oscar Zeta Acosta's benchmark Chicana/o novel *The Revolt of the Cockroach People* (1973) demonstrates this tension between transnational and local political thinking during a key juncture of its narration. Speaking to the events of the Chicano Moratorium on August 29, 1970, in Los Angeles, California, Buffalo Zeta Brown (the novelist's alter ego) recalls a formative moment that culminated in large-scale demonstrations of over thirty thousand protestors a year later.[33] He says:

> I remember a winter day in 1969 when I marched with some five thousand along the same route [in Los Angeles], in the rain. We took to the streets without any fanfare. And by the time we reached Laguna Park, with rain and thunder and lightning and ice-cold wind at our faces, the crowd started to disperse. It wanted no speeches. It wanted warmth and comfort.
>
> I remember jumping up on a park bench and grabbing a bullhorn and telling the people to return, to listen to the voices of the thunder and lightning: we may be the last generation of Chicanos if we don't stop the war. If we don't stop the destruction of our culture, we may not be around for the next century. *We are the Viet Cong of America. Tooner Flats is Mylai* ... The Poverty Program of Johnson, the Welfare of Roosevelt, Truman, Eisenhower and Kennedy, the New Deal and the Old Deal, the New Frontier as well as Nixon's American Revolution ... these are further embellishments of the government's pacification program.
>
> Therefore, there is only one issue: LAND. *We need to get our own land. We need our own government.* We must have our own flag and our own country. Nothing less will save the existence of the Chicanos.
>
> And I let it go at that. (200–201, my emphasis)

With inclement weather threatening to disperse the moderate-sized crowd that has gathered to protest the disproportionate numbers of Chicanos serving and dying in the American War in Vietnam, Brown makes a brief yet powerful transnational and interracial analogy, one ostensibly effective in coalescing a withering Chicano/a political voice: "We are the Viet Cong of America. Tooner Flats is Mylai." One can easily decode the metaphor, and perhaps this is why his statements prove effective in unifying the Chicana/o protesters, whose commitment is being tested by the rain and cold. Declaring that "Chicanos are the Viet Cong of America," Brown draws a direct analogy that calibrates the anguish of the Vietnamese people at the hands of the US government as the suffering of the Chicana/os fighting the same institution. Concurrently, his metaphor conceptualizes the Viet Cong—the oppositional Vietnamese army defending its nation against US imperialist aggressions—as the growing army of Chicana/o protesters fighting its community's own cultural destruction, if not its very extinction. In this sense, Acosta adopts the same interracial and intersubjective strategy Valdez deploys in *Vietnam Campesino*, for his text conceptualizes Vietnamese soldiers and peasants, and Chicana/o families and activists, "as the same."

To bring the metaphor of racial conflation to bear, the flattening of intersubjective difference also operates to conflate the spatial differences between distinct global geographies. In this instance, Brown conceptualizes a Mexican American subdivision of Los Angeles, Toomer Flats, *as* My Lai: a small village in South Vietnam where US forces massacred approximately five hundred unarmed civilians in 1968—mainly women, children, and the elderly—and then covered it up.[34] Unequivocally, Brown's motivational speech in an East Los Angeles park compresses Vietnamese and Chicana/o identities; then it conflates a Chicana/o barrio where residents accuse the Los Angeles Police Department of murder with a small Vietnamese village where the US military has slaughtered hundreds of noncombatant civilians. Rhetorically, this gesture fashions a militant Chicana/o political attitude while also calibrating violence in Los Angeles as a local inflection of the bloodshed in Asia. Yet this conflation of local and third-world space not only culminates in a militant form of political resistance that the novel's hero adopts as the narrative progresses; it also galvanizes and ensures the cohesion of a Chicana/o political body in the future, one which, the novel tells us, amasses in the tens of thousands of animated protesters one year later.

While Brown's rhetorical gestures of racial and spatial conflation prove effective in unifying Chicana/o protesters into an organized and massive presence, they also generate a set of troublesome contradictions. Deconstructing racial and national differences through an act of third-world racial and spatial fusion, Brown simultaneously articulates the need for a distinct and differential nation-state, one exclusively for Chicana/os, with "our own land . . . our own government . . . our own flag and our own country." This nation-state, the text makes clear, is Aztlán, deployed in this instance to signify not only the ancestral homelands of Aztec Indians, but also the *future* nation-state of Chicana/os. In this regard, the text encodes the experiences of the Chicana/o protestors within the time-space of Vietnamese freedom fighters struggling for national freedom in Southeast Asia. Yet it also generates its ideological force by articulating the need for a distinct nation in the US West, one which seemingly excludes the Asian figures that rejuvenate the Chicana/o protestor's political will—and which, the text tells us, Chicana/os have in effect become.

To be sure, Brown's nationalist sentiments consider his community's disenfranchisements transnationally and cross-racially—between Asia, Asians, the US West, and Chicana/os—thereby constructing a conceptual cultural-political geography one might call "Southwest Asia." As an analytic term that considers the transpacific and interracial discourses of Chicana/o texts, which conflate local territories with those across the Pacific, "Southwest Asia" speaks to the imaginary topographies of culture that enable the emergence of new types of Chicana/o identities and that construct powerful political ideas beyond the national. Still, this transnational and interracial conceptual territory is unmistakably transitory, marked by a shift in narrative focus toward both local political redress and the ethnically specific needs of a future Chicana/o nation-state. Indeed, Acosta's text, like Valdez's, moves quickly from a circumpacific political sensibility toward the articulation of Chicana/o nationalism proper, which often served, in the words of Abelardo Delgado, as a "prerequisite to assert our proper roles in our communities . . . [to implicate] those who stole the lands that belonged to our abuelos . . . [and] to nationalize the second largest minority in the United States."[35] In other words, Brown's transnational and interracial cultural geography inevitably takes a nationalist form so as not to dilute its political emphasis on the issues plaguing Chicana/o communities of the 1970s, including those expressed in Chicana/o narratives that imagine the formation of a Chicana/o nation-state in the future.

In this regard, the narrative progression in *Revolt* represents a common process of coming into political being for Chicana/os in the 1960s and 1970s. This sequence is marked by the affirmation of a distinct national, cultural, and political identity, one that, as Frantz Fanon notes in a similar context, "shrinks away from that Western culture in which [subaltern groups] risk being swamped."[36] Yet this process of nationalization, Valdez's and Acosta's narratives teach us, also entails transformative instances of imagining the community's proximity to the suffering of Vietnamese subjects, and of enacting political ideas that extend well beyond the nation. Recalling the words of Chicano poet Alurista, *Vietnam Campesino* and *Revolt* both illuminate how the American War in Vietnam "establishes the conditions for Chicana/o literary production and its [political and aesthetic] processes of poetic signification."[37] Both Valdez's and Acosta's narratives articulate an emergent Chicana/o identity by addressing global threats of injustice committed by the US government in Vietnam, yet they conclude with a fervent commitment to social change by imagining a nationalist homeland that is largely underwritten by local and indigenous values. In other words, these texts articulate nationalist sensibilities by routing Chicana/o political enthusiasm back to the precolonial era represented by Aztlán, while simultaneously moving through the contemporary violence in Southeast Asia. As such, these works demonstrate how Chicana/o cultural nationalist politics, like other nationalist movements that "relentlessly determine to renew contact once more with the oldest and most pre-colonial springs of life of their people,"[38] entail an imaginary project of conceptualizing fleeting, albeit powerful, associative constructions across the Pacific for the purpose of articulating a future political community. Indeed, Valdez's and Acosta's projections of Aztlán cannot be disassociated from their transnational political elements that speak to the injustices of the American War in Vietnam, for their narrative emphasis on the global operates as a critical means for focalizing the community's oppositional attitudes on the local.

For this reason, the lack of narrative weight dedicated to exploring the historical details of the American War in Vietnam and to fleshing out the ethnic particularities of the Asian subjects—who both Valdez's farmworkers and Acosta's protestors have momentarily "become"—is telling. The instances that imagine equivalences between Chicana/os and Asians in *Vietnam Campesino* and *Revolt* may appear isolated, yet when taken together, they begin to reveal a consistent pattern of transformative Asian influence in terms of the political—and of Asian textual marginalization in terms of the literary. This suggests that the flat, transitory, and even singular instances of territorial and interracial equivalences in Chicana/o narratives are not unimportant. Instead, *their very singularity and consistent marginality speak to their narrative and cultural significance.*

These representational qualities are the symbolic consequences of a larger political attitude in Chicana/o communities, one that communicates its global political interests, on the one hand, and articulates the urgency of mobilizing local ideas, on the other. As a result of its marginal representation, the influence of Asia and Asians on Chicana/o culture is difficult to determine within the representative architecture of any single text. However, looked at collectively, *Pocho*, *Vietnam Campesino*, and *Revolt* reveal a structural repetition in Chicana/o narratives, one that assesses the impact of Asia on Chicana/o political sensibilities before and after the American War in Vietnam, and across disparate regions in the US West, which many

Chicana/o communities call home. These important texts' narrative gestures, which equate Chicana/os, Asians, the US West, and Asia, thus stand as significant cross-racial and transnational elements that reveal how the politics of Chicana/o culture are overdetermined beyond a brown/white dyad and outside of the American hemisphere.[39] Indeed, they point to how Chicana/o cultural forms imagine and describe the interrelated social and political worlds artists recognized locally, in the US Southwest, and globally, in Asia's relationship to the West.

To be sure, the transnational geographies of these texts stand as evidence of their global political value; in many instances, they make possible the articulation of a host of local social ills in Chicana/o communities, including labor exploitation, poverty, racial and cultural discrimination, educational imbalances, and more. These themes constitute the oppositional foundation of many landmark texts of the Chicana/o literary renaissance of the 1960s and 1970s. Among these is Miguel Méndez's groundbreaking novel *Pilgrims in Aztlán* (1974), a text that offers yet another example of how Chicana/o narratives script transpacific equivalences to articulate local political ideas.

Pilgrims in Aztlán

As a non-expository narrative, *Pilgrims* does not give a historical realist account of Chicana/o life in the US-Mexico borderlands, as do many of its contemporaries. Instead, it provides life impressions by navigating the deep physiological recesses of its individual characters, similar in style to Tomás Rivera's unforgettable *Y no se lo tragó la tierra* (1971), a text that also forfeits modes of linear plot progression.[40] To this point, Méndez's narrative announces in its opening pages that "The complicated need to arrange memories in chronological order was now of no use [to Loreto Maldonado, the novel's protagonist]" (3). Despite the text's temporal ambiguities and the ways a host of Chicana/o figures take turns occupying the narrative's focus, Loreto emerges as its organizing consciousness, bearing witness to, and meditating on, the testimony of others from across seventy years of borderlands history.

Moving sporadically between the eras of the Mexican Revolution (1910–1920) and the early 1970s, the narrative thus confounds common conceptions of temporal and spatial experiences. Indeed, the past is no longer the past, nor is history an ossified category with no direct bearing on the day-to-day lives of contemporary borderlands inhabitants. As such, *Pilgrims* constructs a narrative space that José Pablo Villalobos calls "transgeographic," for its settings fluctuate across seven decades of history and between both sides of the US-Mexico border.[41] These settings include the regions between San Ysidro/Tijuana, Yuma/San Luis, Mexicali/Imperial Valley, and Tucson/Nogales. Collectively, these individual landscapes, which dot different points along the US-Mexico border, constitute a broad cultural topography on which to tell the narrative's memorable stories of "twice-exiled pachucos at home on neither side of the border."[42]

According to Mary Vásquez, it is this overlaying of US and Mexican territories that collectively "constitute[s] the novel's primary narrative space" and makes possible the communication of its primary thematic concern: Chicana/o alienation. Loreto functions unmistakably as the organizing figure in this transgeographic narrative universe; it is he who gives the Chicana/o characters who live here a sense of community. Having lived through the Mexican Revolution and the contemporary era of Chicana/o politics, Loreto bears witness to a fragmented borderlands history constituted by various social actors and conflicting political ideologies with a temporally and geographically dilated perspective, and in doing so, he serves as the character in which disparate times, spaces, and experiences in the novel coalesce. In this manner, Loreto serves as a figural image of what Mikhail Bakhtin calls a "chronotope," for his meditations between the past and present at the US-Mexico border unmistakably construct the narrative's "connectedness of temporal and spatial relationships."[43]

The most prominent temporal and spatial "connectedness" that coalesces in the text is undeniably the geographical region between Arizona, USA, and Sonora, Mexico. However, this may not be the most impressive fusion of geographical spaces in the text. Although hardly regarded by its generations of critics, the novel's inclusion of Vietnam in the borderlands geography it imagines powerfully communicates the anterior and posterior pain of Chicana/os and their ancestors, a transtemporal theme at the heart of the larger narrative itself. Villalobos argues that the novel's construction of narrative space recovers and communicates the anguish of border-dwellers from historical invisibility.[44] Should this be the case, then the narrative's doubling of the US-Mexico border regions and the Vietnamese jungle makes plain how the suffering of contemporary Chicana/os fighting in Southeast Asia is related to the historical pain of their ancestors who have lived on both sides of the border, including Loreto Maldonado.

This intergenerational and transtemporal suffering is best demonstrated by the figure of Frankie Perez, a Chicano youth who literally stumbles into the novel drunk and despairing on the eve of his departure to Vietnam. It is there, over seven thousand miles from home, that his fellow American soldiers (and I would include a generation of literary critics) forsake his "bones in the middle of the jungle" (143). Before Frankie leaves for war, however, the text imagines this Chicano youth sitting with Loreto in a curious moment of intersubjective reflection. It is during this tender moment that the text recalls the suffering of Frankie's childhood, including the "slavery" (139) he and his family endured as agricultural laborers. Méndez writes:

> His childhood in the sight of the symmetry of the fields, where he had stood deep in thought so many times, channeling the nostalgia of mysterious epochs that he only intuited beyond the wall of lettuce and the bitter beds of the cotton fields that stretched out like vast shrouds. The cursed vineyards that imprison with their tentacles. And that oven! The infernal oven that squeezed streams of sweat from them, sweat that coated the watermelons and cantaloupes, while they, the Chicanos, became dried out like leftover cane stalks. His tragic joy of an undernourished child had only recently been alleviated, living in the filth imposed by poverty, breathing a humid, living breath that drew its greenness from the plants that grew vigorously, growing like soldiers. Now he moved his arms in the jungle of bitterness, when his perspective as a dreamy child had been so different. (140)

Here the narrative analepsis, or flashback, regards Frankie's youth as a child laborer. In doing so, it articulates his insufferable past and hints at his tragic future in Vietnam, both collapsed briefly in an ossified moment of transtemporal contemplation. Frankie's meditation on his lifelong suffering characterizes what Méndez identifies as the ways his writing emanates "emphatically from the pain of a powerless person, from the humiliation and humility that exists on both sides of the border."[45] However, Frankie's meditations do not relate economic realities of farmworker life simply by collapsing geographical spaces on both sides of the US-Mexico border; for his introspective deliberations of the past also generate meditations on his tragic future in Asia. Indeed, the "humid jungle of bitterness" that is the farm where Frankie slaved as a child ultimately mutates into the muggy wilderness of Vietnam, where he dies "as a cell of the gringo army" (139).

Situated between his own dreadful past and his unlived tragic future, Frankie occupies a nebulous timespace in which the narrative articulates its oppositional politics across two hemispheres. This temporal and spatial maneuver ultimately allows Loreto, once a soldier and idealist of the Mexican Revolution, to voice his own contemporary political values, including his opposition to the labor injustices suffered by Mexican Americans like Frankie, and a fervent protest of the unjust colonial war in Vietnam. The palimpsest of images surrounding these issues, moving between the agricultural fields in which Frankie lost his childhood, and the Asian jungle in which he eventually loses his life, thereby conditions a third timespace in which Loreto articulates his own experiences as a young soldier fighting in the Mexican Revolution. Ultimately, these three distinct timescapes fuse into one; when he speaks to his own historical pain, *Loreto eventually becomes an image of Frankie*, both having become a reflection of each other's suffering as poor soldiers.

In this way, the transnational and transtemporal space Frankie negotiates between the United States and Vietnam links the complaints of contemporary Chicana/os to those of an earlier generation, all of which reveal a painful history of a minority group that has been exploited during times of war. The narrative marks this moment of geographical and intersubjective flattening in a memorable scene:

> Frankie sat down trying to remember the place [of his childhood, the humid landscape which is also the place of the war he has yet to experience]. The crippled Indian [Loreto] continued for several seconds in the *same position. He had lived a similar scene far away, very far away, as far back as his youth.* He sat down at the cement wall contemplating the Chicano and the past. All avenues of his life had led to sadness. Suddenly, his tired heart began to pound like a train full of revolutionaries. . . . Memories that frantically tore away the yellowish webs of oblivion, in shreds, hacked away with a machete blade, the loud voices and the fever, the fever and the cannon shots that assaulted your eardrums. (142, my emphasis)

The palimpsest of images regarding two wars and two hemispheres conditions the occasion for the text to reveal small details of Loreto's war experiences as a Yaqui Indian in Mexico, including the suicidal mission that cost him his leg and left him with a wooden peg in its place. In this instance, Loreto's historical pain, Frankie's childhood suffering, and the latter's future anguish in Vietnam become anchored in the present, for in Loreto's mind, "The shouts [and] men blown to smithereens [in both the Revolutionary War and in the American War in Vietnam]" become "fixed in blinding flashes" (142), while Frankie bears witness to "the horrendous slaughter of bombardments, thousands of children, women and old people burning like coals, impregnated with napalm, and screaming horribly" (151). Fusing the violence of two separate wars in two distinct hemispheres, the narrative makes clear that Frankie has inherited the suffering of Loreto, who is now his narrative double from a "similar scene far away, very far away."

A few critics of *Pilgrims* who have examined this instance of narrative doubling of identity and space have confused the force of this formalist gesture. For example, Charles Olstad mistakenly notes that *Frankie Perez* "returned from Vietnam minus a leg," when upon close examination, it is apparent that Loreto is the only veteran between the two who returns from war missing a limb.[46] What is not confusing, however, is that this narrative loop around the violence of the American War in Vietnam and the Mexican Revolution—coupled with the narrative doubling between Frankie and Loreto—both generate an intergenerational and circumpacific history of Chicana/o pain.

This anguish, however, crosses not only crosses temporal and geographical borders, but also racial boundaries, when Frankie establishes powerful sympathies with the Asian soldiers who shoot him down. At the moment of his future mortality, the narrative once again flattens the spaces between the US-Mexico border and the jungles of Vietnam to explore the details of Frankie's death. To be sure, the inclusion of Frankie's narrative about Chicano soldiering in Vietnam not only signals the novel's antiwar critique, but it also generates a fleeting yet intense instance of interracial recognition between Frankie and the Asian soldiers who capture and kill him.

To be sure, the narrative's antiwar message initially emerges through its tone, which describes sarcastically "noble" and "honored" US politicians who, in their mandate to send young Chicanos to Vietnam, "could not take up arms themselves" or send their own sons to fight in this war (146–147). However, the full force of the novel's oppositional values is generated from the aesthetic processes of constructing interracial semblances and interethnic political sensibilities between Frankie and the Vietnamese who end his life. To bring this point to bear, the novel tells us in the final pages of Frankie's narrative that "his intimate suffering, which no longer fit his soul, was now the suffering . . . of his friends among his people, the Chicanos, even of his [Vietnamese] executioners" (152). Having recognized his anguish and misery as that of Loreto and other Chicana/os, Frankie now senses his suffering relative to the Vietnamese, whom he once imagined as the enemy, "stupid" and "short on smarts" (147). At this critical juncture, Frankie not only senses that he has inherited the anguish and wretchedness of poor Indians and Mexicans like Loreto, but also he recognizes that his sorrows are not unrelated to the decades-long suffering of the Vietnamese peasant fighting European and US colonial aggressions thousands of miles away. Indeed, Frankie comes to know that his childhood misery is but an expression of both Loreto's historical pain as a Mexican Indian *and* of the suffering of the Asian figures against whom he must wage war in the future.

In this way, Frankie's cross-temporal and cross-racial anguish speaks to the common suffering between Chicana/os and Vietnamese, and it configures in no ambiguous terms the narrative's protest against the American War in Vietnam. The text makes this a point of emphasis on the final pages of Frankie's appearance in the narrative, which imagine the exact moment of his future death. In this instance, the text describes cryptically Frankie's final cry of misery in a Vietnamese jungle.

> Poor suffering Frankie Perez. Standing on the place on the earth that has existed for millions of years, exactly at the instant of an opprobrious death whose scream of pain joins the echo of the massacre. Frankie was enthralled looking at the moon. When he sought in the moon a reason for his anguish, a cosmic giant, armed with an enormous club, came along and struck it with such violence that the moon cracked as it bounced. Ah! Poor little moon. Foaming cracks gave off fountains that covered its once luminous face. The moon, its face covered, grew dim from its suffering. A dark cosmos began to swallow it up. It fell. . . . Until the final little light . . . went out! Then it sank into the red water borne by the cursed riverbeds. Frankie called out, Mommy, Daddy, but his shouts turned to marble. He was unable to bear the jungle which cried all night long . . . as though wanting in a single night to denounce all human injustice. How the rivers moaned, how the roots of the plants writhed in pain, with what suffering the wounded beasts roared over the death of their offspring, with how much terror the little birds looked at the skies flashing with blood and fire. The winds that travelled from the past, from every direction and era, how disconsolately they cried. The very beasts in their instincts seemed to understand in their startled panic that the earth was inhabited by a being that was all cruelty and viciousness. (152)

In this instance, Frankie's interracial sensibilities that link his lifelong suffering to the pain of the Vietnamese who kill him assume a transpacific scope, one that includes not just "his [Asian] executioners," but also the Vietnamese landscape itself. Within the "living thicket" of the jungle, Frankie envisages his death through an image of a moon cracked by the club of a cosmic giant and drowning under fountains of its own blood, until its luminous face slowly but inevitably expires. This scene of cosmic chaos, which Frankie imagines, explodes above a screaming Asian jungle writhing in pain, where napalm and fire bombs torch plants and animals alike, until the blood-red sky burns and its winds cry inconsolably. Vividly staged, Frankie's suffering is now not only intersubjective (experienced between himself, Loreto, and Vietnamese soldiers). It is also anthropomorphic, for he experiences both the pain of his decimated body and the destruction of the southeastern Asian jungle, which is itself screaming in misery. His final shouts of protest and pain then solidify in the dead space that remains; unheard, "they turn to marble," hardened and unrequited in a world "that was all cruelty and viciousness" (152).

And so Frankie's exit from the narrative is made inevitable. He is left to cry helplessly in the jungles of Southeast Asia, alone until the finality of his death. His brief narrative thus begins with a warm embrace with Loreto, yet ends having traversed four distinct thresholds: one, the geographical space between the US-Mexico border and the Vietnamese jungle; two, the temporal space between his own past as a child laborer and his future death in Asia; three, intersubjective racial differences between himself and the Vietnamese against whom he must fight; and four, differences between his own wrecked body and the devastation of an Asian ecology. As such, it is a mistake to characterize this critical gesture of temporal, topographical, and intersubjective flattening as a means to articulate clean parallels between the US Southwest and Vietnam. Indeed, the transnational geography the text constructs serves as an oppositional critique slightly more nuanced than Acosta's and Valdez's claims that the US West is the "same" as Vietnam. Although *Pilgrims* imagines the relationship between local environments and US structures of power in Asia, its political topography instead articulates the complex tensions between the United States, Mexico, and Asia as they begin to take shape across various Chicana/o communities—in the past, the present, and their projected futures.

This critical tension between the past and present, and between the United States, Mexico, and Asia, begins and ends, curiously enough, with Loreto hugging Frankie warmly. Recalling Loreto's early embrace of Frankie before his departure to Vietnam, it becomes clear then that this moment of consolation anachronistically marks a "symbolic wake over the [forgotten] body" of this young Chicano, for "nine months later, when he fell in Vietnam, no one accompanied his lifeless body [home].... A party of his American soldiers removed the metal tags with his identification number when all that was left of him were bones in the middle of the jungle" (143). Loreto leaves a severed leg on the battlefield at the US-Mexico border during the Mexican Revolution; Frankie's party of American soldiers leaves the shattered bones of their Chicano comrade in the devastated Vietnamese jungle six decades later. Indeed, the narrative confirms that Loreto's early embrace of Frankie made the former understand that "he was symbolically praying for Frankie and his posthumous honors" (149).

That Frankie's body remains in Vietnam where it falls dead finalizes the narrative's damning antiwar critique. Still, his forgotten bones communicate yet another significant cultural message: they mark the trace of a largely forgotten relationship between a generation of Chicana/o youth that comes of political age by protesting the American War in Vietnam, as well as the intersubjective sympathies they often imagined between their own communities and Vietnamese populations from half a world away. That the narrative abruptly ends Frankie's story as it proceeds to explore figures that critics have identified as more worthy of literary critique, contributes to the forgetting of the Chicana/o's circumpacific and interracial sensibilities. Yet the narrative seems to anticipate the forgetting of Asia and Asians in literary critiques of this novel, and of Chicana/o culture generally, by bringing Frankie's spectral qualities to bear. Indeed, in the final pages of Frankie's story, the narrative imagines him as an ethereal and ghostlike figure whose body his fellow soldiers—like Chicana/o literary critics generally—have abandoned in Vietnam, where "all that was left of him were bones in the middle of the jungle."

Vietnam Campesino, *Revolt*, and *Pilgrims* each creates a palimpsest of images between the US-Mexico border and Asia to articulate the social ills plaguing Mexican American life, thereby constructing complex political values that crisscross the Pacific Rim. These transnational features illustrate how the ethnic focus of Chicana/o culture often materializes in the contexts of multiracial and global political interests. To be sure, this "transversalism"—to borrow the term Françoise Lionnet and Shu-Mei Shih coin to capture the movements of cultural identity between global spaces— "produces new forms of identification that negotiate with national, ethnic, and cultural boundaries [that allow] for the emergence of the minor's inherent complexity and multiplicity."[47] Moreover, the cross-racial equivalences and transpacific spaces in *Vietnam Campesino*, *Revolt*, and *Pilgrims* challenge the very ethnic and nationalist boundaries each text conceptualizes in order to comment on the material conditions of the US-Mexico border. Indeed, these transnational narrative elements bear the trace—like the bones of Frankie Perez's forgotten body in Vietnam—of a complex cultural imagination, which, even its nationalist modality, regularly negotiates issues of local injustice interracially and on a global scale.

2

Forging and Forgetting Transpacific Identities in Américo Paredes's "Ichiro Kikuchi" and Rolando Hinojosa's *Korean Love Songs*

> Each of us in some way has been both the oppressed and the oppressor.
> —Cherríe Moraga, *Loving in the War Years*

Inspired by Ernest Renan, Benedict Anderson has famously argued that in order to fashion a sense of national identity, a community must engage in cultural processes of forgetting to engender a "deep, horizontal comradeship" among its constituents.[1] Chon Noriega concurs. He reminds us in a Chicana/o context that this ethnic group can only imagine itself as part of the US national fabric by forgetting the historical pain of the Alamo, for example, at the precise moment in which passionate declarations to "remember the Alamo" reverberate resoundingly in historical constructions of the US-Mexico border.[2] In other words, for the Chicana/os to imagine themselves as full-fledged members of the US national community, they must *forget* the Alamo, including the historical pain of the Texas Revolution, the US annexation of the Republic of Texas, and the more than one hundred years of segregation in Texas that ensued.

To this point, Chon Noriega notes that structures of Chicana/o memory function similarly to those of dominant sectors of Anglo America that have produced standardized histories of the nation. For example, he rightly notes that the nationalist formation of Aztlán is characterized by significant contradictions that rely heavily on cultural discourses which must overlook the past in order to legitimize various, and even incongruous, struggles as they take shape in different political contexts. Daniel Alarcón makes a similar point, arguing that Chicana/o political struggles enable, and often require, an ideologically charged historical memory to address material problems of race, class, and gender. For this reason, he notes that Chicana/o artists and political leaders have deployed the term *Aztlán* to forget and to obscure important issues surrounding Chicana/o identity, "in particular the significance of intracultural differences."[3]

With a significant degree of influence, Chicana/o literary forms have undeniably participated in this community's cultural process of obscuring intraethnic differences, especially during the nationalist era of the 1960s and 1970s. Literature of this period reveals how the cultural processes of eliding difference operate according to complex and oftentimes contradictory constructions of an imagined ethnic community, one whose political and cultural values are regularly communicated by reductive nationalist ideals. At the same time, however, Chicana/o literature has worked to elucidate and embrace distinctions in order to imagine its communities as broad and socially *inclusive* with respect to issues of race, class, and gender, especially during the postnationalist phase of the 1980s. In other words, Chicana/o literature is a *primary* site for expressing inclusions within, and social exclusions from, this ethnic community, including how it imagines its shifting racial and cultural boundaries.

To be sure, the contradictions of community that Chicana/o culture has imagined—as simultaneously inclusive and exclusive, and concurrently both assimilative and oppositional—manifest themselves repeatedly during historical moments of stark political upheaval. As noted in the previous chapter, the American War in Vietnam, for example, produced powerful transnational political attitudes at the same time that it generated intense nationalist values in Chicana/o culture. Chapter 1 has shown that this moment of striking community cohesion and oppositional political advocacy corresponds to a culture that regularly embraced images of Vietnamese revolutionaries while also imagining cross-racial equivalences. Indeed, the Asian others that appear regularly in the margins of foundational texts of Chicana/o literature raise important questions regarding this culture's processes of eliding and forgetting racial distinctions when imagining a national community within interracial and global political contexts. Moreover, these representations of racial difference elicit important queries regarding Asian others in Chicana/o culture's rich literary past, for the American War in Vietnam is certainly not the first instance in which this community imagined its political identities transnationally in the context of a US-Asian conflict.

For example, after the Japanese bombed Pearl Harbor in 1941, many Mexican Americans experienced a radical shift in how they imagined their communities. Yet as Richard Griswold del Castillo notes, many did so by *not* considering their alignments with enemies of the United States. Although certainly not without dissenting voices, large numbers of Mexican Americans instead imagined themselves as common and dedicated members of the US national fabric, *despite* their lived experiences of legal segregation, endemic poverty, and political disenfranchisement.[4] This renewed sense of national allegiance had a significant impact on this community's historical constructions of political and social identity, particularly for its US servicemen and women (see figure 5). In this context, Griswold del Castillo notes that fighting in the Second World War presented Mexican Americans with a range of "opportunities for mobility and economic advancement," allowing many veterans to imagine their US inclusion by "improv[ing] their lives" financially and socially.[5] According to del Castillo,

Fig. 5. Family photo of author's grandfather, Private Samuel G. Gonzales of New Mexico. This photo was taken on January 30, 1947, in Tokyo, during the US occupation of Japan. In his hands, Private Gonzales holds a painting of the author's grandmother, Emma Gonzales (later Emma Eres), on a silk scarf. The scarf is signed by artist "Kozo, Tsuda" of Tokyo. Private Gonzales labored in the mines of New Mexico before enlisting in the US Army; he was a tank driver during the war years. For his service, he earned the World War II Victory Medal and Army Occupation Medal, Japan. According to my grandmother, he and his friends served proudly; during her life, it was clear that she was very proud of him.

World War II generated the opportunity for Mexican Americans to better their lives broadly, but most importantly, it conditioned the occasion for them to imagine their full-fledged inclusion in the nation's social and political fabric.

The numbers of Mexican Americans who accepted their conscription into the US armed forces during the Second World War speak to their internalization of US nationalism generally, which, in the words of Benedict Anderson, "makes it possible . . . for so many millions of people, not so much to kill, as willingly to die for such limited imaginings."[6] Rudolfo Acuña estimates that as many as 500,000 Mexican Americans participated in World War II.[7] Maggie Rivas-Rodriguez considers this a modest figure, estimating that as many as 750,000 Mexican Americans served in the US war effort both domestically and abroad.[8] It may be impossible to pin down the exact number of Mexican American servicemen and women.[9] But what is certain is that large numbers of Mexican Americans participated in World War II, with many having *volunteered* for service after the Japanese attack on Hawaii.[10]

Many did so despite their civilian experiences as second-class citizens. Michael Gambone notes that at the onset of the war, Mexican Americans occupied the lowest rungs of regional socioeconomic ladders in the US West and Southwest, with a median income that reached just over half that of whites.[11] For example, Gambone argues that in Texas, a state from which tens of thousands of Mexican American servicemen enlisted voluntarily or were conscripted in the draft, as many as 47 percent of their children received no schooling during the war years.[12] Mario García adds that severe educational injustices and school segregation policies directed at Mexican American children at the onset of the war ensured this community's ongoing poverty.[13] In the face of these widespread injustices, many Mexican American civilians and organizations such as the League of United Latin American Citizens embraced the occasion to demonstrate this community's patriotism, duty, and honor by serving in the US armed forces.[14] As such, military service presented the primary *opportunity* for Mexican American communities to imagine and to demonstrate themselves to be loyal citizens of the nation, despite widespread and systematic forms of their subjugation.

Looking back on the history of this community's commitments to armed service relative to its consistent experiences with democratic shortcomings, US senator Diane Feinstein recently noted that the country should "honor these brave Americans and their families. Indeed, Latinos are changing the way America looks at itself. . . . I commend the Latino community for its courage and persistence and want to warmly acknowledge the contributions and vitality this community brings to our nation."[15]

Mexican Americans' commitment to armed service during the World War II era demonstrates how members of this community imagined themselves as full-fledged members of the US nation-state by fighting willingly, and in great numbers, for democratic freedoms abroad—while eliding, if not forgetting entirely, many democratic deficiencies at home (see figure 6).

For this reason, Feinstein's declaration that Latina/o and Mexican American armed service has changed the way "America looks at itself" is only partially true. Instead, testimonies from a large number of World War II servicemen and women show how Mexican Americans often changed the ways *they looked at themselves* during the war era. Indeed, statements by service veterans on their commitments to the US nation-state reveal that many Mexican Americans did not imagine themselves as members of a distinct ethnic community, nor did they see themselves in the image of US enemies. Instead, their stories reveal that many imagined themselves as equal, if not common, members of US society. Raul Morin, a veteran and

Fig. 6. Photo of Veteran's Memorial Wall at Dona Ana County Memorial Park in Las Cruces, New Mexico. All veterans from Dona Ana County, including the author's grandfather, Narciso "Smokey" Eres, are represented with their names on bronze plaques that line the marble wall. Only sixteen years old when the United States entered the Second World War, Smokey volunteered for service and lied about his age in order to fight. He eventually committed to three tours in the US Army. The overwhelming number of Spanish surnames on the wall demonstrates the commitment of ethnic minorities to the US Armed Forces throughout many counties of the Southwest. Photo by the author.

historian of Mexican American distinctions in the field of battle, emphasizes this point in his early research on World War II servicemen. Speaking for himself and his friends, Morin states that "Most of us [Mexican Americans] were more than glad to be given the opportunity to serve in the war [after the bombing of Pearl Harbor]. It did not matter whether we were looked upon as Mexicans; the war soon made us all *genuine* Americans."[16] Morin notes that despite the US general public's tendency to view Mexican Americans as outsiders to the national community, soldiers often regarded themselves as legitimate members of the nation, and in the words of Benedict Anderson, served "willingly to die for such limited imaginings."

Publications of the VOCES Oral History Project at the University of Texas, spearheaded by Maggie Rivas-Rodriguez, echo Morin's sentiments. For example, interviews with José R. Zaragoza of Los Angeles, California, and Armando Flores of Corpus Christie, Texas, reveal that the Japanese attack on Pearl Harbor consolidated a firm sense of patriotism and national inclusion for these two soldiers and their respective communities. Zaragoza testifies that after the bombings at Pearl Harbor, "Everyone [in the neighborhood] was ready to go. . . . Everyone was patriotic."[17] In the same context, Armando Flores recalls in an interview with Roberto Suro that, as a soldier of the US armed services, he recognized himself as an "American," as did his army superiors. He states that, "I had been called a lot of things . . . wetback and spick, and greaser. . . . [My time in the armed services was the] first time in my life that I had been called an American."[18] Organizers of the VOCES Oral History Project conclude their examinations of this interview (and hundreds of others) by asserting that Mexican American soldiers and their families regularly generated a firm impression of national belonging during the war era across many impoverished communities that dotted the US-Mexico border. This feeling of inclusion was mobilized by a strong sense of national pride, despite Mexican Americans having had their democratic rights regularly denied in civic society or having experienced racial challenges while conscripted into the military ranks.[19]

For example, Ignacio Servín of Miami, Arizona, confirmed for himself this sense of national inclusion and patriotism by having imagined the United States as world exemplar of democratic freedom, in spite of having had worked as a field laborer as a small child and only having had the opportunity to finish the fourth grade as a result of discriminatory educational structures in his home state. After volunteering to crawl inside a tunnel-like cave to destroy Japanese munitions, an assignment that only one other soldier of his unit was willing to assume because of the extremely high risk of death, Servín testified that he understood well the risk, and that he completed the mission by telling himself: "If I die, it will be for a great country."[20]

This perception of US national inclusion crossed gender lines as well; and it often regenerated itself years later during the Korean War (1950–1953). For example, the late historian Ronald Takaki shares that Victoria Morales, a Mexican American war worker, testified that she had supported the war effort strongly, and that her generation "went proudly to war" because "the Japanese had attacked our country. I say 'our country' because I was born here."[21] For Joseph Alcoser of Melvin, Texas, the sense of national belonging began during the World War II era and then renewed itself during the US military conflict in Korea. According to Alcoser, these conflicts generated the conditions for entire Mexican American neighborhoods to envisage their inclusion in the US nation-state through the military service of their sons and daughters. After the Japanese attack on Pearl Harbor, Mr. Alcoser and his friends immediately volunteered for enlistment, and they did so again after war broke out in the Korean peninsula. On this matter, he shares that members of his community "had an obligation to defend *their* country."[22] Echoing the sentiments of many other veterans, Morales and Alcoser imagined themselves as full-standing members of the US national body during World War II and the Korean War. They did so by asserting their birthrights in the United States, claiming their custody over the protection of the nation, and oftentimes eliding personal experiences of their social marginalization.

Juxtaposed to these testimonies and interviews, writings by foundational Chicana/o writers on the US occupation of Japan and the Korean War complicate the ideologies that linked Mexican American identity to US nationalism during this period. For example, Américo Paredes's "Ichiro Kikuchi" and Rolando Hinojosa's *Korean Love Songs* instead represent early instances of the circumpacific and interracial conceptualizations of Chicana/o identity unpacked in the previous chapter of this book. Paredes's and Hinojosa's respective narratives examine how early wars in Asia conditioned alternative forms of self-identification for Mexican American servicemen, forms which counter the image of the patriotic solider who becomes fully woven into the US national fabric. As Mexican Americans fitted in the uniform of US power that exerts itself relentlessly in Asia and yet also oppresses them at home, the protagonists of these respective texts speak critically of their situation, generating what Homi Bhabha calls in a related context "jagged testimony [that] changes the direction of Western history."[23] Indeed, Paredes's and Hinojosa's texts both challenge the linearity of Mexican American narratives about this community's patriotic participation in early US wars in Asia, and they deconstruct national historiographies concerning Mexican Americans who fought to "sow the seeds of democracy in Japan" and to "curb the spread of communism in Korea."

In undoing the neat narrative of Mexican American participation in early US wars in Asia, Paredes's and Hinojosa's texts destabilize the totalizing image of a patriotic community eager to demonstrate its national commitments. In its place, these texts offer nothing less than highly stylized literary testimonies of a masculine "oppressed-oppressor": the Mexican American subject who, instead of imagining his idealized inclusion in the US nation-state during his military service, must perpetually negotiate the contradictions of race and power on both local and global scales. In these instances, the oppressed-oppressor is nothing short of the Mexican American who becomes an armed functionary of US power, one who considers deeply the stakes of risking his life in Asia and who remains critical of fighting on behalf of a nation that subjugates him at home. Caught between the contradictions of US state and ideological power, on the one hand, and embodying an irreconcilable combination of both the oppressed and the oppressor, on the other, the protagonists of Paredes's and Hinojosa's texts thus highlight how Chicana/o literature communicates, in an Asian context, the Mexican American's precarious position in the US national community decades *before* the American War in Vietnam.

Indeed, these texts contain some of the first images of a Mexican American who fashions his oppositional identity in Asia, all in what would become a long history of US involvement in Pacific Rim conflicts. To this point, Paredes's and Hinojosa's texts demonstrate an ideologically charged process of interracial and transnational thinking not marked by a protagonist who imagines itself as a "genuine" American soldier or by self-identifying strictly as a Mexican "other" excluded from the US democratic project. Instead, the processes of subject formation in these writings are characterized by a complex process of interpreting the self in the image of a projected Asian double, one whom the Mexican American encounters over seven thousand miles away from home.

"Ichiro Kikuchi"

Were it not for the fact that it predates the Chicana/o literary renaissance of the 1970s by more than two decades, critics might see in Américo Paredes's short story "Ichiro Kikuchi" an assessment of how cultural forms of the era often established and then ignored interethnic unions between Mexican Americans, Asians, and Asian Americans. Written between 1948 and 1949, but not published until 1994, "Ichiro Kikuchi" instead *anticipates* the ways elements of Chicana/o cultural nationalism would come to repress associations between Mexican Americans and Asians, and how Pacific Rim conflicts could shape a proto-Chicana/o's processes of seeing and knowing itself.

To begin the story, the eponymous Japanese Mexican hero addresses an unnamed Mexican American reader, one who he does not believe will accept as true his remarkable story of interracial recognition. Ichiro begins by outlining for his Mexican American counterpart his personal history: he was born in Cuernavaca to a Japanese father and Mexican mother; he immigrates with his family to Japan; he gets drafted into the Imperial Army after World War II breaks out in the Pacific; and he ultimately survives capture and an ordered execution at the hands of US armed forces. In the course of this action, Ichiro reveals that his Mexican mother baptized him "Juan Guadalupe" in honor of the spiritual mother-saint of Mexico, this to the dismay of his Japanese father who "was very angry when he found out" (151). On her insistence, Ichiro dons on his neck an emblem of the Lady of Guadalupe, a symbol that ultimately saves his life once the Mexican American soldier ordered to execute him recognizes it as a shared cultural icon.

The narrative's emphasis on Ichiro's face-to-face encounter with this Mexican American soldier shows that the impetus of Paredes's story is not to expose horrendous US and Japanese war crimes.[24] Instead, Paredes imagines in "Ichiro Kikuchi" nothing less than the development of Chicana/o political agency in a circumpacific context and relative to what proves to be an uncomfortable encounter with an Asian other. In the Philippines, in the most unlikely of landscapes, the fates of two young soldiers—one a Japanese Mexican, the other a Mexican American—collide, with the effect of constituting a preliminary step in the latter's political and social identity. After his company's capture while fighting in the Philippines, Ichiro says:

> We were taken as prisoners of a unit that had seen much fighting, from the looks of them. The man who was in command was talking to another, a sergeant. The sergeant was arguing, it appeared, but finally he saluted and came to where we were. *He looked familiar somehow.* He picked out a dozen of his own men, and they took us back some fifty meters toward their rear. . . . When we stopped, the Americans guarding us took their spades from their packs and dropped them on the ground in front of us. Then they moved back and made signs to us that we should pick them up. . . .
> We were ordered to dig a long, narrow trench. (155, my emphasis)

Caught in a war fueled by vicious racial abstractions and infused with strong nationalist sentiments promulgated by both the Japanese and American armed forces, Ichiro momentarily deconstructs the dehumanizing rhetoric of the enemy, for at the order to dig his grave, an unnamed American soldier "looked familiar somehow."[25] This cross-racial encounter provokes intense interracial recognition when the US sergeant reciprocates Ichiro's gaze after noticing an emblem of the Lady of Guadalupe hanging from the POW's neck. Paredes writes:

> The sergeant came up to me and shouted, "Hey, you! What is that you're wearing?"
>
> I looked up at him, and now that he was close to me I saw why he had looked so familiar. He was Mexican. *Like you. An American Mexican.* So I answered in Spanish, "A medallion. La Virgen de Guadalupe."
>
> "Put down that spade," he said, also in Spanish. "Get out of that hole and come with me."
>
> I was trembling as I climbed out of the hole, trembling and praying, giving thanks to La Guadalupana and to my mother, who had put the medallion around my neck when I was home for the last time.... The sergeant led me away, to the rear where I was put in a pen with some other prisoners....
>
> I heard somebody call the sergeant Melguizo, that's how I know his name. (156, my emphasis)

Ichiro's fluent Spanish and his religious medallion affirm his cultural multiplicity, underscoring for the Mexican American sergeant his own hybridity to the extent that he recognizes himself in the image of the Asian prisoner. As a result, the American soldier defies the immoral order of his Anglo superior and experiences a destabilization of the US ideologies that work to standardize American perceptions of the self and of the other he is commanded to murder. Although he spares only Ichiro and not his company, the US sergeant is forced to reconsider constructions of "ally" and "enemy" and to rethink his national identity. Ultimately, he succeeds in differentiating himself from the nation's discourses that seek to homogenize American self-perceptions, and the narrative marks this constitutive moment of identity formation by finally assigning this soldier a proper ethnic name: Melguizo.

Ichiro's biracial identity allows Melguizo to recognize the contradictions of his own life, deconstructing the binary oppositions between US American/Japanese and ally/enemy that structure ideologies of this war. Still, the contradictions of Mexican American life, magnified by its proximity to Asia and Asians, prove far too much for Melguizo to negotiate. Confronted by the reality of his racial and national differences—and having recognized himself in an Asian subject—Melguizo cannot imagine how to resolve the epistemological problem that arises when the signifiers "Mexican," "American," and "Japanese" can no longer represent how he recognizes himself or the other against whom he must take up arms. This symbolic insufficiency thus situates Melguizo in an epistemological no man's land, yet it also anticipates in an Asian context the political possibilities yet to take shape in the United States years later under the signifier "Chicana/o."

The narrative postpones this future promise formally through Melguizo's own textual marginalization, for he walks out of the story during the American occupation of Japan unaware of how to reconcile his powerful encounter with his Asian counterpart. Ichiro says of Melguizo:

"I didn't see him again in the Philippines. It was only recently that I met him at a street corner here in Tokyo.
"'¡Melguizo!' I said. 'Qué gusto de verte!' [It is great to see you!]
"*He stared at me.* 'I don't know who you are,' he said in English and walked away.
"It was the same man, I am not mistaken. *I wonder why he pretended not to know me.*" (156–157, my emphasis and translation)

Seeming to reduce him to an unverifiable presence, the narrative actually affirms Melguizo's Mexican American identity during his feigned moment of interethnic blindness, which his Asian opposite sees through ("It was the same man, I am not mistaken."). Uncomfortable with this cross-racial situation, Melguizo does not fail to recognize Ichiro's face so much as repress its significance; the narrative confirms this position by testifying that his encounter with Ichiro is one that "he does not want to know" (152).

Melguizo's final meeting with Ichiro brings to the surface an uneasy sense of Melguizo's own racial dilemmas within US social structures both at home and abroad, and his silence on the matter highlights the lack of a transnational political vocabulary at this point with which to address these problems in Chicana/o cultural history. To be sure, the image of an Asian other occasions a lasting, albeit uncomfortable, shift in Melguizo's emergent political identity. Yet by suppressing the moral good he demonstrates when saving Ichiro's life, Melguizo also reveals that this Asian image represents the racial limit to how he will come to remember his oppositional experiences of the war and the US occupation of Japan.

Certainly, Melguizo has legitimate reasons to suppress the transgressive interracial alliance he establishes with his Japanese counterpart. Because the risks are high, Melguizo cannot sustain his interracial allegiance to Ichiro. First, to acknowledge Ichiro in this final instance of the narrative is for Melguizo to concede to the vicious war crimes in which his company participated. Second, to confirm his relationship with Ichiro is to raise doubts about Melguizo's loyalty to the United States and, in doing so, draw dangerous attention to his "hyphenated" Mexican American identity. To this point, one must recall that President Theodore Roosevelt had warned the US public before the First World War that the "politico-racial hyphen is the badge and sign of moral treason."[26] For this reason, Roosevelt and other patriotic zealots interpreted US allegiance and identity using the slogan "100 percent Americanism." This ideology impacted domestic policy years later, during World War II, most notably in the case of the US government's incarceration of over one hundred thousand "hyphenated" Japanese Americans. In this context, Paredes's text raises serious questions concerning Anglo-Saxonism as the normative default of US identity. Moreover, it highlights the precarious position of Mexican American soldiers like Melguizo, who were living in a historical era underwritten by an ideology of racial absolutism that scripted soldiers and civilians alike as either 100 percent American or as the treasonous other.

For these reasons, Melguizo's encounter with Ichiro, in which he recognizes himself in the image of the Asian other, not only deconstructs ideologies of "100 percent Americanism," but also it raises questions regarding the racial limits for articulating Mexican American identity generally. Melguizo's rejection of Ichiro on the streets of Tokyo elides their history of interracial recognition, a story that distinguishes the latter from a "common" Japanese soldier and the former from a "genuine" American one. However, the formal arrangement of the story conveys that this transnational alliance, which transcends racial and national boundaries, is unsustainable for Melguizo, for his newfound Asian identity immediately threatens his status as a "genuine" American soldier, *as well as* the oppositional Chicana/o politics he represents in the future.

This issue is brought to bear most clearly through the story's character distribution, which establishes *Ichiro* as the primary narrative figure while reducing Melguizo to a marginal one. Indeed, Melguizo only appears in the story to save Ichiro's life before he exits the narrative, *having denied his own presence* in that very course of heroic action. Put another way, Melguizo is a "flat character" in the story whose oppositional political actions the narrative ultimately represses. This is not to suggest, as E. M. Forster reminds us, that excessively flat characters misrepresent life.[27] Paredes himself shares that the impetus of Ichiro's story is based on an actual experience of a friend.[28] Instead, the narrative's stylistic treatment of character, which privileges an Asian consciousness over the proto-Chicana/o's, represents a cultural strategy that is hardly viable for a community struggling to articulate Mexican American identities and to communicate day-to-day dilemmas of historical life at the US-Mexico border.

In this sense, the character system of the text, which relegates the proto-Chicano to a marginal position, impacts the story's referential stakes to the degree that the narrative is unable to explore the dominant themes that would come to characterize Chicana/o literature throughout the 1960s and 1970s. Juxtaposed to the ways the narrative rounds out Ichiro's uncommon family history, the text does not provide epistemic access to Melguizo's own transnational identity and personal story. Rather than privilege Melguizo's cultural past or imagine in detail the political and racial issues that would become dominant themes of Chicana/o literature during its renaissance years, Melguizo's encounter with Ichiro instead seems to speak to *postnationalist* critical fashions of engaging the Chicana/o's transnational affinities. Whereas landmark texts of the Chicana/o literary renaissance address ideological issues of cultural nationalism or articulate the racial struggles of quotidian life for Chicana/os locally, "Ichiro Kikuchi" does neither, opting instead to critique the interracial elisions of Chicana/o literary culture globally.

For this reason, the significance of the text's first-person autodiagetic narrator who delivers the story of intersubjective recognition between Ichiro and Melguizo cannot be overstated. As both narrator and character, Ichiro articulates his remarkably story, almost in epistolary fashion, by addressing, in the second person, "An American Mexican" "like you" (156). Comparing Paredes's voluminous body of literary works, one quickly notices this to be a convention rarely duplicated in his other prose narratives.[29] In this instance, the text's second-person appeal to "you" (designated as an anonymous Mexican American addressee) draws attention to Paredes's unique system of narration. In doing so, it establishes clearly the racial qualities of its characters and their function in the text's representative apparatus: Ichiro (Japanese-Mexican, narrator); "you" (Mexican American, addressee); Melguizo (Mexican American, minor character). Yet Ichiro's second-person appeal does more than establish the text's narrative structure and the function of its characters. It also breaks down the narrative's diagetic plane, or its "story-world." As such, the appeal makes the implied receiver of its final petition somewhat indistinct, for Ichiro's parting query directs itself both to the unnamed Mexican American addressee—*and to future Chicana/o readers and critics.*

If Melguizo symbolizes an early instance of a Chicano who identifies with an Asian subject, then Paredes's story not only challenges Mexican American testimonies that promote ideologies of "100 percent Americanism," but it also anticipates how powerful segments of the Chicana/o Movement would come to marginalize its interracial and transnational features during the 1970s. For this reason, Paredes's midcentury story of a proto-Chicano's refusal to acknowledge its Asian self-image, not to mention its own belated publication history, demarcates what racial associations and cultural products must be ignored for a nationalist consciousness to develop as it did during the height of the Chicana/o Movement.[30] In this sense, Ichiro's parting query, "I wonder why he pretended not to know me" (157), appeals not only to the narrative's anonymous addressee, but it is also directed to future scholars of Chicana/o letters, prefiguring by more than fifty years current critical efforts in investigating the multiracial encounters of the Chicana/o literary imagination and the rich transnational identity politics of Mexican American social relations.

Korean Love Songs

Published nearly three decades after "Ichiro Kikuchi," Rolando Hinojosa's *Korean Love Songs* (*KLS*, 1978) offers another image of how Chicana/o consciousness develops politically and ambivalently across national and racial differences in Asia. As the fifth installment of Hinojosa's famous Klail City Death Trip (KCDT) series, *KLS* recounts its central protagonist's experiences of the Korean War, thereby establishing a relationship between this conflict and race problems along the US-Mexico border. Indeed, to read *KLS* against earlier texts in the KCDT sequence, one notes how the series moves between two settings—the 1960s US-Mexico border and 1950s Korea—by exploring the protracted impact of this Asian war on Chicano soldiers and their families.[31] Although the formal features of the book are distinct from Paredes's signature poetic markers, this text about the United States' "forgotten war" in Asia similarly represents "jagged testimonies" that are oppositional to ideologies of absolute Americanism. In addition, this collection of narrative poems promises to theorize further the marginalization of Asian relations in Chicana/o literature, including their underexamined impact on this community's cultural consciousness.

KLS first critiques standardized ideologies of absolute Anglo-Americanism by establishing a semblance between Mexican Americans and Chinese in the poem "The Eighth Army at the Chongchon." Like *Pocho, Vietnam Campesino, Revolt, Pilgrims*, and "Ichiro Kukuchi," this narrative poem shows how images of Asia work counterintuitively to articulate an ideological epicenter for expressing Chicana/o political and cultural concerns. *KLS* illustrates this point when Rafa Buenrostro, the text's central protagonist, recalls how General Walton H. Walker had sought to animate army morale in the face of a relentless Chinese army. Given the numerical advantage the Chinese hold over Rafa's regiment, one already decimated by months of fighting, Walker undermines the spirit of his soldiers; and in doing so he also succeeds in confirming Mexican American differences within his ranks. Hinojosa writes:

> And those who survived
> Remember what he said:
> "We should not assume that (the)
> Chinese Communists are committed in force.
> After all, a lot of Mexicans live in Texas."

And that from the Eighth Army Commanding
Himself. It was touching.
And yet, the 219th
Creating history by protecting the world from Communism,

Brought up the rear, protected the guns, continued the mission,
And many of us there
Were reminded who we were
Thousands of miles from home. (11)

General Walker's comments represent a racialized attempt to boost the spirit of his unit by highlighting the Texas War of Independence, including the numerical disadvantage Texas soldiers faced during the decisive battle against the Mexican Army at the Alamo.[32] General Walker's logic, which I paraphrase here, is clear: "US soldiers in Texas, like US soldiers in Korea, were vastly outnumbered, yet they fought valiantly against all odds."

Despite his motives, General Walker's intentions are woefully misdirected, for they are infused with racial animosities that bring to the surface the uneasy history of Texas for Mexican Americans like Rafa and his friends. For them, General Walker's speech on Texas history conflates Mexicans and Mexican Americans ("A lot of Mexicans [still] live in Texas"), and then it conceptualizes how to regard these so-called foreign populations by equating them with the Chinese enemy before them.[33] General Walker's remarks on the supposed similarities between Chinese, Mexicans, and Mexican Americans thus highlight for Rafa and his friends their tenuous position as US citizens by reminding them of Texas annexation and by shuttling them back to the realities of racial discrimination in the places along the US-Mexico border that they call home. In other words, how General Walker fuses the historical and racial differences between Chinese, Mexicans, and Mexican Americans during the Korean War and the Texas Revolution generates a sense of sameness between these categories of people, while confirming a sense of difference between Mexican Americans and Anglos, despite their sharing a common uniform. Rafa brings this point to bear in the conclusion to this poem, when he testifies that after having witnessed General Walker's speech, he and his friends "Were again reminded who we were/Thousands of miles from home" (11).

The construction of racial similarity (Chinese and Mexicans) and difference (Mexican Americans and Anglos) reveals that this text's oppositional politics emerge not only through Rafa's signature sarcasm, but also through a series of racial, temporal, and geographical juxtapositions embedded in its paratactic architecture. Clearly, Rafa lacks sincerity when he responds to General Walker's speech with posture, saying, "It was touching . . . . / Creating history by protecting the world from Communism" (11). Still, the full force of *KLS*'s political critique is generated through the paratactic structure of its three dozen poems, many of which juxtapose in fragmented form a series of discontinuous images and storylines, often without a clear connection. This narrative architecture demands that readers consider deeply the connections between its casual representations of distinct geographies and the racial populations of the temporal spaces it places side-by-side. William Arce comments on this readerly effect of Hinojosa's paratactic prose in several texts of the KCDT series, including the novel *Rites and Witnesses* (1982). Juxtaposing the discontinuities of two fragmented plot lines—civilian life in Klail City and the military experiences of Mexican Americans fighting in Korea—this narrative, Arce argues, generates the story's primary political theme: "the gross ethnic injustice of sending young Chicano men to die in an imperialistic war while the white corporate structure . . . increases its wealth and power in Klail City."[34]

This novel's juxtapositions of its two time-spaces, the fragmented representation of its many events, and their seemingly random and recurring sequencing operate similarly, albeit less intensely, in *Korean Love Songs*. It articulates irregularly distinct experiences of Rafa's life between 1949 and 1952 to generate a coherent critique of the racial inequalities of Mexican American life at the US-Mexico border. Yet it does so, on more than one occasion, in a manner that emphasizes the racial flattening between Mexican Texans and Asians found in General Walker's failed motivational speech. In other words, the random sequencing of narrative events and the seemingly arbitrary appearance of the numerous storylines generate powerful instances that conflate Mexican American and Asian identities with the effect of bringing to bear the text's larger oppositional critique of Mexican American life in South Texas.

For example, in the poem "Nagoya Station," the narrative of *KLS* shifts from fragmented stories of Rafa's war injuries and recurring news of the horrific deaths of his friends to the story of his visit to Colonel David "Sonny" Ruiz. This poem reveals that Sonny has shed his US ethnic identity and has secretively assumed a Japanese one in order to abandon a hellish life in the US Army along the deadly frontlines in Korea. By the same act, he also has foreclosed his imminent return to the oppressive conditions of the fictional Klail City, located in Lower Rio Grande Valley. Since this action occurs in key passages of the poem, I cite it at length:

> It's eight forty, and the Tanaka Tea Gardens, a mile off,
> Is where I'm to meet Sonny Ruiz,
> Who these many months,
> Has been AWOL (and reported missing sometimes, and dead at others).
> They'll never find him; to begin with,
> To Americans he looks Japanese; For another,
> No one really gives a damn, one way or another. The Army,
> For all its pretense,

Is not led by divine guidance.

Sonny of the *old*, old 219th and twice wounded, made corporal and
   stopped;
One day he filled out and signed his own Missing-In-Action cards,
Just like so much equipment;
He personally turned them over to battery HQ,
Then simply walked away to the docks.

Army efficiency being what it is immediately produced a replace-
   ment . . .
Not long after, cards started to arrive from Nagoya and signed
By Mr. Kazuo Fusaro who, in another life,
Had lived as David Ruiz in Klail City,
And who, in his new life,
Was now a hundred and ten per cent Japanese.
There he is, punctual as death; Business suit, hat, arms at his side,
And as I approach, he fills the air with konnichi wahs,
As he bends lower and lower, arms still at his side, smiling the while.

He and I are the only ones left:
   Charlie Villalón, Joey Vielma, Cayo Díaz,
   And a kid named Balderas
Have all been erased from the Oriental scene . . .

Business is fine, and he is marrying later in the fall;
A schoolteacher, no less.

And home?

"*This* is home, Rafe. Why should I go back?"
He has me there. Why, indeed? (43–44)

Sonny's narrative about a Chicano soldier gone AWOL shows how he and Rafa consider home at the Lower Rio Grande Valley according to shifting Mexican American and Asian identities on a transnational scale. Sonny deserts the US Army and becomes "one hundred and ten per cent Japanese," romantically assuming an Asian self without conflict and assimilating seamlessly into Japanese society. The narrative's mathematical rhetoric that impossibly quantifies Sonny's new ethnic makeup unmistakably parodies President Roosevelt's idioms of "100 percent Americanism." Yet this portrait of an American turned "one hundred and ten per cent Japanese" does not represent a utopian image of racial transformation as much as it spotlights a historical crisis between North Korea and South Korea as the means to highlight the realities of social injustice along another national divide: the US-Mexico border. Sonny's query to Rafa ("Why should I go back?") and the latter's response ("He has me there. Why, indeed?") call attention to standing racial inequities in South Texas. In this manner, Hinojosa fires a political critique of Anglo-Mexican relations far from the actual narrative events of the poem. While the action in *KLS* takes place exclusively throughout Asia, the text's exploration of Mexican American war experiences in Korea and of Mexican American–Asian encounters in Japan both show how race relations of a particular time and place function in the political assessment of race relations in another.

Unfortunately, Sonny's escape from life at the US-Mexico border requires that he deny his Mexican American identity in order to enjoy the rights of national citizenship in Japan, which confers benefits he cannot secure as a member of a minority living in the United States. Rafa, however, must *deny his friend's Asian self* in order to assert possibilities for Chicana/o advancement back home in the Lower Rio Grande Valley. Hinojosa emphasizes this issue of erasure when Rafa must testify before the US Army Board of Inquiry regarding Sonny's disappearance.

> The Board of Inquiry wishes to ascertain
> Facts relative to
> The matter of Cpl. David Ruiz's death
> In battle action in the summer of 1951.
> On a Government Issued bible, I swear
> That, to the very best of my knowledge
> Cpl. Ruiz is dead.
>
>
> At parade rest,
> > Before the Board,
> > I think of old, mad Tina Ruiz, the widow of Ortega,
> > Who lost another son, Chano,
> > On a sixth of June, a few years back.
>
> > She's Sonny Ruiz's sole beneficiary, and she's worth a
> >   howitzer or two;
> > And so I lie. (49)

Far from the US-Mexico border, yet firmly conscious of its racial structures, Rafa rejects the Board of Inquiry's authority and withholds information regarding Sonny Ruiz. Indeed, he must repress his friend's Asian identity in order to ensure that his family at the US-Mexico border receives his death pension. Rafa concludes that honesty is "well and good. /But, Tina Ruiz needs something to eat and to live on" (49). Sonny's Asian identity thus represents the limits of racial recognition in Rafa's efforts to ensure Mexican American gains back home. His figurative death and his new adoptive identity as "Mr. Kazuo Fusaro" thus open up new questions about what can be known and represented, and about what must be purposely elided in order for Chicana/os to focus on the material problems of day-to-day life in the borderlands.

Sonny's story of a Mexican American turned Asian therefore not only highlights his precarious subjectivity as both the oppressed and the oppressor, but also brings to bear Rafa's own uncertain position within the US military power structure. To be sure, his denial of Sonny's adoptive Asian self for the benefit of Tina Ruiz demonstrates his commitment to address long-standing racial problems in South Texas with political guile rather than "With His Pistol in His Hand."[35] As a well-regarded US soldier, Rafa is decidedly not Gregorio Cortez, the famed figure that early *corridos* (border ballads) celebrate as a result of his heroic armed struggle against Anglo American injustice. Instead of being an open enemy of the state, Rafa (whose last name translates as "Good Face"), is a distinguished agent of its government, one willing to exploit his good standing in his company "as one of the best" in order to achieve immediate political and material gains. He explains:

> You see, I'm what's considered to be
> "A good man." In their view,
> One who won't cry, carp, complain, cower, or crap in his pants.
> A good man. Yessir. One of the best.
> And so, I lie.
> . . .
> The Board could hardly be interested in anything resembling sense,
> So I continue my starring role as "A good man,"
> Who's believed; and well he should be, you see,
> He's been hit twice,
> And he's back for more. (49–50)

Rather than overtly rejecting US hegemonic forces, Rafa adopts the role of a "good man" who learns to work within the system of injustice in order to undermine its power structure. To use words that Paul Laurence Dunbar uttered in a distinct, yet similar context, Rafa must "wear the mask that grins and lies" in order to realize immediate political gains, even if this means denying his friend's adoptive Asian self.[36] Ramón Saldívar has argued "Gregorio Cortez and his solitary armed resistance . . . invented a narrative community, a complete and legitimate Mexican American *persona*, whose life . . . was worthy of being told."[37] If this be true, then for politically committed Mexican Americans like Rafa, Sonny Ruiz Fusaro represents an *illegitimate* Chicana/o-Asian figure whose life and identity *cannot* be told. In this sense, Rafa represents a political consciousness—one mobilized more by cunning than armed force—that recognizes the benefits of strategically *forgetting* the Chicana/o's transnational Asian identity for the purpose of attaining community gains along the US-Mexico border.

Unmistakably, we are now in a global age in which the destinies of subaltern groups across the world are crisscrossing, overlapping, and becoming intimately conjoined. In accord with these global shifts, postmillennial literature about the US West and Southwest has begun to examine explicitly everyday life underwritten by powerful and oftentimes vicious economic and political forces that link these places to the rest of the planet, including Asia. However, the texts examined up to this point reveal this crisscrossing as more than simply a contemporary phenomenon.[38] Instead, they point to a long history of convergence between Asians, Asian Americans, and Mexican Americans in the production of Chicana/o cultural ideologies, which, for purposes of political mobilization, too often has become obfuscated or ignored. Indeed, the range of racial figures in *Pocho, Revolt, Vietnam Campesino, Pilgrims,* "Ichiro Kikuchi," and *Korean Love Songs* show that cross-racial relations are not a recent trend in Chicana/o literature. Instead, these texts reveal that, despite their consistent marginalization in a larger narrative structure, cross-racial encounters are key elements in the ideological work Chicana/o literature performs, including the articulation of this community's "jagged testimonies" of US democratic inclusion, and its long-standing ideological opposition to Anglo injustice.

3

Conquest and Desire

Interracial Sex in Daniel Cano's *Shifting Loyalties* and Alfredo Véa's *Gods Go Begging*

> By loving me she proves that I am worthy of white love. I am loved like a white man. I am a white man. Her love takes me on the noble road that leads to total realization. I marry white culture, white beauty, white whiteness.
> —Frantz Fanon, *Black Skin White Masks*

The previous two chapters have revealed that US military engagements in Asia produce intense transnational and interracial political attitudes in Chicana/o literature, while also generating strong and narrow nationalist sensibilities. The contradictions of community that Chicana/o literature has imagined—as simultaneously transnational and local—manifest themselves repeatedly in the narrative forms and themes of Chicana/o texts that engage historical moments of US-Asian political turmoil. For example, the literal character space manufactured by Chicana/o narratives, coupled with the collapsed identities and geographical places they conceptualize, establish the oppositional politics at the core of much of Chicana/o culture, including issues of educational discrimination, labor rights, cultural erasure, economic injustice, and racial equality. Addressing these recurring themes in key Chicana/o texts, this book has highlighted that Chicana/o literature, paradoxically enough, often articulates its political positions on local matters with an interracial and global purview.

Still, the political themes encoded in Chicana/o texts that imagine Asia as the refracted space of US territories or that regard Asians as a racial equivalent against which to imagine an oppositional identity are not always progressive.¹ This chapter reveals that the very stylistic maneuvers of racial and spatial conflation that mobilize discussions of Chicana/o culture's oppositional themes actually operate in some instances *to perpetuate* values of US imperialism in Asia. I show here that despite the overt oppositional ethics inscribed in both Daniel Cano's *Shifting Loyalties* (1995) and Alfredo Véa's *Gods Go Begging* (1999), the formal treatment of race, space, and gender in these texts undermines their oppositional ideals by reproducing the material violence of US imperialism on female Asian bodies.

The liaisons these narratives fashion between Chicano men and Asian women, I reveal, allegorize US acts of conquest through the former's sexual domination of the latter. Protesting and then reproducing US imperial power, these texts thereby demonstrate the durability and resiliency of US hegemony by revealing these texts' internal constraints on the Chicano protagonists to resist US colonial ideals. In other words, these texts negotiate the unique subject position of the "oppressed-oppressor"² occupied by Mexican American soldiers, revealing how US power implicates Chicana/o literature in the reproduction of imperialist violence, even in instances of its staunch opposition.

In order to assess this power dynamic at the intersities of race, gender, and nation, it is useful to speak of the sexual dominance of Asian women in Cano's and Véa's novels in the context of trauma, for the Chicano's domination of the female body in these instances arises in no small part from the former's psychological stress. To be sure, both novels signal the traumas of minority soldiering in Southeast Asia in the context of private interracial sexual encounters, thereby conflating the boundaries between a Chicano's violent experiences of fighting on behalf of a larger imperial project and that soldier's experiences as a gendered and raced individual.

To make this point, I start with a short theoretical remove, beginning with Sigmund Freud. Freud has revealed that the ways in which a subject negotiates a traumatic group situation, such as war, depends largely on its psychological history, including its sexual past.³ E. Ann Kaplan has reiterated this point by emphasizing the social contours of one's subjectivity in a traumatic situation. She argues that in order to regard one's trauma, one must account for the subject's specific positioning vis-à-vis the incident as an individual who is already a repository of an accumulation of lived experiences on the one hand, and who is a member of multiple imagined communities on the other.⁴ Freud and Kaplan note that in order to come to terms with a traumatic occasion, both one's sexual history and one's social positioning impact how the subject negotiates, masters, and communicates lived experiences of violence and terror generally, and of war specifically.

To add to this, Anne Cheng's work on "racial injuries" reveals how a subject dealing with trauma must negotiate not only its sexual and social histories, but also how it must negotiate the dynamics of *racial difference*. Reading Toni Morrison's novel *The Bluest Eye*, for example, Cheng theorizes that the psychic construction of an African American subject—including its production of "white desire" and its internalization of a "white ideal"—cannot be delinked from the minority's experiences with the uneven values of race in US social structures, all of which overwhelmingly privilege whiteness at the top of nearly all of their hierarchies. Cheng writes:

> Underneath the pop-psychological insight of an "inferiority complex" lies a nexus of intertwining affects and libidinal dynamics—a web of self-affirmation, self-denigration, projection, desire, identification and hostility. To claim that racial difference on the part of the racialized subject provokes self-shame that leads to compensatory white preference drastically foreshortens the complex process of coming to racialization/socialization. *The pedagogy of discrimination is painfully installed in multiple stages*. White preference is not a phenomenon that simply gets handed down from society to black women and then to black girls; instead it travels a tortuous, melancholic path of alienation, resistance, aggression, and *then, finally, the domestication of that aggression as "love."* Is not the conversion of the grief of being black into the enjoyments of whiteness a very *cultural* lesson of mastering displeasure as social pleasure?[5]

Here, Cheng challenges and then debunks racial theories that identify white preference and racial self-loathing as biologically determined, or even spontaneous. Instead, she argues that both racial melancholy and racial violence manifest themselves collectively in white idealism through a long process of an "education of racism [that] is the education of [white] desire."[6] In other words, the minority's *social* experiences of racial difference engender intrapersonal racial grief, which the psyche negotiates through anger, rejection, and finally, the desire of the white ideal, after having learned time and again the privileges of whiteness as a social signifier. For this reason, Cheng notes that white preference is not simply passed down from parent to child genetically, nor is it an essentialist characteristic of racial biology or ethnic psychology. Rather, white desire is a *pedagogy*, she argues, one "painfully installed in multiple stages" wherein the subject, having recognized the debased value of racialized identities, manages to convert its anger and frustration of ethnic difference into white adoration, desires for racial conversion, and ultimately white love.

Shifting Loyalties and *Gods Go Begging*, I argue, dramatize these painful stages of the minority's social education in racial preference and its social production of a white ideal. However, by emphasizing

Chicano soldiering in Asia, these novels complicate Cheng's notions regarding the pedagogy of white desire in two ways. First, they situate the Chicano's racial education on white preference within the context of unimaginable horrors of war against a racial population. Second, they negotiate the soldier's psychic production of white desire through a cross-racial liaison between Chicano men and Asian women, with the latter becoming proxies of white idealism for their male counterparts. For these reasons, these texts emerge as two exemplars of what were common experiences for Chicano soldiers coming of sexual and political age during the 1960s: the experience of their childhood pedagogy on white idealism in a pre–civil rights era, and the development of libidinal sexual desires in the context of a brutal colonial war in Asia.

In this sense, how these novels produce images of Chicano masculinity is not so much linked to recovering the history of the US-Mexico border between 1846 and 1915, when violence between the two nations established their political frontiers.[7] Nor does it emerge from having lost and then having to remember so-called "traditional" pre-Cortesian values, a project that consumed much of Chicana/o politics of the late 1960s. Indeed, Cano's and Véa's novels do not regard the emergence of Chicana/o political identities relative to the historical trauma of modernity at the US-Mexico border, nor to the history of internal colonialism in that region.[8] Instead, these texts offer a glimpse of the social and psychic dynamics of this political identity having emerged *from Asia*, and in the historical context of violent US colonial enterprises against its peoples.

Shifting Loyalties

It is in both Vietnam and Thailand that Cano's narrative tracks closely the experiences of six Chicano soldiers before, during, and after US military engagements in Southeast Asia. These soldiers are: Danny Rios, "a religious, easygoing baby-faced Chicano from Redwood City, California" (79); David Almas, a lower middle-class Chicano from Los Angeles; Hector Medrano, a "tall good-looking guy" from Culver City, California, who loses his brother and his own life in the war; Joey Serrano, also from Los Angeles, who grows up with a father who becomes a drunk after his own service in the Korean War; Charley Yañez, "from Modesto, or Stockton," who was "into history, raza politics. . . . And always talking about white broads" (103); and Manny Cardoza, "a cholo" from Hollywood who loses himself to drug addiction after his return from the battlefield. Through painful installments that explore the lived experiences of these characters, the narrative communicates the protracted trauma of war for Chicano soldiers and their families. In doing so, it codes its staunch antiwar ethics, inscribing its oppositional politics collectively in the image of a community thoroughly devastated by decades of institutional racism and by years of war in Vietnam.

Among the more memorable of the text's satellite characters is one who works to inscribe the narrative's dissent: "Little Rodriguez" from Brownsville, Texas. He notices that Chicanos "die left and right," while Anglos get less dangerous war duties. "Little Rod," as he is affectionately known to his friends, also wonders why Chicano soldiers must risk so much, given they have received so little as a result of the overwhelming poverty they and their families endure in South Texas. Adding his voice to this antiwar protest is Maimonides, Joey Serrano's uncle, who is angered because there are not "too damn many congressmen and senators sending their kids off to fight wars. Nope they're off at Harvard, Yale, Columbia" (263).

But perhaps the strongest tone of protest among the secondary characters manifests itself through the ghostly specter of Jesse Peña of San Antonio, Texas—despite his never appearing in the novel. Jesse's friends reveal that one day this highly regarded soldier disappeared from his combat company, presumably having gone AWOL. Although many soldiers believe Jesse deserted the US Army in order to join the Viet Cong—a tale that echoes between each of the novel's major figures—the narrative makes clear this story is a fable, a "sort of military anti-war protest" (91). Hector Medrano declares Jesse's imagined departure as the ultimate act of protest, saying:

> The dude's got balls. I don't know how, but that guy Peña understands that everything here [in Vietnam] means nothing. It's all fantasy, a joke, a big fuckin' lie, man. I ain't never met the guy, but I been thinking about him a lot. . . . I heard Peña lived in San Antonio, in some rat hole that he couldn't afford to buy because the bank wouldn't lend him the money. I heard that in the summer when it hits a hundred, him and his neighbors fried like goddamn chickens because they couldn't afford air-conditioning. So now they send him here to fight for his country, for his land! Wow, what a joke, man. (98)

Interrogating the intersections between race, patriotism, and privilege, Hector and the other primary figures in the novel begin to highlight not only Jesse's "shifting loyalties" away from the United States, but also the disillusion of an entire community all too cognizant of the contradictions between the racial structures of US society and the call to fight and die for those structures in Vietnam. In this way, the narrative's oppositional political ethics hardly waver from a portrait of the shared suffering of an entire community, one in which the distressed fate of each individual materializes in an unheroic and inescapable tragedy of collective injustice.

However, the narrative's exploration of interracial sex complicates its staunch, yet thinly coded objections to war, thereby undermining its protest of US imperial power and of the exploitation of poverty-stricken Chicano soldiers. In the most powerful instance, the text's oppositional ethics are destabilized by David Almas's relationship with Shiu: a Thai massage girl who fashions her body in the image of white Hollywood starlets for purposes of her sexual consumption. To be sure, this interracial relationship between this young Chicano and the Asian woman turned white marks an element of the text that reproduces US imperialist values, for David's sexual possession of Shiu affirms how the Chicano's social education on racial difference manifests itself in the desire of a white ideal, and ultimately, its conquest. David's interracial desires link his childhood racial neurosis and late-adolescent war traumas to his adventures of sexual conquest across the Pacific, revealing the resiliency of US hegemony as it reproduces itself seamlessly within a text overwhelmingly coded by political opposition to US power.

This issue manifests itself most clearly while David is on "R&R" (Rest and Recreation) in Thailand. There, Shiu quickly becomes the object of his masculine gaze, which reduces the Asian women around him into a series of sexualized anatomical parts: "Many looked like starlets, beautiful, long legs, flat stomachs, small shoulders, silky hair" (204). However, Shiu denies David's initial advances. She firmly asserts her difference from the rest of the Asian ladies on display by telling the young Chicano desperate for female comfort: "I not toy. I not bar girl" (235). Unable to accept her rejection, David's desire is further inflamed by Shiu's protests, turning his lust into an obsession to conquer and to sexually dominate what remains beyond his possession. He asks, "If I pay your boss what he wants, will he let you go with me?" (217). Immediately, the narrative makes clear that David's attempts to subjugate Shiu depend on how he yields his economic buying power not only in a heterosexual relationship, but also in a homosocial one between himself and *Shiu's boss*. In this way, the story establishes David as a rival to Shiu's manager, whom the narrative immediately discloses to be her fiancé.

David's desire to govern both Shiu and her fiancé generates a psychic projection of himself as full-fledged American colonialist, one that mimics and fantasizes about an imperial obsession to subjugate the Asian other. In a narrative unambiguously oppositional to the US war in Vietnam, David's sexual experiences in Thailand deconstruct those antihegemonic values by reinscribing US power in his determined conquest of an Asian family. This reproduction of domination demonstrates what Edward Said identifies as the "Orientalizing process" of imperialism, including "the will . . . to control, manipulate, even to *incorporate*" the East through nonmilitary forms of "political power in the raw."[9]

Said reminds us that colonial domination over the East can hardly be reduced to violent and bloody expressions of military might. His readings of Orientalist discourses in Western culture, ranging from Aeschylus's *The Persians* to Gustave Flaubert's *Salammbô*, note that not only does colonial control entail nonmilitary forms of power, but it also demands the feminization and "incorporation" of the other, including the symbolic (if not the physical) penetration of the colonized body. As a member of the armed forces, David symbolizes US efforts to dominate the body politic of Vietnam, while his gender and buying power in the Thai sex market represents imperialism's masculine subjugation of female Asian bodies. If Orientalism as a discourse expresses a desire to "incorporate" Eastern difference—that is, "to put (one thing) in or into another so as to form one body"—then in order for David to imagine himself as a constituent of US colonial power, he must deploy both his economic and physical domination over Shiu's sex.[10] In other words, dominating Shiu (which in effect emasculates her fiancé) is contingent on David exerting economic *and* sexual control, both of which allow him to envision himself in the image of a US white ideal that he learned to conceptualize as a young child.

An early portrait of David's childhood portrays this construction of his white desire well before his arrival in Thailand, demonstrating an instance of the Chicano's traumatic pedagogy in Anglo idealism. An opening chapter whose title is suggestive of David's conquests of Shiu later in the narrative, "Planting the Seeds" depicts David's father's association of social mobility for Chicana/os with ethnic shedding, racial distancing, and finally, white idealism. For example, this chapter depicts how Mr. Almas mandates that his son play Little League Baseball "in the rich part of town [although] he could barely pay the registration fee," despite his son's protests and wishes to "do what all the other guys in the neighborhood did . . . go to the neighborhood school, [and] play [ball] at the neighborhood park" (22–31). Clearly, Mr. Almas's directive to David limits his son's interaction and development with his Mexican American friends. Moreover, it demonstrates his devaluation of their Mexican American community and his preference for Anglo interaction. More importantly, however, is that David's early Anglo encounters reveal for him the urban and suburban realities of de facto racial segregation in the United States, including having learned the social privileges of whiteness as he comes of age playing ball with kids who "lived in Mandeville Canyon, Westwood, and Bel-Air" (26). In order to bring to bear this lesson of segregation and racial privilege, the narrative makes clear that when it came to playing baseball in these areas, "David was the only Mexican" (26), emphasizing that he, like his modest family car parked among Jaguars, Mercedes-Benzes, and Lincoln Continentals at the baseball fields, was "[well] out of place" (26).

Significantly, Mr. Almas links his son's lessons on the racial dynamics of upward mobility and ethnic shedding to ideologies of masculinity, particularly when he shares with David his personal admiration for the famous US Army paratroop unit, the Screaming Eagles. Mr. Almas reminds his son that this unit made the first jumps behind enemy lines in World War II. He also references the Screaming Eagles as part of a pep talk to enthuse his son before big games, telling him that the soldiers "were scared, but one thing stayed in their minds. They were there to do a job, do their duty, to do the things men do" (25). In another instance, Mr. Almas undermines his wife's opinion that "the important thing is that [David] is having fun," for he interrupts her to reiterate for his son the values he ascribes to the famous paratroop unit: the important thing is not that David enjoys recreational sports, Mr. Almas says, but rather that he will "learn to be a man" (29). Collectively, Mr. Almas's lessons on masculinity and his strategies for social mobility introduce his son to the gendered dynamics of Chicano patriarchy and to the racial lines that constitute the stark economic divisions between East Los Angeles and the more affluent West Side.[11]

To be sure, the narrative makes plain that David's childhood lessons on de facto segregation and on the differential values attached to race are not lost on him, or on his friends. These boys note that each of the teams from the West Side always boast new uniforms; they play ball exclusively on manicured grass and with the best equipment; and their players are taxied to games in the finest of sports coupes and luxury sedans. In short, the young, impressionable boys notice that all the rich kids are white, and, as one says with sharp resentment, "rich kids get all the breaks" (30).

David's pedagogy on the economic discrepancies of de facto segregation and on the social values of race set in motion for him a complicated process of psychic negotiations, particularly with respect to his emergent libidinal desires, which ultimately inform his relationship with Shiu and her fiancé.[12] Yet early manifestations of his father "planting the seeds" of both white idealism and patriarchal values impact the young Chicano's sexual desires almost immediately. For example, David shares that he often feels uncomfortable about being the "only Mexican" playing baseball on the West Side, but he still appreciates the encouragement and cheers of the white mothers, especially Mrs. Silverstein, a team mom who had become "a fantasy in his dreams" (28). Although she is presumably Jewish, the text never specifies Mrs. Silverstein's ethnic particularity. Still, her whiteness is made unmistakable, and David learns to desire her as such. To be fair, Mrs. Silverstein, whose whiteness affixes itself to David's libidinal desire at an early age—and whose name denotes a precious metal of high economic value—does not introduce David to racial difference and financial privilege, per se. Instead, her figurative representation of whiteness and wealth highlights how Mr. Almas's lessons on patriarchy intertwine with his son's emergent libidinal energies as matters of his everyday racial pedagogy. In this regard, Mrs. Silverstein represents an early image of David's desire for a white ideal, for she symbolizes how he has come to learn US dynamics of race and class, and to understand the gendered contours of Chicano patriarchy across distinct racial spaces of Los Angeles. Put shortly, David's social and cultural lessons on race reveal how "the education of racism is [also] an education of desire."[13]

Yet it is not until David goes to Thailand as a member of the US armed forces that he can fully live out his repressed fantasies of whiteness. Dressed in the uniform of the US Army and loaded with the purchasing power of American dollars, David experiences for the first time a sense of economic freedom with which to consume anything he desires, including Shiu, a "tall, thin woman whose hair bobbed. She reminded him of an Asian Natalie Wood" (204). Significantly, David recognizes Shiu both as Asian and as a surrogate image of "Hollywood" whiteness. For him, she is an exotic body to be purchased and conquered; yet she is also an icon of Anglo beauty to be sexed and possessed. In other words, Shiu's body will become the object onto which to deploy his masculine and financial power, and from which to express his repressed sexual and racial desires.

Straight away, the text links David's growing sexual adventure with the Asian/white woman to his first experiences of financial power. On his first night in Thailand, David stays at a luxury hotel and experiences for the first time the lavishness and comfort he had only witnessed as a young boy playing ball on Los Angeles's West Side. As he dons the uniform of the US armed forces, the colonial war in Southeast Asia resituates David's position in a global economic system into one with immense buying power. No longer inhibited by economic and social proscriptions, David's learned yet repressed desire for the American white ideal resurfaces. He focuses exclusively on Shiu, for whom he is willing to pay any price, despite her fiancé's staunch objection.

In this sense, Shiu is the ultimate test of David's economic autonomy; she is also the commodity whose purchase will satisfy David's childhood desire for the Anglo American ideal once represented by Mrs. Silverstein. Purchasing and sexing Shiu, a proxy of American whiteness, thus allows David to participate fully in a US colonial fantasy *and* to transcend his minority status, for she represents both the Asian to be conquered overseas and the Hollywood starlet to be rescued from an Asian rival. As such, the psychological stakes of David's racial and masculine identity are significant, yet they are fully contingent on intersubjective and cross-racial rivalries between himself, Shiu, and her fiancé.

The consequences of commodifying and purchasing Shiu, therefore, exceed a biological desire for sexual release; and these stakes are raised when both she and her fiancé repeatedly refuse the seduction of David's charm and the allure of his growing financial offers. Shiu tells David indignantly, "You Americans think you can buy all the things you want" (235). Realizing that money alone will not win over Shiu, David develops another strategy: he says to the interlocutor between himself and Shiu's boss, "[Tell him] I'm not like other guys. Sometimes I feel Thai. Look at me, my face, my eyes, my skin color. Do I look American? Maybe I am a Thai man" (233–234). Distinguishing himself from the hordes of American soldiers wielding outrageous sums of money in a sex market that its colonial army sustains, David deploys his race as a form of capital in order to realize Shiu's purchase. Unlike the protagonists in *Vietnam Campesino*, *Revolt*, *Pilgrims*, "Ichiro Kikuchi," and *Korean Love Songs*, who conflate their racial identities with Asians in order to inscribe oppositional politics, David articulates his sameness in order to realize Asian domination. In other words, conflating racial difference between Chicana/os and Asians for David does not inspire resistance to US power, but rather it becomes a new strategy for *perpetuating* its authority. If race once signaled David's psychological and social affliction, a mark of his economic and national difference as a boy, it now signals a potential advantage for securing his conquest over Shiu's body and his domination over her fiancé.

As an imaginary Thai companion, David refuses, however, to acknowledge his subjugation of Shiu as a matter of imperial conquest. Instead, he romanticizes her conquest within a Western fantasy of love and domestication, one modeled explicitly after a cultural figure that Vijay Prashad identifies as a powerful allegory of Western colonial power: James Bond, "that overarmed agent of US-UK imperialism,"[14] whom Western filmmakers made sure merged his domination of the Eastern villain with his love of the exotic female. Indeed, after having asked her to imagine his Asianness, David immediately takes Shiu to a James Bond film. Together they watch Sean Connery get his man and his woman in the classic *You Only Live Twice*. Afterward, David admits that the film "stayed with him, the love story between the Asian woman and James Bond, the conflict with the villains. He could see the [interracial] love scenes [between Sean Connery and Mie Hama], he heard Nancy Sinatra's voice and the music, subtle and beautiful" (233). Inspired by an allegory of Western conquest, and stimulated by its romantic depiction of love and lovemaking with the Asian other, David proposes the unthinkable to Shiu's fiancé: He makes an open offer, telling the interlocutor between the two men, "I don't care how much they want for her" (233).

Shiu's mysterious fiancé (who never appears in the novel) becomes the focus of the young Chicano soldier's negotiations, emerging as a sort of Hollywood rival during the young American's Bangkok adventures. The narrative inscribes his villainy unequivocally when the local interlocutor tells David that Shiu's boss is a "tough man, like Mafia man. Keep close watch on the girls, afraid of V.D. Shiu beautiful woman" (223). With the main characters of his Western fantasy in place—including the Asian villain and the exotic Eastern female—David pays a handsome sum for an evening with Shiu in a market when "most girls went for ten dollars, all night" (234).

In the face of tremendous purchasing power, Shiu's fiancé succumbs to David's demands. He allows the American GI one night with her, during which she confirms his triumph over the Asian villain in his Western fantasy. She tells David: "Life very hard in Thailand. . . . My fiancé sacrifice. Right now he feel terrible" (237). Armed with a strong financial arsenal and motivated by a memorable colonial allegory, David subjugates the will of the Asian villain. What remains is his "incorporation" of his lover's body.

To do this, David continues to consider carefully the figure of James Bond. In the process, he structures his conquest over Shiu's sex according to narratives of romantic love and protection, which this Western character allegorizes. Although Shiu recognizes the rendezvous for what it is—an example of exploitation of third world women by both local and colonial men—David demands that Shiu participate in her sexual subjugation through a wedding fantasy. He commands, "I want you to pretend . . . that you have great feelings for me. I want you to pretend that this afternoon, you and I were married, your family was there and my family was there. We all had a wonderful time, and Shiu and David are going to be together always. This is the first night. I have never been with another woman, and you have never been with another man. We are in love" (240). Having been paid for handsomely, Shiu submits. David forces her to mask her prostitution and pain with a love narrative that is born both from David's interracial desires and from his childhood lessons on race and masculinity. Imagining his domination of Shiu—now a proxy of American whiteness and middle-class values—according to a romantic Hollywood script, David finally enacts mastery over his childhood desire for an Anglo ideal.

To be sure, David's domination of Shiu not only affirms his own masculinity, but it also forges for him a symbolic and ideal image of his own imaginary whiteness in both heterosexual and homosocial contexts. Gwen Berger reminds us that women in an interracial colonial relationship must always be regarded in relation to men, for colonized female bodies enable "the differentiation of masculine subject positions according to race."[15] Indeed, David's sexing of Shiu, and the economic power he deploys toward her fiancé, exemplifies what Gayle Rubin characterizes as the patriarchal and capitalistic economies of colonialism, for both allow David to act on his *heterosexual* desire of the white ideal in a *homosocial* colonial situation.[16] Assuming the role of the US imperialist, this Chicano wields his economic authority in order to subdue Shiu and her fiancé, thereby mastering his psychological desire for whiteness, and resembling at the individual level what Prashad sees on a global scale: that "US imperialism [in Asia] was like a poison. Apart from the napalm, the United States used its arsenal of finance capital to undermine the sovereignty of nations of the Third World."[17] To this point, Cano's novel demonstrates how political domination is reproduced at the level of social experience, for David's interracial relationships with Shiu and her fiancé reveal in a Chicana/o context how "[psychological] intrasubjectivity exists as a form of [social] intersubjectivity."[18]

Fashioning their bodies according to images of Hollywood actresses such as Natalie Wood, Shiu and the countless women like her who survive in the Asian sex industry reveal that US colonialism impacts not only geopolitical relationships between nations, but also the significance of race. Indeed, US colonialism has established and perpetuated a commercialization of desire across Asia according to *Western fashions* and tastes, all with radical consequences for how ethnic soldiers like David, as well as comfort women like Shiu, regard their racial identities. Ramón Saldívar reminds us that Asian comfort women who worked during the US occupation of Japan aggressively refashioned their bodies according to Western values of sexual appeal, thereby articulating "early stages of the postwar commodification of desire."[19] If this is so, then Cano's depiction of Vietnam and Bangkok as the background of David and Shiu's sexual transaction reveals that these structures of commercial desire in Asia have reached unprecedented heights. Tavivat Puntarigvivat writes that "there were . . . during the Vietnam War, a half million prostitutes in Saigon [alone]. But R and R [rest and relaxation] centers outside of Vietnam also had to be offered. Alternative sites of mass prostitution were established in Thailand [specifically], where up to 70,000 soldiers visited annually."[20] Puntarigvivat notes that the number of prostitutes and their American clientele skyrocketed above their already high figures when the United States increased the number of military bases in the country in the 1970s, putting its country's sex trade on the scale with dominant sectors of the national economy.[21]

The market of recreational sex not only highlights the financial power of the industry; it also makes plain the relationship between race and US imperialism more broadly. Indeed, the sheer number of women who resorted to prostitution in Thailand during the American War in Vietnam speaks to the desolation and poverty of the region, and it reveals how imperialism and its rising commercial and recreational markets embody a racial code. According to Puntarigvivat, this growing market of "images of exotic, alluring, and docile Asian women" morphs into the landscape of ever-widening consumer culture, one which ultimately fails to distinguish between Western commodities and the "exotic" bodies of "Westernized" Asian women.[22]

At the conclusion of David's sexual conquest, the narrative addresses the issue of commercialization and commodification of which Puntarigvivat speaks, particularly with respect to the racial dynamics imperialism engenders. Following David's shopping spree in Bangkok's black market after his sexual domination of Shiu, the novel depicts David downtown, walking the "crowded sidewalks, stopping to look at window displays, seeing nothing other than a blur of clothing, women's apparel, men's suits, children's clothing. He walked through the department stores, and was sickened by the replicas of Sears, May Co., Penny's, and Broadway. He thought: is this what the war is about? To force America on the rest of the world? The cheap clothing? The junk?" (241). Shopping in Bangkok's commercial center on the eve of his return to Vietnam, David stands before his own reflection, initially "seeing nothing other than a blur of clothing." Having not noticed his own image refracted back to the self among a collage of cheap merchandise, the novel comments on what Walter Benjamin describes as the devaluation of the subject in a marketplace, one which exploits reflective showcase windows to obscure the relation of the subject to its environment and to commodities put on display for sale.[23]

Yet David's series of rhetorical queries complicate further this confused relationship between the subject and commercial goods. In this instance, David realizes, all too late, that the American War in Vietnam and its export of brand commodities in Thailand blends reflective "images of exotic, alluring, and docile Asian women" seamlessly into a landscape of consumerism, producing a marketplace of desire infused with new social and racial formations. In this sense, this scene in downtown Bangkok comments on how the dynamics of Western consumerism in Asia distort local values of Thai society, including notions of "filial piety" under which Asian women now fashion themselves as sex objects in order to bear the burden of family responsibility during times of economic stress.[24]

Yet this curious scene also reveals how this distortion of local values is complemented by a *distortion of racial formations*. The "exotic Asian woman" now becomes a proxy of US whiteness. Her purchase allows Chicano soldiers like David to deal with psychological traumas of race and war, and to bridge the gap between minority self-perceptions and the white ideal they learned to desire as children. Shiu's Asian/Anglo sex allows Chicano soldiers like David to imagine an Anglo colonial self that conquers the Asian other while also possessing her projected white perfection. As such, the sexual consumption of the Asian women turned Anglo assuages the Chicano's traumatized consciousness by allowing the racial subject to imagine himself fully, as Fanon describes it in a similar context, as "a white man."[25]

Gods Go Begging

Like Cano's novel, Alfredo Véa's *Gods Go Begging* is staunchly oppositional, at least thematically, to the US imperial war in Vietnam. Yet how this narrative explores sexual exchanges begins to highlight a pattern of Asian sexual dominance in Chicana/o novels that protest this conflict. Véa's text explores deeply the moral abomination of this war to reveal how state domination of a foreign population reproduces itself at the level of the individual, particularly in the context of the Chicano's sexual control over female Asian bodies. In order to bring this point to bear, I begin this analysis by examining the ways Véa's text critiques the monstrosities of the American War in Vietnam—including the protracted trauma of Chicano soldiers—before moving on to an examination of how Chicano-Asian sex in the text replicates the forms of state-sanctioned violence that the narrative seemingly stands to scrutinize.

The narrative's protest of the American War in Vietnam and of local racial injustice largely materializes through the ways it conflates this violent history with the day-to-day lives of poverty-stricken minorities in the United States. I agree with Patrick Hamilton's critique that it is through the novel's "breaking across" geographical borders between the violent spaces of Vietnam and the violent spaces of urban America that the narrative produces its oppositional political ethics.[26] Indeed, the narrative's overlaying representations of bloodshed—including scenes of gruesome chemical warfare in Vietnam during the 1960s and a rampage of cold-blooded murders in the ruined neighborhoods of Northern California years later—highlight how minorities suffer structures of violence domestically and abroad. This narrative structure makes little distinction between nations and neighborhoods at war, thereby mapping the horrors of US racism by imagining the violence in the lives of minorities "chosen to bear the discomfort of their country" both in Asia and at home (196).

In this sense, the geographical flattening between the violence in Vietnam and the racial violence in California operates according to a literary strategy already established in Chicana/o literature, as I examine in chapter 1. In constructing a conceptual space that I have identified throughout this study as "Southwest Asia," *Gods Go Begging* compresses geographical differences across the Pacific Rim to articulate its protest against US racial violence on a transnational and transtemporal scale—one that makes little distinction between the local and global, and the past and present.

Perhaps the most significant instance of the novel's geographical and temporal flattening occurs when protagonist Jesse Pasadoble speaks of the horrific battle in which he loses his good friend Amos Flyer in Vietnam, which is juxtaposed with the murder of Flyer's wife three decades later in San Francisco. Jesse says to his girlfriend:

> "Here and there, where the world has shifted and cracked open, one era will touch another. And once upon the rarest time, human hands and eyes from the distant past can seek out and find . . . search for and contact . . . hands and eyes of the present time . . . our time. . . .
>
> "I know you might be skeptical. You don't believe that such things can take place. . . .
>
> "Believe me, it happened. I am a living witness. It happened here in this city, on Potrero Hill [in San Francisco], and on a hill near the eastern edge of Laos. I was there, at both places . . . almost three decades after that enemy sapper ran up that hill in Vietnam, at the very same instant in time that his [Amos Flyer's] body flew towards its own doom [on the battlefield], Persephone Flyer looked up to see two boys [her murderers] standing in front of the glass door of the Amazon Luncheonette [in San Francisco]." (282–283)

As one of the few critics to assess this text, William Arce notes how its temporal and spatial overlays are metaphors for ways that Jesse's war traumas "cannot be contained by memory."[27] The violence of the past perpetually plays itself out in the present, producing a problem of history that his psyche can never fully process on account of its inability to situate the site of its injuries.[28] The structure of trauma in which Jesse's experiences of war and urban violence play out perpetually in the present is nothing short of the temporal structure of the narrative proper, for the novel regularly lacks clear historical markers to highlight discrepancies between time and place. In this way, the narrative communicates Jesse's experiences of a brutal war in Vietnam and the racial violence in San Francisco decades later as occurring "at the very same instant" (283).

Still, the historical structure of the narrative and of Jesse's psychology should not be understood solely as a single traumatic event experienced in one place and time manifesting itself in another place and time in the victim's psyche. Instead, the temporal conflations between the past and present manifest themselves as material matters for Jesse, for the racial dynamics of the bodily carnage he experiences in Vietnam are nothing less than an expression of the *same* racial bloodshed he witnesses in America's inner city. In other words, the problem of historical placement in the novel is nothing less than an expression of a pattern of violence repeatedly experienced by US racial minorities at home and abroad. This means that for Jesse, his trauma endured in the hills of Vietnam wreaks havoc on his capacity to calibrate time and place. Yet it also produces for him a *type of knowledge* with which to understand and to experience vicariously the violence enacted toward others across time, space, and race. For this reason, Jesse declares himself a "living witness" to his African American friend's death at the hands of a Vietnamese soldier, and to the murder of that friend's wife by two disenfranchised youth thirty years later, saying, "I was there, at both places" (283).

Yet Jesse is decidedly *not* present at either of these scenes. Instead, he understands—or better yet, his traumatic experiences *have taught him to learn to recognize*—that the racial violence in Vietnam is not unrelated to other US wars, including the one being waged by and against ethnic minorities on America's poverty-stricken streets. To bring this point of equivalencies to bear, the narrative configures Jesse's historical memory of Vietnam according to the carnage playing itself out in US ethnic neighborhoods, and it ultimately formulates his racial identity itself in the image of an ethnic North Vietnamese prisoner of war, Hong Trac.

Jesse meets Hong during the latter's incarceration in a prison yard in Da Nang, Vietnam. What begins as a rare opportunity to see an enemy solider alive eventually evolves into an instance of cross-racial recognition between two minorities, for Hong himself is an ethnic figure fighting on behalf of a nation that has historically subjugated him and his community. Indeed, this moment of intersubjective identification affirms Jesse's and the prisoner's mutual experiences of a global war being waged against ethnic minorities within and beyond US borders. The text reads:

> The NVA soldier smiled broadly, almost childishly, then reached up to grab a shock of his own hair. With his other hand he pointed at the American sergeant [Jesse].
> "You same-same me," he said in pidgin. . . . He released his hair, then ran his fingers over the brown skin of his cheek, then over his brown, sunburned forearm. "You same-same me," he repeated. . . .
> "You," said the NVA, still trying his pidgin. . . . You Español?"
> "Habla Usted Español?" said Jesse excitedly.
> "No. Poco, poco. Beaucoup Españoles en Marseille."
> "Marseille? Français? Parlez-vous Français?"
> "Mais oui," said the regular . . . Êtes-vous Español?"

"Non," answered Sergeant Pasadoble, immediately caught up in the common language, "Je suis Mexican, Mexican-American...."

"In the north of my country, the children are told in school that all people of color in the United States live in a separate country.... And do you live in a separate country?"

Sergeant Pasadoble placed his right index finger on the center of his own forehead. "We do," he said.

"Ah," sighed the regular, "je comprends!" He nodded his head. "I am a Chàm," he said. "Some people say we came from India long, long ago. Some say we came from Indonesia. We have a completely different way of writing and we speak a dialect that is like no other in Southeast Asia. Any radio communications between our troops—if we have a radio—is done in Chàm, since no Vietnamese, north or south can decode [it]. Centuries ago we were conquered and then subjugated by the Vietnamese. Since that time we have never had an equal place in this country.

"Because I am Chàm, I must sit alone in this yard." (79–81)

Like Jesse, Hong Trac is an ethnic other fighting for the interests of a nation-state that has historically discriminated against its minority populations. From this brief dialogue, both soldiers recognize in the other their own respective situations, their repression at the hands of their own particular governments, and their complicity in fighting a ruthless war on the states' behalf. As such, this interracial encounter marks a radical shift in Chicana/o literature's constructions of racial and political symmetries between Mexican Americans and Asians. The Chicana/o is no longer, in the words of Valdez, "the same" as the generic image of a Vietnamese freedom fighter; and while Acosta's narrative claims that "Chicanos are the Viet Cong" of America, they are decidedly *not* in Véa's text. No longer "the same" as a Vietnamese revolutionary, the Chicana/o is now the "same-same" as *another* minority ethnic group, one of Indonesian descent that has been victimized for hundreds of years by the very Vietnamese figures that repeatedly inspired Chicana/o counterpolitics during the 1970s. To be sure, the racial symmetry Véa's novel produces in this instance generates a more complex equation of racial relations by inserting the Chàm as an ethnic group for Chicana/o political consideration. In this sense, Véa's narrative highlights the ideological fallacy in previous forms of Chicana/o culture that idealizes oppositional identity by pairing it with a romantic image of North Vietnamese resistance.

Underscoring this issue is Jesse's own position as a US soldier. Like Melguizo in Paredes's "Ichiro Kikuchi," Jesse comes to realize the contradictions of his political standing as an enlisted military combatant, and not as a civilian political protestor. When Jesse encounters Hong's body after their initial meeting, he realizes that his counterpart had been tortured and murdered while in US captivity by having a screwdriver plunged slowly into his brain through the ear canal. John Alba Cutler rightly recognizes that this murder episode "underscores Jesse's complicity in the violence of the war, resisting a complete analogy between Chicano and Vietnamese soldiers."[29] Still, Jesse's discovery of Hong's murder by the army with whom he shares a uniform does less to highlight the fallacy of interracial sympathies than does the interiority of the Asian figure that the narrative constructs. No longer a one-dimensional image of opposition to US hegemony, the Vietnamese soldier is now a complex figure with a biography and political consciousness all its own; one whose own ethnic particularity challenges his standing with its Vietnamese peers. Hong's narrative of Chàm history and his personal story regarding his life in Marseille contrast sharply with the romantic abstractions of Asian singularity produced in early Chicana/o narratives, including the flattened brand of oppositional ideas they represent. In this regard, Véa's narrative surveys the historical intricacies of the Vietnamese other to the degree that Hong represents not the implied idea of resistance, but rather a global structure of ethnic oppression that undermines the stopgap politics in Chicana/o culture that have largely romanticized Chicana/o-Vietnamese sympathies.

Having refrained from scripting a flattened brand of political equivalences, the narrative navigates possibilities for regarding complex contours of Chicana/o identity vis-à-vis a broad range of subaltern populations. Indeed, Jesse explores his political affiliations and stark interracial sympathies with a number of US minorities across a broad spectrum of racial difference. Yet it is another Mexican American soldier's shifting sense of self that brings to bear the manifold categories that constitute and complicate Chicana/o political identity during times of war: Guillermo Moises Carvajal.

Having deconstructed the values that idealized images of the Vietnamese other once enabled in Chicana/o culture, Véa's novel introduces Guillermo Carvajal. Carvajal's complex ethnic history, like Hong's, highlights the ideological limitations of racial conflation, and in doing so, challenges the very viability of the sign "Chicana/o" as a signal of an oppositional identity. This sounds progressive enough, for it seemingly undermines Chicana/o cultural practices that appropriate flattened images of Vietnamese in order to construct flattened images of Chicana/o political resistance. However, the impetus of this liberating force for Carvajal stems from his explicit incorporation of the Asian female, resembling the gendered dynamics of interracial sex between David and Shiu in *Shifting Loyalties*. In this instance, an Asian prostitute named

Cassandra destabilizes for Carvajal shorthand practices for establishing Chicana/o political identities, but in doing so she also serves as a sexual conduit for this chaplain of the US Army to rearticulate and to perpetuate US imperialist ideologies. The narrative emphasizes this point by revealing Carvajal's racial syncretism as a form of Mexican mestizaje that escapes nearly all forms of political categorization, yet it only does so after he penetrates an Asian woman and reconfigures her sex according to his own culturally informed desire. In order to make this point, it is first necessary to revisit Carvajal's identity crisis.

Born Guillermo Carvajal in Mexico, later named Father William Calvert in the United States, and still later named Vô Dahn by his Asian lover Cassandra in Vietnam, this figure's varied eponyms signal the permutations of his racial, national, religious, and political identities. To account for these shifts, Cassandra's final designation of her lover as "Vô Dahn" (which means "anonymous") appears to infuse this Chicano's unsettled identity with an Asian persona. However, the racial dynamics at play here are very different from those literary strategies that simply conflate one ethnic identity with another, or that imagine utopian forms of political solidarity and racial transfigurations. To be sure, Carvajal's new Asian self is very much *unlike* David Ruiz's, who in *Korean Love Songs* assumes a Japanese identity in order to experience democratic rights unavailable to him as a Mexican American. Carvajal's/Vô Dahn's identity is also unlike that of the Chicana/o marchers in *Revolt* who self-identify as Viet Cong to inspire street-level protests; and his cross-racial self is still different from the farmworkers in *Vietnam Campesino* who recognize Vietnamese villagers as a reflective image of their own political body. Instead, Carvajal's Asian identity radically *negates* the affirmation of simple political alignments. Rather than affirm racial and political coherencies, Carvajal's Asian self signals a seemingly irresolvable crisis of Chicana/o identity: he is literally "no one," a designation that leaves in limbo his very racial, political, and national categorization.

Cassandra brings this point to bear after their lovemaking. After sex, she shares with Carvajal the little she knows about his personal history, revealing to him that "Vô Dahn" does in fact translate as "nobody." She ascribes this name to him on account of his inability to recall his life before, during, and after his traumatic experiences in the jungles of Vietnam, including his prior life as a Sephardic Jew in Chihuahua, Mexico. In this sense Carvajal/Vô Dahn symbolizes not the cohesion of racial and political differences consolidated in the consciousness of one subject. Instead, he represents the ambiguities and emptiness of national signifiers, given the sheer brutality of war, and the political limitations of common markers of identity to account for the complex ethnic makeup of various cultural selves.

Although Carvajal only has erratic psychological access to his own past, the narrative provides the particulars of his war experiences for the reader. This story includes his having learned of a gruesome battle, knowledge that eventually ruptures his memory and untethers him from reality. As a chaplain of the US Army working with Catholic soldiers, Carvajal abandons his regiment on the eve of a bloody firefight in which his platoon is decimated by the North Vietnamese Army. Having learned of the gory deaths of so many young boys, Carvajal's faith is corroded beyond repair, the consequences of which include him going insane and walking away silently into the jungle.

While in a deep cataleptic stupor, Carvajal falls into the Mekong River. Like the ebbs and flows of the river's eddying waters, Carvajal's mind begins to float randomly between memories of his childhood past and the brutal battle in which most of the young soldiers of his unit suffered gruesome deaths. The narrative reads:

> One hundred kilometers behind the floating padre were the deep brown eyes of Corporal Tiburcio Mendez scanning the heavens above for some absurd object—for some insane reason. . . . Poor Cornelius was there [too], impossibly still, lying and dying in his chrysalis next to the stiffening body bags of a Midwestern boy and Jim Earl. . . .
>
> Both boys had been cracked open, their scrambled innards draped, painting the dirt a deep aubergine and red. Both had suffered terribly before finding the ultimate comfort. . . .
>
> The padre was free of it all now, his flimsy legs and knees striking an occasional rock or tree stump. His wild, confused, and careening mind—even more turbulent than the water—was far, far away from the Mekong River and that unspeakable war. . . .
>
> The chaplain's body, saturated by water to within an inch of his bones, traversed a small rapids, his back and chest striking several sharp rocks. A rib cracked beneath his fatigue jacket. Like so many other injuries, this would not heal for years. Perhaps it would never heal.
>
> *The Mennonites of his youth refused to tell him of his origins, nor would the disdainful nuns and priests of the local cathedral.* . . .
>
> As he bobbed in the wake and backwash of a passing rice boat, the lieutenant wondered if the pain he was feeling was the deep ache of a broken rib bone or the sad pang of a memory. . . .
>
> Two hundred miles down the Mekong the wind had pushed the lieutenant toward the bank, where he was rudely prodded by oars. He responded with half groans and semi-gestures that spoke the whole truth about the war. . . . A bird landed on the chaplain's forehead and

began to peck at insects that clung to his hairline, *and still, the padre dreamed of Chihuahua*. (197–204, my emphasis)

With the structures of his consciousness shattered by the brutality of war, Carvajal struggles to cling to stunted memories of his past that float aimlessly in his mind. These memories are vacuous, "free-floating signifiers" if you will, for Carvajal, the narrative tells us, has never learned of his family origins before his upbringing by the Mennonites of Mexico. Dreaming of his childhood in Chihuahua, Carvajal is unable to anchor any specifics of that era beyond echoes of faint village gossip that his father and grandfather "were reputed to be . . . famous hermit-misers that pretended to suffering abject poverty but who in reality possessed wealth beyond Midas" (202). Without a clear sense of his family origins and with only a dim impression of his own biography, Carvajal represents to himself what Jacques Derrida has referred to in a linguistic context as a "trace": the presence of a sign that "displaces and refers beyond itself."[30] Indeed, as the novel scripts Carvajal's reveries and the details of his bodily injuries as he floats down the Mekong River, it simultaneously enacts his own dislocation and narrative erasure. This erasure is marked by the imposed silence of the Mennonites who raised him and by the amnesia he suffers as result of the war, both of which contribute to his displaced sense of self and his inability to articulate a coherent social or political identity.

Carvajal's having become the figure of "no one" brings the processes of his narrative effacement to bear, for it marks an injury to his identity that perhaps "would never heal" (201). Yet the injury to his identity marked by his war trauma and by his childhood silence decidedly *does* heal. Carvajal miraculously recalls his birth name, regains his sanity, and remembers the details of his youth and family origins at the moment of his sexual penetration of his Asian partner, Cassandra. The text designates this moment with a breach into the narrative itself, one marked by a literal blank space. After this caesura the text affirms without ambiguity the origins and contents of Carvajal's biographical life:

> When after an unknowable time had elapsed—perhaps months or perhaps years—and he finally woke from a drowning dream, he was sweating, naked, and breathless, his erect male member inside a woman who called herself Cassandra.
>
> "Why did you stop?" Her large eyes were open now, her heavy breathing had slowed.
>
> "Vô Dahn, *mon cher*, you're beginning to remember things, aren't you? . . .

"This is our apartment, Vô Dahn.... We met in a refugee camp in Thon Buri, Thailand. If you think hard, you will find that you speak some Chinese, French, Vietnamese and Thai...."

My name is a lie, he thought to himself.... Now he remembered the useless land (in Chihuahua) the Mennonites had purchased from his father had turned them into rich apple growers. It made them gentlemen farmers, and to assuage their guilt, they had given the poor Mexican boy a luxurious name in repayment. They had always known the real value of the property and had paid his father next to nothing for it.

"Do you know who you really are, Vô Dahn?"

"... I am a [Mexican] Jew." (207–213)

If the encounter between Jesse and Hong deconstructs imaginary political equivalences between Chicana/os and Vietnamese by complicating the latter's ethnic constitution, then Carvajal's Jewish-Mexican self—one that speaks Yiddish, Spanish, English, Chinese, French, Vietnamese, and Thai—obliterates Chicana/o culture's image of its indigenous political identity. Specifying Carvajal as polyglot Sephardic Jew, the narrative challenges Chicana/o authenticity as it has been culturally posed during the 1970s. Instead, it imagines him as an embodied form of mestizaje that exceeds utopian possibilities of racial and cultural accumulation beginning with Mexico, or even the Aztecs. In this sense, Carvajal represents an image of Mexican mestizaje that Rafael Pérez-Torres describes as breaking from "a vexed tradition in which race mixture sustains an uninspired teleology leading from the subjugated Indian, African, and Asian Other to a new mestizo agent in history."[31]

To be sure, what Hong Trac's ethnic Chàm identity and Carvajal's Jewish-Mexican self reveal is not the formative force of Chicana/o-Asian encounters that contextualize their emergence. Instead, they expose the mythology embedded in images of Vietnamese and Chicana/o revolutionaries that have become incorporated into Chicana/o literary culture since the 1960s. As such, these "un-Vietnamese" and "un-Chicano" figures illustrate—in the words of Homi Bhabha—how "identity is never an a priori, nor a finished product; it is only ever the problematic process of access to an image of totalities."[32] Indeed, Hong and Carvajal symbolize the contradictions and deletions that take place in a literary culture committed to articulating an image of a Chicana/o self when it is forced to contemplate its own political marginalization and its own social erasure.

For this reason, Hong Trac and Carvajal represent a significant instance in the pattern of Chicana/o-Asian encounters in Chicana/o literature, for they are marked by radical complexity and nuance, rather than a flattened brand of oppositional equivalences. No longer one-dimensional political types of racial otherness, both figures represent a form of "mestizaje... that embodies the idea of multiple subjectivities."³³ Véa's narrative makes this point plain, especially for Carvajal, whose markers of identity—including his name, race, religion, and nationality—constantly shift throughout the story. He is alternatively identified as "Padre," "William Calvert," "a white Unitarian military chaplain," "Guillermo Calavera," "an immigrant," "a Mexican Sephardic Jew," "Vô Dahn," and upon his return to the United States, "Mr. Homeless."

Still, the significance of this figure's sexual encounter with an Asian woman cannot be overstated, because while Carvajal's name, race, ethnicity, class, religion, and nationality prove malleable, his gender and sexuality remain resolute. The narrative emphasizes this point when it constitutes Carvajal's complex and nuanced political self at the *exact moment* of his having sexually breached the female Asian body.³⁴

In this sense, the process of complicating an "authentic" Chicana/o identity is enacted through the penetration of the Asian woman, thereby *reaffirming* Chicano masculine values at the same time that it deconstructs a flattened image of its political ideal. The narrative highlights this point on the rigidity of this Chicano's masculinity through its depiction of Cassandra's own shifting sexuality, one expressed through her romantic liaison with an African American woman decades later in the United States.

Comparatively viewed, Carvajal, like David in *Shifting Loyalties*, reclaims his masculine self and affirms his subjectivity through the physical act of heterosexual penetration of an Asian prostitute. And like David, Carvajal frames the female Asian body according to his own culturally informed desires. David fantasizes Shiu as a James Bond girl in order to imagine his own colonial authority, while Carvajal refigures Cassandra as a white Hebrew woman in order to consolidate his newly discovered Jewish self. In this instance, and with a scopophilic gaze that reduces Cassandra to a set of disembodied parts, Carvajal "stared at the lovely face of the woman beneath him—at her rising and falling breasts, at the glistening patches on her skin where their sweat had mixed.... She was as striking as Tirza, as bright as Jerusalem. Her breasts were like twin fawns feeding amongst the water lilies" (214). Carvajal's refashioning of Cassandra not only speaks to his culturally informed desire of a white Jewish ideal, but also it masks the historical materiality of her own tragic life as a refugee and prostitute.³⁵ Similar to how David imagines Shiu as a proxy of American whiteness and as a figure of his repressed colonial desire, Carvajal fantasizes Cassandra as a sexually disembodied Hebrew woman and as a figure of his own repressed ethnic heritage. Indeed, Carvajal imagines the Asian woman whom he sexes "as striking as Tirza," a Hebraic figure of the Torah whose name means "my delight."³⁶ In this way he confirms his possessive gratification over her body and over her very cultural and racial identity.

This contrast between Carvajal's regenerated masculine Mexican identity and Cassandra's own ethnic erasure takes hold in yet a final moment of their naming, one that mimics a perverse ballet dance that the novel calls "*une pirouette dehors.*" Carvajal says to Cassandra,

> "The name my father gave was Guillermo Calavera, but that name is a lie too, like everything else in my life."
>
> He inhaled as his muscles swelled. His hands tightened on her tiny midriff. She flexed her lovely legs. Still confused and a bit awkward with her own nakedness beneath the robe, she turned first to the right and then to the left, *une pirouette dehors.* Her long hair leapt from one shoulder to the other. Then, following the force of his hands, she jumped straight up. He carried her back to the bed and laid her down once more.
>
> "My name is not really Cassandra. I've had a Thai name, a Chinese name . . . so many names. . . ."
>
> "Me llamo . . . my true name is Guillermo Moises Carvajal" (209–210).

Choreographed according to the postures of a ballet, this give-and-take dance on identity between Carvajal and Cassandra concludes with the former positioning himself forcefully over the Asian woman, on their bed. In this instance, Carvajal recovers his true name, while the identity of the lover over whom he gazes remains largely concealed. Properly named, Carvajal reveals to himself the details of his childhood and family origins, including secrets that he could hardly unveil without having firsthand experiential knowledge. The sexual encounter with the Asian woman fleshes out Carvajal's personal and family histories, laying bare for him a complex past constituted by a tapestry of racial, linguistic, and cultural mixtures. Still, in this moment of identity reformation that untangles Carvajal's identity and his past,³⁷ *Cassandra's identity remains obscure*, especially to him. During their give-and-take dance on identity, Carvajal abruptly abandons his partner on the bed, and in a last effort to possess the sight of her body "he tried to memorize her beauty. He [then] turned to walk away, never asking for her true name": Mai Adong (214).

To be sure, Mai's mystification forms the basis for much of the narrative's plot, for it is her and her African American girlfriend's murder, anachronistically represented in the opening chapter, that sets in motion the detective work of its protagonist, Jesse Pasadoble. While Jesse pieces together relationships between his past acquaintances on the war-torn hills of Vietnam and his contemporary contacts on the war-torn hills of San Francisco, Mai Adrong remains largely anonymous to Carvajal, the figure for whom she has restored a sense of self. This point on her anonymity and misrecognition is brought to bear in the narrative's closing moments. Almost three decades after their love affair, Carvajal takes refuge in San Francisco, reappearing in the story to comfort Mai on the city streets as she lies dying, her body riddled with bullets just like those of the boys with whom he served in Vietnam. In this fleeting moment between the life and death of Mai Adrong, Carvajal acknowledges her presence, lovingly so; yet he cannot speak her true name. Instead, he can only misrecognize her one last time at this moment of her mortality as "my dearest Cassandra" (291).

Chicana feminists have long noted how much of the community's culture often deploys hyper forms of masculinity in ways that inscribe oppositional politics on the bodies of female figures. Critics and cultural brokers like Gloria Anzaldúa, Cherríe Moraga, and Lorna Dee Cervantes, for example, have shown how female bodies often serve as sexual conduits for affirming masculine values in Chicana protest culture.[38] According to Anzaldúa, hyper-masculinity among Chicanos is both part of an inherited ideology with origins in Mexican patriarchal culture and a psychic response to the social emasculation of Chicano men within US political structures that subjugate them.[39] Lorna Dee Cervantes agrees with Anzaldúa's position, a point that emerges from her memorable poem "Para un revolucionario." This piece notes that the oppositional politics paraded by Chicano revolutionaries code and then calcify hierarchies of gender on the backs of their female counterparts. In addition, Cervantes notes that the political identities this community produced for itself during the Movement era were too often predicated on affirming a hyper-masculine self that lays its claim and safeguard over a hyper-sexed Chicana body.[40]

David's sexing of Shiu in *Shifting Loyalties* and Carvajal's penetration of Mai in *Gods Go Begging* recapitulate the heterosexual imperative of which Anzaldúa and Cervantes speak. However, these texts complicate the important critical interjections these thinkers make by imaging the gendered dynamics of interracial unions between Chicano *soldiers* and *Asian* women. Unlike the revolutionaries of whom Cervantes speaks, the Chicano in these instances is a US military combatant, and not a political radical; and the woman whom he incorporates is an Asian commodity available for sexual purchase, not a social protestor. These political and racial details highlight how Chicano patriarchy reproduces uneven gendered relations beyond the community, outside the hemisphere, and in relation to another subaltern population with which it often sympathized. Indeed, Shiu's and Mai's sex, and not their ideas, link their respective Chicano lovers directly to the political identities each represents, providing interracial instances of what Anzaldúa, Moraga, and Cervantes voiced decades earlier, namely, that reconfigurations of Chicano identities and their formation of liberating critical sensibilities routinely rest upon the confirmation of masculinist values.

Understood in this way, the Chicano-Asian sexual encounters in Cano's and Véa's texts represent an interracial variant of the gendered critique that has come to define Chicana feminism for much of the last four decades. Indeed, the Chicano-Asian encounters in these texts open up possibilities for regarding the "Chicano" according to alternative political relations, if not more progressive critical perspectives. Yet it also cements ideologies of selfhood that depend on traditional and uneven gendered values. David's sexual encounter with Shiu highlights the former's injurious social education on racial difference, and it makes plain for him—albeit much too late—the ideologies of race and free-market capitalism for which he unwittingly fights. Similarly, Carvajal's sexing of Mai regenerates for him a memory of his childhood pedagogy on the unequal values of racial and cultural difference in Mexico; yet he fails to recognize the unequal value of gender in the process. Indeed, both David's and Carvajal's sexual encounters with the Asian woman symbolize the contradictions that take place when the Chicano's trauma of having learned the unequal values of race intermingle with the trauma of fighting an imperial war against another subaltern population. In other words, these interracial sexual connections make plain the resiliency of the Chicano's pedagogy on racial difference by revealing his complicity in perpetuating imbalances of power. This theme is too often buried within the oppositional ideologies of much of Chicana/o culture, including Cano's and Véa's own respective antiwar narratives.

4

Through Mexico and into Asia

A Search for Cultural Origins in Rudolfo Anaya's *A Chicano in China*

> The civilization of ancient Mexico was not entirely original: no specialist denies the relationships and influences between the cultures of the north, south, and Mesoamerica. On the other hand, American man is of Asiatic origin. The first immigrants, who would have arrived in North America during the end of the Pleistocene, without a doubt brought with them the rudiments of a culture. Between those rudiments one finds seeds of a world vision—something infinitely persistent and which, as a result of being passive and unconscious, resists technical, philosophical, and institutional social change. The Asian origin of the peoples of the Americas perhaps explains the numerous similarities between pre-Confucian China and the civilizations of the Americas.
> —Octavio Paz, "Dos apostillas"

With various cultural and political motivations, writers across Latin America began to embrace Asian poetics in the early twentieth century. This movement generated a reverent regard for the "Orient" in the Latin American literary traditions across the hemisphere. It also marked a drastic shift in the politics of many Latin American cultural agendas, which once insisted on indigenous designations in order to articulate cultural origins.[1] Erik Camayd-Freixas notes, for example, that poets of this period often looked idyllically to Asia in search of the exotic, seeking inspiration to refine their respective national poetic sensibilities.[2] These writers include Rubén Darío (Nicaragua), Julián del Casal (Cuba), Julio Herrera y Reissig

(Uruguay), Enrique Gómez Carrillo (Guatemala), and Guillermo Valencia (Colombia).³

In addition to the allure of the exotic, which Asian culture provided Latin American writers, poets in the hemisphere also found themselves compelled to address new evolutionary theories, which posited that founding groups of Asian migrants made their way across the Americas between thirteen and sixty thousand years ago. Placing less emphasis on recent waves of Asian immigration to the Americas during the nineteenth and early twentieth centuries, and rather than indicting contemporary Asian migrants for economic conditions in the region, a new literary vogue interested in theories of non-European origins in the Americas emerged. As a result, the region's most important literary brokers began to dedicate intense poetic energies to coming to terms with theories of pre-Columbian migrations from the East and the cultural impact of the first inhabitants of the Americas: Asians.

For this reason, figurehead poets from across the Americas not only began to venerate Asia as a muse for poetic refinement, but they also began to look to Asia as a means for identity building, particularly in the mid-twentieth century. Thus, the 1950s witnessed a literary trend in which Latina/o writers engaged Asian/Amerindian connections as a source for negotiating new cultural foundations. In doing so, this literary vogue did not reconfigure the Orient as a category of Western hegemonic discourse, as Said famously theorizes, but rather it produced a discourse of the East from a region of the planet that itself had been plagued by hundreds of years of European and US colonialism.⁴ Among the Latin American writers intrigued (and oftentimes troubled) by theories of Asian migrants as the first to populate the Americas was Mexico's foremost national poet, Octavio Paz. Indeed, Paz spent a great part of his career vested in Asian cultures for purposes of articulating Mexico's non-European roots, thereby seeking to imagine an alternative national identity.⁵

Paz's and his contemporaries' work concerning theories of Asian migration to the Americas uncovered drastic differences and intriguing similarities between Asian and Mesoamerican cultures, particularly in terms of their respective cosmologies. On these relationships, Paz writes:

> The differences [between these two cultures] are less disturbing than the similarities: one would say [their views of the cosmos] deal with distinct versions of the same conception. *These analogies [including their similarities] do not confirm direct influence of Chinese civilization in America.* Chinese worldviews predate the era of the Confucian reform, which is to say, they belong to a period in which the limited advances in navigation technology prevent us from engaging

the possibility of maritime relations between both continents. As a result, it is fair to say that the [similarities] *are independent developments of the same seed.*[6]

In one of his many essays written in the 1950s and 1960s, Paz conceives of the possibility of locating an Amerindian kernel of knowledge planted by prehistoric Asians in Mexico. According to Paz, one might harvest this kernel by regarding Asian cultures closely, and then studying the foundations of American civilizations that developed in relative isolation after water levels rose in the Bering Strait and severed further intercontinental contact. Since European conquest destroyed the codes for interpreting pre-Cortesian cultures entirely—including the art of reading Aztec glyphs—Asia represents for Paz the opportunity to identify the seeds of a precolonial Mesoamerican worldview, ones planted by prehistoric migrants, yet cultivated in relative seclusion until their near complete destruction by Europeans thousands of years later.[7] Put another way, Asian cultures represent the possibility of unearthing a kernel of Mesoamerican knowledge that predates the colonial era, and they provide a means with which to identify an indigenous consciousness that must have developed in relative isolation after rising water levels cut off migration routes from the East.

Clearly, for Paz, his decades-long work on Asia underscores a desire to redeem lost native civilizations by interpreting Amerindian values via Asia, instead of through contemporary cultural remnants tainted by Europe. According to Camayd-Freixas, "This was Paz's unavowed poetic agenda: to posit an Asian Amerindian seed; to read it via poetry, supplying the missing worldview by means of an archeology of knowledge, a regression *ad ovo* along the continuity of Eastern thought in order to arrive at the shared archetype on which to ground the symbolic reconstruction of a bridge of continuity linking original Amerindian culture with modern Latin American poetics, as though the Conquest had never taken place. This would in fact be a poetics of counterconquest, a countercolonial Orientalism."[8] Put another way, Asian ideas and poetry represent for Paz nothing short of keys for unlocking the mysteries of pre-Cortesian cultures in the Americas, including their views of the cosmos and their inhabitants' relationships with it. Particularly attentive to structural semblances between pre-Cortesian and Asian cosmologies, Paz's surrealist poetics become the methods by which to reconstruct and make intelligible what Raymond Williams has called, in a different yet related context, a "structure of knowledge."[9] This transpacific structure of knowledge, for Paz, is the key to reconstituting and to identifying foundational relationships between original Amerindians and contemporary Mexicans, all while using Asian cultures as an operative intermediary. For this reason, Paz's compositions of this era are often organized according to archetypal semblances between Chinese and Mesoamerican values, particularly with respect to their emphases on religious dualisms and a mystic cosmogony.[10] Put in Derridian terms, poetry for Paz is the vehicle for discovering a "transcendental signified" that marks the absolute meaning of culture for Mesoamerican societies and pre-Columbian ideas.[11]

Paz's prose on this matter reveals that he understood well the difficulty of undertaking such a poetic agenda; his personal notes on this issue highlight his ambivalence. Locating a shared kernel of cultural knowledge between Asians and Mexicans across fifty thousand years, and then organizing this wisdom into a poetic system with which to *first uncover it,* is a troubling paradox, no matter the depth of the poet's intellect or the finesse of his linguistic skills. Yet Paz's greatest impediment may not have been a lack of literary ingenuity or the archeological contradictions of his poetic strategy. It may have very well been his doubt. For Paz, healthy skepticism on this matter eventually came into play once he began to consider dispassionately the complex global routes of cultural and commercial exchange across modern and ancient history. Most problematic, however, is Paz's recognition of the work of anthropologist Claude Lévi-Strauss, who regarded the binary structures of cosmological myth (on which Paz based Asian-Mesoamerican cultural semblances) as a potential *universal* dualism found in civilizations across the planet.[12]

Still, the Asia-Aztec theory piqued Paz well into the later phases of his career. He writes: "How to explain [the cosmological] semblances [between America and Asia]? I don't know. I don't mean to suggest the Asiatic theory [of a rudimentary culture] is false: instead I affirm that the hypothesis is weak and the proof insufficient. . . . The Asiatic theory doesn't convince me, but it does move me. If my reason rejects it, my sensibility embraces it. And the testimony of the senses, for me, is no less decisive than that of judgment."[13] Intrigued, yet not convinced, Paz's speculations sharpen his critical judgments on this matter, and they reinforce his values anchored in surrealist aesthetics. Indeed, he posits that perhaps he sees one world melded into another through the suspended continuities of time between Asian and American cultural landscapes *because his imagination constructs it so.* As a committed surrealist, Paz forfeits absolute values of truth and surrenders to art, subjectivity, and the imagination, concluding that "veritable realism is [always] imaginary. . . . Beyond truth an error—the discussion remains open—the Asiatic theory forces us to see ancient American works of art through a different lens."[14]

Paz's decades-long intellectual relationship with Asia is worth exploring in this book on Chicana/o-Asian encounters because it highlights the cultural value of a text by one of Chicana/o literature's most widely read authors, *A Chicano in China* (1986) by Rudolfo Anaya. In this text, Anaya dedicates himself, like Paz, to emergent theories of Asian migrations to the Americas in the context of cultural inheritance and national identity. Whereas Chicana/o writers like Luis Valdez, Miguel Méndez, Oscar Acosta, and others all worked to establish political identities in the image of peasants and contemporary freedom fighters in Vietnam, Anaya works to construct Chicana/o cultural identity according to a relationship with prehistoric Asians who first inhabited the Americas. In this respect, Anaya's meditations on Asia articulate Chicana/o identity by participating in literary fashions of Latin America, instead of by practicing those of local protest culture that underscored a link between Chicana/os and Vietnamese as colonialized populations. As such, *A Chicano in China* expresses a common desire to privilege the Chicana/o's relationships with Latin American and Native American cultures over its Anglo-American and Spanish influences, yet it does so by insisting on this community's *Asian roots.*

Best known for his popular novel *Bless Me Última* (1972)—which as of 2015 has gone through more than twenty print runs and has sold more than 360,000 copies—Anaya has established himself as one of Chicana/o literature's most recognizable figures. Critics have rightfully noted that *Última* has enjoyed almost worldwide positive acclaim as a result of its "self-conscious drive to attain to 'universal' significance," despite "its [specific] social and geographical parameters set around rural New Mexico."[15] Rich with local legends and ripe with regional mysticisms, this text, according to Vernon Lattin, marks a "paradigmatic instance in American literature [as a result of its] transcendental desire to recuperate the separation between man and nature."[16] Indeed, Anaya's prized novel deploys local cultural values and regional cultural tongues in order to speak to a universal theme: man's alienated relationship with his environment.

If *Bless Me Última* attains universal significance by exploring the common theme of man's severance from nature, then *A Chicano in China* seeks to attain local significance by exploring Latin America's severance from its Asian roots. This latter text—far from exploring the mystic significance of nature according to patterns of high literary technique—instead reads as a prosaic journal of daily impressions on the author's two-week journey across China, a place which he identifies in the introduction as "the birthplace of the Asiatic people who thousands of years ago wandered over the Bering Strait into the Americas" (vi). From these opening pages, Anaya's narrator announces straight away that he imagines his travels as a pilgrimage to China; it is a journey to the Chicana/os' native land, which will mimic the migratory patterns of this community's earliest ancestors—in reverse.

The trip, therefore, is motivated by the narrator's desire to discover his roots by laying claim to his cultural heritage. He affirms his cultural and ethnic identity at the moment he embarks on his voyage, making clear in the narrative's opening pages that he is a "native son of the Mexican community of the United States, one who also takes pride in that part of [him] that is Native American" (vii). In this way, the text registers the reader's own departure into the story by confirming that the significance of the narrator's journey is to "seek out the history and thought of the Americas [specifically]" (viii). Indeed, the text emphasizes that the narrator's travels across China are nothing short of a prescribed cultural journey in identity formation; it is an Asian pilgrimage for understanding a Chicana/o and Native American heritage to which he has already laid claim—and confirmed. In other words, Anaya's narrator flies to Asia to shed his European past and to find his true native self, one which he has *already* reinvented as Chinese.

Significant here is the narrator's stopgap approach for regarding the value of China in coming to terms with his contemporary Chicana/o identity, including the erasure of his Spanish roots. Asserting a false positivism, the narrator notes:

> This is not a trip to Europe, or Mexico. . . . China is part of the old Asiatic world that sent its migrations of people across the Bering Strait thousands of years ago; those people were the *real source* of the Mesoamerican populations, the Native American. . . . [This is] a visit to the *origin*, that is, the origin that does *not* belong to Spain. (3–5, my emphasis)

Recalibrating Chicana/o racial and cultural mixtures away from Europe, Anaya's narrator fantasizes a return to Native American origins by crossing the Pacific Ocean—and not the Atlantic—thereby bracketing over five hundred years of colonial history. Having already affirmed himself as a "native son of the Mexican community of the United States," one who also "takes pride in that part of [him] that is Native American," the narrator therefore romanticizes his indigenous self, not as an assemblage of European and Mesoamerican racial mixtures, but rather as a *direct* ancestor of Asian migrants.

In this sense, the narrator establishes a curious and circuitous route of identity formation that traces the roots of contemporary Chicana/o culture back to a prehistoric Asian source. The text's point of departure does not simply mark the narrator's enplanement for Asia. It also establishes a conceptual frame through which to see and to reconstruct relations between early Amerindians and contemporary Chicana/os, using only the cultural tools and influence of the Chinese and dismissing those inherited from the Spanish colonialist. In other words, as the narrator travels the plenary routes of his itinerary from New Mexico to mainland China to discover the roots of his non-European origins, he constructs a fantasy heritage that redeploys the logic of uninterrupted cultural inheritance between Chicana/os and Native Americans to include ancient Chinese before them, as if the conquest had never occurred, or had only minimal impact on indigenous cultures.[17]

This reading is elucidated by Anaya's own public musings on the significance of "New World Man," the name with which he configures a sense of authentic identity that is local to the US Southwest and is severed from its Spanish past. In a public interview, Feroza Jussawalla asks Anaya to elaborate on this sentiment, particularly with regard to statements the author had made concerning the identification of his roots in New Mexico. Anaya responds: "What I am trying to do in my work and when I talk to people, is—by having them look down at their feet and their roots, at the soil of the New World—to take a meaning and identification from it. *We don't have to go to Europe or to Spain to find our roots. We have finally become New World persons.* I think if we don't do that, we will never meet our authentic selves."[18] If understanding the "authentic" Chicana/o self entails accentuating the new world and the local, while deemphasizing the European and the Spanish, then *A Chicano in China* reveals a problematic element of this imaginary counter-colonial genealogy. In order to become finally a "new world" person of the Americas, the Chicana/o subject must now recognize itself as "old world" Chinese.

Clearly allured by romantic fantasies that identify Native Americans and Chicana/os of the US Southwest as authentic and original descendants of the Chinese, the introduction to *A Chicano in China* thus scales down significantly, if not erases entirely, the social complexities and violence of Chicana/o and Native American histories. The almost unimaginable brutalities of Spanish colonialism and the ongoing civil rights struggles of Chicana/os become replaced by the mysteries of ancient Chinese symbols as the matters for regarding contemporary cultural and political identity. In this way, Anaya's emphasis on the "authentic" and "local" problematically demands the simultaneous erasure (Spain) and the romantic inscription (China) of the global, both at the expense of the stuff of material history.

This process of privileging symbolic semblances between Chicana/os and Chinese over matters of material history facilitates the narrator's faculty for imagining his new "Chinocano" self, so to speak, once he arrives in China. In particular, the narrator notices the symbol of the dragon repeated across the palace grounds of Beijing as a sign of the Asian origin that he seeks. "The dragon is everywhere" (21), he says, and it reminds him immediately of the feathered serpent in the Aztecan pantheon, Quetzalcoatl.[19] Inspired by the semblance of the Mesoamerican symbol reiterated across the palace grounds, the narrator links other archetypal features of China to Mexico, all to the degree that he imagines the Chinese palace as a contemporary iteration of Teotihuacán, a pre-Columbian city in Mexico.[20] He says of the palace grounds:

> The dragon is everywhere. That is why I have dragons in my dreams. Now I know. Now I see. Something about the vast courtyards between the buildings reminds me of Teotihuacán in Mexico. The walls, the smells, the sprigs of grass and weeds on the grounds. The dragon is everywhere, the flaming Quetzalcóatl of Mexico. I am on the right track. The face of the fierce dragon looks out at me from walls, from gargoyles, from decorative pieces, almost exactly as the serpent head in the pyramids of Mexico. This is my first clue. *This is the door I seek.* In the faces of the people it is written: the migrations of the people from Asia across the Bering Strait, down into the Americas, thousands of years ago. Those Asiatic people came bringing their dragon dreams. (21, my emphasis)

Clearly, Anaya's narrator places much value on the perceived semblances between the Chinese and Mesoamerican dragons in their respective cultural cosmologies. However, he highlights less that this is a shared archetypal symbol and emphasizes more the *sensation and sensibility of sameness* generated by the Chinese palace. "Something about the vast courtyards between the buildings [of the palace] reminds me of Teotihuacán in Mexico" (21), he says, mystified. For the narrator, his visit to the palace arouses in him a strange sensation of surprising familiarity. Beyond the semblance of certain formal elements between the palace grounds and Teotihuacán—including the recurring dragons, and steep and stepped architecture (which signify the layers of the universe in Chinese and Mesoamerican cosmology)—there arises in Anaya's narrator a powerful sensation of cultural similitude, an overwhelming structure of transhistorical and transpacific *feeling*.[21]

Convinced that this feeling is indeed the unnamed seed of the Chicana/o's secret origin, the narrator immediately begins to imagine his Chinese hosts as Chicana/os, and to re-remember Native American friends of New Mexico as Asian. For example, at the palace, he misrecognizes Mrs. Wang, his group's tour guide, as a familiar woman from Laguna Pueblo, a Native American tribe of New Mexico (21). Shortcutting dramatically the material, cultural, and subjective particularities of his Chinese host, Anaya's narrator enacts a process of epistemological transgression not only on the Chinese, but also on a good friend back in Taos, New Mexico. Anaya writes:

> I had a friend in the Taos Pueblo, the commune of the Taos Indians. Cruz, an old man who taught me to hunt. Now I think I see his face in the pine trees [here in China]. Cruz, old man of the pueblo, governor, cadre, hunter, farmer, communal man, man of power. Now I know the power he carried in him, the power we carried in the mountain on the hunt, the hunt to provide for the Pueblo. He was a dragon man. He knew how to balance his energies. Thousands of years separated from the Orient, separated from Asia, thousands of years since the migration from Asia and he still carried the supreme sense of the dragon in his soul. (46–47)

In possibly the most egregious instance of appropriating another's ethnic identity, Anaya's narrator refashions Cruz's selfhood according to a curious racial logic. This logic borders between the philosophy of a shared cultural seed among Native Americans and Chinese on the one hand, and biological essentialisms that resemble the very discourses deployed in the service of Native American subjugation on the other. As one of the few critics to regard *A Chicano in China*, Jeffrey Cass argues that this scene in which the Pueblo Indian is retrospectively turned Asian "transforms Chicana/o [and Native American] history into a rhetoric of eugenics."[22] Cass's point is well taken, yet perhaps somewhat overstated, for one cannot overlook how the narrator's interest in Cruz's Asian identity resuscitates for him the *spiritual sensation* of Native American and Chinese sameness, one stemming from a cultural seed that seemingly nourishes their common soul. According to Anaya's narrator, Cruz's relationship with the land and "his power in the hunt" testify not to his biological constitution, at least not exclusively, but rather to "the supreme sense of the dragon in his soul." In this regard, the narrator's interest in finding the "genetic material for [decoding] New World Man," as Cass argues, is not so much the result of racial essentialisms as it is a result of the narrator's negligible approach (if not his desperation) to assert Native American and Chinese cultural equivalences.[23] In other words, Anaya's narrator haphazardly establishes interracial semblances across the Pacific based on his appropriations of the Chinese dragon he sees surreptitiously etched across Asia's cultural landscape, as well as across Mexican prehistoric landmarks that are carved deeply in his memory.

This rush to judgment leads the narrator to see the Chinese not as the other, per se, but rather to recognize the Asian as a foundational other within. To be sure, the Chinese do not represent a referential political figure for Anaya's narrator to assert oppositional political action. Instead,

"Chinese" emerges as a concept, one with which the narrator molds transpacific equivalences according to loose interpretations of Asian cultural traditions and Native American symbols. If, as Edward Said notes, Orientalism is a "system of knowledge about the Orient, an accepted grid for filtering through the Orient into Western consciousness," then Anaya's text itself is a system of representation, one which seeks to affirm Chicana/o and Asian identities by romanticizing Chinese culture as the projected image of the Chicana/o's.[24]

The one-way projection of this cultural agenda is brought to bear by the narrator's own admission that his hosts do not recognize him as Chinese, much less an ancestral relative from across the spans of land and time. Whereas the narrator imagines the Chinese he encounters as contemporary Pueblo Indians who have inherited an Asian soul, the Chinese decidedly do not recognize him as a spiritual next of kin. Instead, they see him for what he is: a Western tourist. For instance, street vendors greet him "with awkward stares and some surprise" (66), for they have never seen a Mexican American. Whereas the narrator believes he "is no longer American" (67), and stops speaking English in order "to remove [himself] from the group of [Westerners]" (91), the Chinese fail repeatedly to recognize him as a spiritual cousin. This intersubjective gap marked by a lack of mutual self-recognition is not insignificant; and at one point a group of Chinese mistake the narrator for an Arab (28).

Unnerved by the lack of mutual recognition, Anaya's narrator proceeds to refashion haphazardly his own identity in a romanticized cultural image of China that largely ignores its own ethnic diversity. "How simple it is for me to relate to these brown [Chinese] men and women I see bent over rice fields and vegetable gardens" (40), the narrator declares as he moves about the country, imagining moments of false intersubjective recognition between himself and the locals he encounters. Indeed, this pattern of identity appropriation largely organizes the narrative proper: as he moves about the country, the text insists on bringing to bear the narrator's life as a manifestation of the people he views from a distance. "Perhaps," he says,

> *I feel close to China because I have lived in that peasant, rural culture during my formative years.* A hard life, but so full of rewards that I would not trade it for another. Perhaps, in a past life I have lived in China; I have lived in the villages. I have seen the Mongolian warriors swoop down from the north or I have been a poet in the court of some emperor. Who knows? Certainly, there is a strain in my memory that feels connected to the collective memory of these people. *I see myself in their eyes and the color of their skin.* (94–95, my emphasis)

Once again treading the boundary between cultural relativity ("Perhaps I have lived in that rural culture during my formative years") and biological essentialism ("I see myself in their eyes and the color of their skin"), Anaya's narrator moves from misidentifying Asians as Chicana/os to imagining himself as a self-declared "Chicano Chinaman." In this curious and abrupt instance of identity transformation, the narrative initially marks the narrator's Chinocano identity with an element of doubt marked by the subjunctive mood (*"Perhaps*, in a past life I have lived in China"). Quickly, however, the narrative sheds the subjunctive mood and imagines in the present indicative mood the narrator's and the Chinese's common sensibilities. For the narrator, this commonality stands as hard evidence of a shared identity: it is born of the same seed of absolute consciousness, reinforced through the assumption of a collective memory, and finally rediscovered by insisting on racial symmetries ("Certainly, there is a strain in my memory that feels connected to the collective memory of these people. I see myself in their eyes and the color of their skin").

Along this trajectory of identity transformation, the Chicano's Asianness manifests itself not by plotting political sameness between subjugated populations that resist Anglo American hegemony (as Chicana/o writers often did during the Vietnam War). Rather than conflate racial particularities according to idyllic projections of transnational political solidarity, *A Chicano in China* instead fashions a brand of Chicana/o-Asian sameness by seeking cultural codes that unlock a collective cultural memory. History has locked away these unnamable cultural codes after the prehistoric migrations from East to West; yet apparently, they are easily recovered by tracing migrations from West to East, at least for Anaya's narrator. He insists on unearthing Chicana/o and indigenous roots by searching for cultural clues scattered along the original routes of the first Asian migrations to the Americas, and he finds them immediately, and often.

Unequivocally, the cultural clue that is impressed upon the narrator most forcefully, and almost singularly, is the image of China's iconic dragon. Although attending to similar harmonies and compositions between Mexican and Chinese music (155) and to semblances between Mexican and Chinese funeral processions (85), and convinced that Southwestern folklore of the Golden Carp originates from the yellow fish he sees swimming in a Chinese lake (152), the narrator pays particular attention to the "content" and "hidden knowledge" contained in the symbol of the Chinese dragon.[25] For Anaya's narrator, the image of the dragon is a synecdoche for China itself. It is a national emblem that embodies the values of an entire country and whose scales code the cultural secrets of Chinese history that he desperately seeks to lay bare.

Coming to terms with the cultural significance of the Chinese dragon, Anaya's narrator notes that variations of the serpent traditionally symbolize potency and the powers to control water, the essential resource of life. He also notes the dragon as the symbol of the emperors of China, representing their godlike supreme being, as well as their natural earthly incarnations. Most significantly, however, is that the dragon for Anaya's narrator represents energy, a spiritual life force that encapsulates the delicate yet harmonious balance of nature's violent oppositional forces. For this reason the text codes the dragon's energies fugaciously as both masculine (fire, sun, heat, aggression) and feminine (water, rivers, oceans, passivity). These oppositional forces ravish the narrator's soul and morph his spirit into the image of the Chicano Chinaman he so desperately wants to experience. Notably, this transformation occurs during a bout of passionate yet pacifying sex, during which the dragon enters the narrator's body. The narrator says:

> It rained last night. A refreshing rain. This morning the parched earth of China is damp. The sky is overcast. . . . We stay indoors and read and record our thoughts. I sleep, and in my fitful sleep, a dragon enters my body. I need this time of being alone and still to feel the thrashing dragon. China is entering me. I am absorbing China. I am making my peace with this giant country and its billon people. It is a fitful sleep, a restless sleep, full of dreams, memories, vague sounds, which echo first in Chinese then in Spanish. It is the power of the land and the people; the yin and the yang which come in the form of the brilliant, twisting dragon to enter my body. Only when I no longer resist does China rest in my heart. The dragon settles itself in me, its eyes breathing fire through my eyes. Its breath the life in my lungs, its serpentine body settled along my spine and heart and liver and stomach. Each dragon scale touching and resting at one of the body's acupuncture points. The tail of the dragon spreads to my feet. The dragon sex now goes into my balls and penis. Finally, it has entered me completely. I am still. I have made my peace with China.
>
> When I awaken, I feel refreshed, a new man. A dragon man. . . . The yin and yang, the opposites, the polar forces waiting for me to use them as I wish. . . .
>
> I have the dragon coiled in my body. I feel I am a new man. A Chicano Chinaman. (45–47)

Juxtaposed to other instances in which "China is a jealous woman-in-the-blood: a dragon, which once experienced will never let go" (79), and still others in which China is a "she dragon" (100), the instance above highlights a masculine image of a sexually charged dragon that ravishes, penetrates, and then impregnates the narrator's body. Jeffrey Cass notes that the image of the dragon in this moment operates as a "colonialist metaphor," one which "incarnates Anaya's own imperialist designs" of "appropriating its physical properties in order to assert an imagined scene for a revitalized and repoliticized Chicanismo."[26] This claim is brought to bear by the narrator's fantasy of absorbing the mythical powers of the Chinese dragon and enlisting a billion "Chinese Brown Brothers" for the Chicano cause, so the two "could rule the world" (17).

However, this image of a dragon penetrating the narrator's physical body also symbolizes thinly his spiritual appropriation and embodiment of a Chinese soul, the cultural seed of which has been replanted in his body through the serpent's dominating sex. Indeed, the morning after this ravishing sexual bout, the narrator feels himself a new man. He is now a self-declared "Chicano Chinaman," with "the dragon coiled in his body." According to the narrator, he now carries in his body and soul what he significantly interprets as a "supreme" sign of culture (47). The Chinese dragon is now nestled firmly in the narrator's belly through an act of satisfying sex; it represents for him the absolute and hitherto lost seed of Chinese culture to be nurtured and attended to in the future by a Chicana/o host. Briefly put, the narrator now carries in his core what for him must be the lost and forgotten kernel of his own cultural DNA.

In this regard, the "supreme" dragon signifies for the narrator a point of reference from which all systems of Chinese and Chicana/o cultural meaning ultimately originate and toward which they inevitably gesture. The dragon is a symbol that marks the origin, where differential traces of all cultural meaning begin and end; Anaya's narrator imagines the dragon as a kernel of absolute knowledge and the genesis of all cultural signification for Chinese and Chicana/os. In this sense, the dragon is not just a key or gateway to knowledge about Chicana/os and Native Americans, but rather it is the symbolic core of all cultural knowledge itself.

Committing himself to beliefs that culture is tantamount to absolute knowledge, Anaya's narrator is able to claim an authentic and otherwise autochthonous Chicana/o identity that is born in ancient China, yet otherwise differentiated from contemporary Chinese. Through a heuristic exercise that underwrites mythologies of Chicana/o cultural autonomy, he claims to have found the original source of both Chicana/o and Asian cultural ideas, knowledge whose respective advancements—he imagines—have developed in almost complete isolation after Asian migrants first populated the Americas in a prehistoric age. In this way, the narrator deflects anxieties about the potentially corrupting elements of contemporary Asia on the integrity and coherence of Chicana/o culture, for he mythologizes a

Chicana/o consciousness that is both essential (unchanged across history) and absorptive (able to incorporate and then discard Asian difference into his fantasies of Native American genealogies). The narrator emphasizes this point by asserting Chicana/o and Asian difference at the conclusion of his trip. He states:

> The journey to China has been made; it will linger in the memory; it will sleep through my thoughts; it will become part of my personal history. . . . I have found myself, I can say that; I have found a small part of myself in the Third World, in the villages and the cities of China, I have been in the arms of my mistress, my bittersweet China; from this fulcrum I do not move the world; I can only move myself. From this space between yin and yang I stretch my muscles and create more space and in that space I describe myself and my history. . . . A Third World man, who in his own time, has moved into parallel planes and times of other worlds *as the Chinese move into the time and reality of [other] new worlds* . . . (183–184, my emphasis)

Despite the shared origin on which the narrator's claims of cultural authenticity rest, Chicana/os are decidedly not Chinese in this instance, at least not contemporary ones. The text achieves this intersubjective remove by means of classic Anayan mysticism, which privileges the spiritual over brute matters of material history. In order to distance himself from the modern Chinese whose cultural history has inspired his new self, the narrator fashions "a space between yin and yang" in order to regard personally "my history." In other words, instead of recognizing his travels as a well-scripted tour, one largely organized by the Chinese government and restricted to highly regarded tourist sites, Anaya insists on having "moved into parallel planes and times of other worlds." It is within the conceptual boundaries of this unnamed dimension that the narrator claims to have discovered the seed of his identity, one that marks him as a cultural relative of *ancient* Asian populations, yet which nevertheless marks him as dissimilar from *contemporary* ones.

As such, Anaya conceptualizes an autochthonous Chicano self with Asiatic origins, while insisting that this identity is unique from contemporary Chinese who, having moved into the "time and reality of new [and different] worlds," have assumed new and distinct identities. What Anaya means by "Chinese," therefore, is not any particular social identity; and certainly he does not mean it to refer to a contemporary set of political experiences in Asia. The signifier "Chinese" in these representative instances that mark the narrator's spiritual awakening is therefore not a sign with which to tease out social relationships between Chicana/o and Asian material histories. Instead, China is a means for the narrator to project onto his political self an indigenous identity without having to claim contemporary social, economic, or political Asian life as matters of his own.

Put shortly, China symbolizes a fantasy. It is a stopgap summary of cultural origins used for ideological deployment in a discourse on Chicana/o identity that already romanticizes its pre-Cortesian beginnings. For this reason, Anaya's text must be seen relative to Chicana/o cultural efforts of the 1970s that fantasize about this community's uninterrupted heritage beginning with the Aztec Indians. Yet in this instance, China is a transpacific cultural idea that the narrator inserts into well-established mythologies that imagine an uninterrupted continuum between pre-Cortesian societies and contemporary Mexican American realities, a continuum he desperately wishes to celebrate. The origin of identity idealized in *A Chicano in China* thus attests to a popular political ideology already circulated widely by cultural elites like Anaya well before his travels to Asia. For decades, this ideology has insisted that pre-Cortesian cultural products are somehow more authentic than those fashioned after colonial contact, and that native lineages are more genuine than European ones. In this sense, *A Chicano in China* codes the *rejuvenation* of a longtime political desire to establish an ancient pre-Columbian identity amid anxieties about European racial and cultural mixtures.

Along this circuitous and circumpacific route for establishing Chicana/o cultural origins, one critical question emerges, however: How has Anaya's narrator managed to discover the seed of Chicana/o cultural knowledge and render intelligible its form and content after its being hidden for tens of thousands of years from the rest of the global community? A note in the text's introduction offers a clue to understanding this important query. Anaya writes:

> For some time I have been seeking those simple secrets that hint at the deeper spiritual and humanistic relationship the pre-Columbian societies had with the Earth and with the deities of the cosmos. The ceremonies still exist, changed as they are by the passage of time and the onslaught of other cultures that have come to call the Americas their home. For those of us who listen to the Earth, and to the old legends and the myths of the people, the ciphers of the blood draw us to our past. But often the secrets are locked away in symbols we can no longer read, in legends we no longer understand, in paintings and in ancient writings that puzzle us. *There is a door we can enter, and in passing through the door illumination fills us and we see the truth* hidden in those symbols and secrets and stories of the past. This is what

the pilgrim seeks: *a key to turn, a door to enter,* a new way to see his role in the universe. (viii, my emphasis)

Despite claims of serendipity, or of his being the beneficiary of Chinese fortune, Anaya's narrator finds special knowledge by carefully calculating his own fate. In other words, he anticipates discovering the seed of Chicana/o cultural knowledge by insisting that a genetic model of Native American cultures survives. He must only travel to China to find it. We must recall that the narrator has already imagined himself a "Chicano Chinaman" in the narrative's opening pages, a form of identity that facilitates—or better yet ensures—that he will unearth the cultural seed of knowledge which he fortuitously unlocks.

Yet it is significant that he "sees" this seed in the symbol of China's emblematic dragon not as a result of poetic intervention or painstaking cultural decoding. His discovery is decidedly not the reward of an archeology of knowledge that uses the tools of language to reveal cultural mysteries. Instead, the narrator recognizes the dragon as a symbolic kernel of Chicana/o origins based on his cultural determinism. Put another way, the narrator locates the seed of Chicana/o culture in Asia because he desires it to exist, having already framed a predetermined and causal relationship between Chicana/o and pre-Cortesian cultures as a matter of his choosing, and less as a matter of evidence or poetic discovery. In this sense, Anaya's interpretations of Chinese culture highlight what Yunte Huang calls in a similar instance "transpacific displacement": "a historical process of textual migration of cultural meanings . . . poetics, philosophical ideas, myths, [and] stories" that inevitably "predetermine what we see and how we see it."[27] Indeed, Anaya's encounter with China and his transpacific interpretations of Chinese symbols corroborate and refine his precalculated view that ancient China represents an image of Mesoamerican cultures.

While Anaya's style and prosaic language do not reveal the secrets he seeks to unlock, they do establish China as a curious metaphor that reflects his cultural motivations: China is a "door" into the past, a gateway to the "old Asiatic world," "the real source of Native America. . . . The real source of the Mesoamerican populations, the Native American Indians, and all the mythology and thought which has intrigued and interested me for many years" (3). Already inflamed by a decades-long desire to discover a common origin to a transpacific culture, one that circumscribes Europe and romanticizes Native America, Anaya insists on having to pass through a symbolic door that will expose the "secrets and stories of the past."[28] This indelible image (and not Anaya's journalistic prose) gestures provocatively to the surrealist poetics of Anaya's predecessors across the Americas, many of whom experimented with structures of language in order to open a door that would allow one to see a Mesoamerican cultural union with Asia.

More specifically, this image of a door inevitably returns us to Octavio Paz, who articulated his transpacific linguistic experiments as a poetic excursion through "doors of time" and back into the ancient worlds of precolonial civilizations. Significantly, Paz's book of essays that speaks to the symbolic relationship between Asia and the Americas is entitled *Puertas al campo: Doors to the Land*. He (or his editor) complements this image by placing René Magritte's 1939 painting *La victoire* on the cover of this collection of writings (see figure 7). A well-known piece of a stand-alone door on a beach, Magritte's *La victoire*, we must recall, is midway open and seemingly fading as if the opportunity for passage is growing faint. On the far side of the door extends a vast blue sea and an indeterminate horizon in the distance. In the foreground, a solitary cloud enters the passageway and cannot be seen as it floats across the second side of the open door, which, oddly enough, frames nothing: the ocean and sky are just as visible within the doorway as they are beyond it. From his construction of China as a metaphorical door back to the Chicana/o's cultural origins, it appears that Anaya knew well this image of Magritte's door, and of Paz's references to it.[29]

Magritte's image brings to bear a significant point that Paz's critics have long highlighted, and which helps to elucidate the theoretical assumptions of Anaya's lone Asian text: Paz understood well that cultural similarities between China and Mesoamerica do not imply a direct cultural continuum *except in matters of aesthetics and the imagination*. Like Anaya, Paz maintained that mythical cultural structures between Chinese and Mesoamericans demanded investigation, and for the latter, this cultural inquiry constituted much of his poetic agenda for over four decades. Paz was to locate the missing Mesoamerican worldview by means of poetic innovation, one that would uncover its ancient Asian origins. Indeed, Paz's innovative poetics *are the journey* back to an archetypal cultural seed; and through a philosophical experimentation with language, the relationship between modern Mexican sensibilities and the ancient world would emerge, as if one had stepped through a mystical door into another place and era.[30]

Understood comparatively, Anaya's *A Chicano in China* stands as a confirmation. It is a conclusion to questions surrounding Mesoamerican cultural origins, juxtaposed to Paz's poetic inquiry of cultural reconstruction. Anaya's travelogue is the stuff of certainty, while Paz's poetry is synonymous with philosophy, for his quest to interrogate the relationship between modern and ancient cultural worlds does not seek to confirm archeological accuracy or to resolve historical debates. Rather, it explores an aesthetic theory of Latin American modernity and pre-Cortesian cultures using experimental and surrealist poetics. For Paz, poetry is the stuff with which

Fig. 7. Cover of Octavio Paz's *Puertas al campo*, featuring *La victoire*, by René Magritte. Published by Seix Barral, 1982.

to construct a door like Magritte's famous entryway on a deserted beach. It does not provide one with access to truth, but rather it frames an optics of knowledge that reveals, as Paz says in the same context, that "true realism is [always] imaginary."[31]

Undoubtedly, Anaya's depiction of China as an open doorway into the source of knowledge between Asia and the Americas is itself related to

Paz's project of reframing a transpacific cultural geography. Yet while Paz understood well that this poetic passageway into cultural knowledge may very well be an illusion—a chimera, like Magritte's depiction of a standalone door on an empty beach—Anaya concludes his text by expressing an unshakable faith in how this passageway has permitted him to establish a direct relationship between Asian and Mesoamerican cultures. For Paz, the image of a gateway to the cultural origins of Mesoamerica is a surrealist image, a symbol of the powers of poetry and the imagination to conceptualize and to structure a cultural critique. For Anaya, the image of a passageway to China is a shortcut, an operational metaphor for confirming the cultural DNA of pre-Cortesian societies and for framing a rhetoric with which to tell "secrets and stories of the past" (viii).

Understood as such, Anaya's text not only makes plain the imaginative spheres of culture on which his ideologies of identity are predetermined, but it also repeats the tropes of racial and spatial conflation found in earlier Chicana/o writings on Asia, *with a twist*. As a self-declared Chinaman, Anaya's Asian self is similar to, yet distinct from, the forms of racial flattening that constitute the circumpacific sameness that I have outlined in Paredes's, Hinojosa's, Valdez's, and Acosta's respective texts. To recall, Paredes's "Ichiro Kikuchi" and Hinojosa's *Korean Love Songs* establish racial equivalences in order to highlight deficiencies of US democracy for Mexican Americans soldiering in Asia, while Valdez's and Acosta's writings conflate racial differences with the effect of projecting romantic ideas about political solidarity between Chicana/os and Vietnamese. *A Chicano in China*, however, fashions a brand of Chicana/o-Asian sameness by insisting on a genetic *cultural* seed, one from which related yet distinct cultural universes blossomed after the first Asiatic migrations to the Americas. For Anaya's narrator, this cultural seed testifies to the Chicana/o's native roots in the hemisphere and to the community's direct relationship to the first Mesoamerican populations. In this regard, Anaya's text resembles not only the efforts of Latin American writers such as Octavio Paz who obsessed over theories of Asian migration to the Americas, but it also resembles the efforts of Chicana/o cultural nationalists of the 1970s who insisted on a continuum between contemporary Mexican Americans and Mesoamerican Indians of a precolonial era.

It is here where the contradictions of Chicana/o cultural ideologies on Asia come full circle: while cultural nationalists of the Vietnam War era romanticized this community's Amerindian heritage by largely *deemphasizing and forgetting* cultural constructions of Chicana/o and Asian sameness, *A Chicano in China* insists on transpacific equivalences in order to fantasize about this *same* pre-Cortesian lineage. As I have shown earlier, cultural nationalism became the primary tool both for imagining

Chicana/o identity and for galvanizing political organization in the 1970s.[32] During this era, cultural constructions of a circumpacific community conflicted with an ideological emphasis on indigenous civilizations, a point of stress that marginalized transnational political orientations for purposes of Chicana/o political cohesion. Political and cultural discourse of this era fantasized about national homelands; it claimed and romanticized pre-Cortesian origins as the means to articulate ethnic pride, and it emphasized these points by deploying repeatedly the image of American indigeneity to legitimate Chicana/o political struggles.

To be sure, establishing the Chicana/o's indigenous roots in the Americas also hinges on the overt romanticization of a pre-Cortesian past for Anaya's narrator, yet it does so by *stressing*, instead of marginalizing, its Asian influences. *A Chicano in China* thus concretizes a cultural identity by incorporating a neoclassical form of indigeneity that absorbs Asia, rather than delimiting it, as do its literary predecessors. Francisco Lomelí and George Mariscal remind us that in the 1970s, a generation of Chicana/o cultural brokers activated cultural identities by making fewer and fewer references to Asia; instead, they fashioned an image of the community based on romantic constructions of Amerindian racial lineages.[33] If this is so, then *A Chicano in China* reveals how, in order to address matters of pre-Cortesian culture, this community must imagine its Asian origins *first*, thereby marking a radical shift in how Chicana/o literature emphasizes and frames discussions on its indigenous roots. No longer eliding transnational difference, the construction of Chicana/o indigeneity in Anaya's text is fully dependent on imagining transpacific equivalences, ones this cultural community once disregarded.

In alignment with Anaya's text, a growing body of scholarship has recently emerged identifying Asia as the "fourth root" of Latin America's racial and cultural heritage.[34] Without disregarding the significance of Latin America's Indigenous, European, and African roots, this historical and anthropological research has begun to rediscover the forgotten stories of Latin America's Asian immigrants, including their significant impact on the region's many cultures. For example, scholars Robert Chao Romero, Julia Schiavone Camacho, and Erika Lee have followed the work of pioneers in this field, such as Evelyn-Hu Dehart and María Elena Ota Mishima, to rediscover and to recollect the histories of Asian immigrants at the US-Mexico borderlands, including the transnational lives they led across two separate hemispheres.[35] As we shall now see, "to rediscover" and "to recollect" emerge as operative verbs for excavating the formative and relatively forgotten histories of Asians in the US-Mexico borderlands and for mobilizing the thematic interests of the concluding text of this study: Virginia Grise's *Rasgos asiáticos*.

5

Chinese Immigration, Mixed-Race Families, and China-cana Feminisms in Virginia Grise's *Rasgos asiáticos*

> If we [Mexicans] reject the Chinese [from the national community], it is because man, as he progresses, multiplies less, and feels the horror of numbers, for the same reason that he has begun to value quality.
> —José Vasconcelos, *La raza cósmica*

As this book has highlighted, Chicana/o literary formations are characterized by significant contradictions that rely heavily on cultural practices that both include and exclude ethnic subjects from the imaginary communities they construct. It is fair to say that perhaps no other text has critiqued these processes of inclusion and exclusion in a Chicana/o context more famously than Gloria Anzaldúa's *Borderlands/La Frontera* (1987). A benchmark of Chicana/o letters, this text deconstructs exclusive constructions of Chicana/o communities by calling attention to their intraethnic differences and by highlighting those whom cultural discourses have obscured for purposes of political cohesion. Primarily tackling Chicana/o culture's nationalist and patriarchal tendencies, Anzaldúa engages rather than elides intraethnic differences with the effect of enabling a discourse with which to address racial, cultural, and gendered pluralities. In this way, her work confronts and exposes *culturas que traicionan* (cultures that betray)—be they Anglo American, Mexican, *or* Chicana/o—thereby signaling a critical shift in Chicana/o literature's postnationalist era and reformulating the gendered, racial, and linguistic borders of this culture's ideological interests.

In one of the many powerful and memorable passages in which she engages contradictions and discontinuities in Chicana/o culture, Anzaldúa writes:

> Alienated from her mother culture, "alien" in the dominant culture, the woman of color does not feel safe within the inner life of her Self. . . . Not me sold out my people but they me. . . . Though I'll defend my race and culture when we are attacked by non-Mexicanos, *conozco el malestar de mi cultura* [I know the ailments of my culture]. I abhor some of my culture's ways, how it cripples its women, *como burras* [like donkeys], our strengths used against us. . . . I abhor how my culture makes macho caricatures of its men. I do not buy all the myths of the tribe into which I was born. . . . The worst kind of betrayal lies in making us believe that the Indian woman in us is the betrayer. We, indias, mestizas, police the Indian in us, brutalize and condemn her. . . . The dark-skinned woman has been silenced, gagged, caged, bound into servitude with marriage, bludgeoned for 300 years, sterilized, and castrated in the twentieth century. For 300 years she has been a slave, a force of cheap labor, colonized by the Spaniard, the Anglo, by her own people. (42–45, my translation)

Calling out Chicano culture for having silenced patriarchy's violence against women, Anzaldúa restructures the hierarchies of her community's constituencies with a feminist neo-indigenous architecture. As such, her work demonstrates how, as Ramón Saldívar notes, deconstruction in Chicana/o narratives inevitably entails a reconstruction of ideas at the site of that which has been undone.[1] From this process of deconstruction and reconfiguration, the community in Anzaldúa's text ultimately emerges as one in constant flux, whose members' identities are plural and never static.

In this sense, Anzaldúa's work follows a tradition in Chicana/o thought that engages a US/Mexico binary to explore how cultural identities constantly intersect and oftentimes clash.[2] Yet her ideas also conceptualize how Chicana/os must negotiate the intersections of other important categories that constitute a sense of self: Anglo/Chicano/Indigenous, American/Mexican; First World/Third World, Man/Woman; English speaker/Spanish speaker; and more. Indeed, it is the perpetual *movement* across racial, national, classed, gendered, and linguistic borders that characterizes the constituents of Anzaldúa's borderlands, itself an analytic term that represents how discursive practices stage new types of Chicana/o identities beyond the realm of the national and the traditional. She writes: "The prohibited and forbidden are its inhabitants. Los *atravesados* [the crossed] live here: the squint-eyed, the perverse, the queer, the troublesome, the mongrel, the mulatto, the half-breed, the half-dead; in short, those who *cross over, pass over, or go through* the confine of the 'normal.'" (25, my emphasis in last instance). To be sure, Anzaldúa's formal border crossings in this text between memoir, poetry, critical exposition, and historiography, and her movement between three languages—English, Spanish, and Nahuatl—communicate and reproduce the interstitial condition that thematizes this passage and the larger text from which it is extracted. In this way, her work is a symbol for and consequence of a *condition of being*, of inhabiting and moving perpetually across the liminal spaces of racial, national, gendered, and linguistic boundaries.

Conceptualized by Anzaldúa and others, the borderlands, then, becomes a "zone of transition," an indeterminate space marked by the never-ending transgressions between many rigid categories of difference.[3] In the words of Rafael Pérez-Torres, to inhabit this space is to move constantly between "intersections of various discursive and historical trajectories," all of which overdetermine the cultural, linguistic, and gendered identities of its constituents.[4] For this reason, "the Chicana/o becomes a fluid condition, a migratory self."[5] Néstor García Canclini concurs, adding that the hybridism that Chicana/o writings often communicate emerges precisely from this capacity of its inhabitants to see the "multitemporal heterogeneity" of day-to-day life in the borderlands regions.[6] Indeed, "liminality," "interstiality," "multitemporality," "migratory," "ambiguity," and "heterogeneity" all emerge as catchwords for describing life at the US-Mexico borderlands, as well as for describing the constant flux of imagining the self in this cultural, national, and linguistic space. These terms may also serve as watchwords for regarding Virginia Grise's recent play *Rasgos asiáticos* (*Asian Traits*, 2011), a work whose formal features make visible the multidimensional and interstitial space of the US-Mexico borderlands on stage.[7]

To be sure, the play's cross-generational conversations, queer rhetoric, interracial unions, and cross-linguistic interplays collectively reproduce the experiential processes of Chicana/o identity with respect to "moving between the worlds of indigenous and European, of American and Mexican, of self and other."[8] However, the play's construction of a circumpacific space that includes the United States, Mexico, *and Asia*, the Mexican/Asian racial mixtures of its characters, and its linguistic exchanges in Spanish, English, and Cantonese reconfigure the borderlands in ways that are much more complicated than Anzaldúa and others have hitherto imagined. Put shortly, one must move in this instance between the worlds of the indigenous, the European, the American, the Mexican, *and the Chinese*.

Calling attention to the relatively forgotten history of Chinese immigrants in Mexico's border history, Grise's piece dramatizes the psychological consequences of imagining oneself as a queer Chinese-Chicana who is detached from her transnational past. As such, the play explores the lives of mixed-race subjects in a cultural universe that has largely elided its own "Asian traits" by romantically transposing native lineages (Aztecs) and hemispheric geographies (Aztlán) onto Chicana/o political thought. In this sense, the play's formal features dramatize the processes of inhabiting and speaking from a space of perpetual movement that has largely gone unrecognized, for the stage becomes nothing short of the site "where identities and cultures intersect" across four generations of women; between the United States, Mexico and China; and within English, Spanish, Nahuatl, and Cantonese linguistic systems.[9]

To begin, the play gives a brief synopsis of itself in order to establish coherency in what becomes a challenging spatial and temporal collage. The play's introduction offers this summation: "A series of conversations across time, between four generations of women who are searching for an understanding of hope, love, and home despite shared histories of violence. A courageous portrayal of love between women, questioning how to let go of binding gender roles" (1). Inhabiting its ambiguous constructions of space, which span nearly one hundred years and cover distances between the United States, Mexico, and China, are the play's six main figures: Hija (born in Texas, 1976); her girlfriend Esa (born in California, 1974); Mother (Hija's mom, born in Monterrey, Mexico, 1944); Maria (Hija's grandmother, born in Sonora, Mexico, 1928); Andrés (Hija's great uncle, born in Canton, China, 1886); and Wong (Hija's great-grandmother, born in Canton, China, date unknown). From this cluster of characters emerges a series of intergenerational and transpatial dialogues that navigate the play's thematic announcements on "hope," "love," and "gender." These conversations across race and space address both national histories that dismiss Chinese immigration to the US-Mexico borderlands and a family's quietude about gendered and racial violence in its community.

Primarily, it is the cross-temporal and intergenerational dialogues that mobilize the play's thematic interests. For instance, act one highlights tender affections between Hija, her girlfriend Esa, and her mother through a cross-generational and transpatial conversation involving all three. Positioned under steady light, Hija says to her mother, who "appears in different lights," "you were the first woman I ever loved," before sharing with Esa (also in differentiated light): "[you are] the first woman I ever trusted" (5). This act proceeds with Hija continuing to converse with her mother and Esa simultaneously, yet from different times of her life. She speaks to her mother tenderly during a moment when she was a young child, while she addresses Esa affectionately as her contemporary adult lover. As mother and Esa take turns speaking with Hija, irregular lighting illuminates their respective places on the stage. Each time one of the women speaks, her words emerge from places of shifting light; when she is silent, she stands in seeming darkness, but ever so present. The vacillating light between Mother and Esa marks distinct time-spaces of Hija's life, and as their conversations become more continuous, so too does the lucid intensity of each woman's presence.

This visual alteration quickly enables the play's transtemporal configurations, for the past and present now clearly collide as a matter of fact. As a result, the three women become conjoined in the present, linked by their shared feminine affections expressed across distinct historical moments. Enabling this temporal bridge, the irregular lighting that accompanies their concurrent conversations casts shadows across the stage, so that the dimness each woman inhabits begins to shift. As such, a visual pattern mobilizes the play's production, for lights mark both the speech and presence of each figure, while her silence is marked by dimness, if not darkness. This is not to suggest that the darkness signals absence, however. To be sure, the variations of light in this act mark the intermittent silences between Hija, her mother, and Esa; but they also symbolize historical differences between the present and Hija's childhood, showing how the temporal distances between these three women both divide them and invariably *connect* them.

From the conversations between these three women, the audience learns that Hija's father insisted her mother have an abortion because she "was too expensive" and "he too old." It also learns that Hija's mother insisted on having the child "with or without him" (6). Further, the audience is made aware of Esa's and Hija's intense lesbian romance, including their deep emotional union. Yoking the mother's affections for Hija to Esa's romantic passion toward this same figure, this initial act bridges the difference between them to form an intense triangulated bond, one marked by the distinct movement from disparate dialogues to concurrent conversations in which Mother, Esa, and Hija begin to speak as one another's echo. For example, Mother and Hija express in chorus their respective desires "to pull [the other] close until there is no space between us"; to which Hija and Esa add synchronously "[until there is] no distance" (6). Unsurprisingly, this temporal transformation is marked visually, for the simultaneity in dialogue corresponds to lighting that reveals at once Hija and Esa in their bedroom, and Hija's mother in the protagonist's childhood residence.

Between these shadows of differential lighting, the audience begins to hear and to see Hija, Mother, and Esa simultaneously and in proximity to one another, despite their having inhabited distinct time-spaces. This formal arrangement reveals that, in order to regard Hija's life, one must account for her transtemporal relations. Indeed, it becomes evident that Hija's past relationships, even with *deceased* members of her family, function as *living* structures of her day-to-day being. To this point, the author notes how intergenerational dialogues and intermittent lighting mark the relationship between the past and present, and between the living and the departed. In her notes to the play's production, Grise writes: "*The living and dead coexist*. Movement between time and space should be seamless and the stage should be transformed via light, sound, gesture or movement, not by set pieces. . . . The ancestors exist in separate spaces/times" (3, my emphasis). Here, Grise insists that the play's temporal and spatial features be configured by shifting light to illuminate how the living and the deceased coexist in Hija's consciousness, while still retaining their respective historical distinctions. Indeed, the conversations in act one show how the play's movements between different temporalities are produced by portraying invisible space as a shared place of marginality that Hija, her Mother, and Esa co-inhabit from particular historical moments. As the play proceeds, these movements across time reveal that the interstitial places between darkness and light—and the past and present—are where these women will inevitably come to recall the painful memories of their lives at the US-Mexico borderlands.

Among these painful memories are the tumultuous relationships between Mother, Maria (Hija's Mexican grandmother), and Manuel Yee (Hija's grandfather, a Chinese immigrant to Mexico). In one of the more memorable acts of the play, Mother and grandmother Maria sit stage side, both illuminated by a single flickering candlelight that casts waves of dimmed yet warm luminescence across the stage (12). From the shadows, Mother and Maria begin to narrate a history of Chinese immigration to Mexico during the early 1900s, including the story of Hija's Chinese grandfather, Manuel Yee. Maria, stage directions tell us, narrates these stories to Mother, while Mother relays them simultaneously to her own daughter, Hija. Stage instructions also remind us that despite their sharing the stage, Mother and Maria tell the "same story [but from a] different time" (13). Mother says, "The Chinese worked in the factories [in Monterrey], in the mines and Mexican plantations, on the railroads. *Sembraban* [They harvested]. They worked for hacienda owners when Mexican campesinos [field workers] went to fight in the revolution. They also worked [and owned] small stores" (13). Maria adds to the conversation, telling Hija they were "green shots and bean sprout merchants in the mercado in Monterrey" (13).

From this brief intermittent dialogue between three generations of women spoken across Mexico and Texas, Esa (and the audience) recognize not only that "the living and dead [simultaneously] coexist in different times and spaces," but also that remembering the forgotten history of Chinese in the US-Mexico borderlands is critical for establishing and maintaining the emotional bond that links Hija, Mother, and Maria. In other words, the pain and endurance of coming to terms with the history of Chinese immigration at the border is tantamount to understanding the pain and endurance that will establish the strong emotional attachment between the women in Hija's family.

In this sense, the temporal convergences in *Rasgos* exemplify what Emily Hicks describes in another context as the "multidimensional perception and nonsychronous memory" of borderlands constituents.[10] To this point, Alfred Arteaga notes that at the borderlands, "two nations are imagined in English and in Spanish and differentiate themselves at a common border, yet Chicano borderspace is a heteroglot interzone, a hybrid overlapping of the two."[11] Indeed, the borderlands space that emerges in *Rasgos* is nothing short of a "nonsynchronous heteroglot zone," to use Arteaga's theoretical vocabulary. However, in this instance, the "Chicano borderspace" that develops is a hybrid overlapping of English, Spanish, and Chinese. It triangulates the US-Mexico border with Asia and is constituted by Hija's "nonsynchronous memory" of her grandmother's relationship with a Chinese man, a story itself embedded in the oft-forgotten history of Chinese immigration to the borderlands region.

Maria's relationships with both Manuel Yee and his friend Andrés function as the play's primary means for excavating this forgotten history. These interracial unions reveal both the violence and sexism the women in Hija's family have long endured, and the racism Chinese immigrants suffered in Mexico in the early 1900s. In this way, the play communicates how Hija's pain begins with Maria's anguish when she marries an abusive husband. Unwilling to tolerate the abuse, Maria solicits Andrés's hand in marriage in order to escape her violent Mexican spouse. Only fourteen years old, yet already embedded in violent patriarchal structures that script her subservience, Maria does the unimaginable in the eyes of society: she leaves her husband, finds an apartment on her own, and then ultimately moves in with two older immigrants from China, one of whom is already married and with a child. She says:

> I move into a small apartment on top of the cigar factory, worse than my mother's home. My apartment has cockroaches and the smell of the cigar factory gets caught inside my chest. . . . Tomorrow, when I go to the market, I will ask Andrés [the Chinese merchant] if he needs a wife. I hear that it is hard for Chinamen to find wives in Mexico and I'm tired of the cockroaches. . . .

> I find out that Andrés has a wife. She lives in China [with their daughter]. I feel shame in my chest where the coughing hurts and I look at my feet but Andrés smiles and says that I should not worry. . . .
>
> Andrés feeds me. . . . He explains to me that he lives with his companion Manuel and because they're Chinamen they can't own anything—the house, their puesto en el mercado [booth in the market] and that he has a wife but Manuel doesn't. (31–32)

And so the story of Hija's Asian heritage and the history of Mexico's Chinese begin to take shape: her grandmother Maria abandons an abusive relationship, eventually seeks refuge with Andrés and his companion Manuel Yee, and finally marries the latter despite his being two decades her elder, all so that he can sign his store's deed in her name (33). From this story emerge two tales of survival, the first of a Mexican woman desperate to escape Mexico's patriarchal violence, and the second of two Asian immigrants desperate to cope with Mexico's racial discrimination against Chinese. When Manuel dies, seemingly of natural causes, Maria and Andrés develop a bond that positions them as agents of their own destinies amid Mexico's growing nationalism and its rigid patriarchal and racial ideologies. And in line with the play's overriding motif of simultaneity and convergence, this drama makes clear that Mexico's gendered violence against its women cannot be dissociated from its nationalist history of racial violence against its Chinese migrants.

To this point, a figure none other than José Ángel Espinoza had linked an anti-Chinese brand of Mexican nationalism to the oppression of the female Mexican body. A leader of several campaigns in northern Mexico to rid the country of Chinese, Espinoza published *El problema chino en México* in 1931 and *El ejemplo de Sonora* in 1932. This second publication in particular includes racist caricatures that portray Chinese as diseased subhumans who threaten the health of Mexican women, whom the text constructs plainly as a synecdoche of the national body (see figure 8). For example, one cartoon in *El ejemplo* depicts a dejected and ailing Mexican bride of a Chinese man alongside her sickly and degenerate offspring, calling the child an "escupitajo de la naturaleza" (a spit of nature).[12] Another cartoon depicts a Chinese merchant married to a robust Mexican woman, entitled "The night of wedding." In an adjacent image, marked "five years later," the Chinese man is seen walking away from his Mexican bride and their mixed-race children, each one frail, decrepit, and ill-looking.

In many parts of northern Mexico, class, gendered, and nationalist ideologies of the revolution (1910–1920) propelled an antiforeigner consciousness that extended beyond the war years, resulting in patterns of extreme violence against Chinese, who by the early 1920s made up the second-largest foreign-born population, behind Spanish nationals.[13] Evelyn Hu-Dehart reminds us that in this period, nationalists made particular targets of Chinese merchants like Andrés who had successfully established themselves as a "petite bourgeoisie."[14] Adding to this, Robert Ham Chande notes that over 97 percent of the Chinese population in Mexico during the first half of the twentieth century consisted of males, many of whom were small-business owners.[15] Among this modestly moneyed and overwhelmingly male Chinese population, interracial marriages with local women were not uncommon.[16] Yoking the modest success of Chinese merchants to their relationships with local women, nationalists like Espinoza constructed a powerful and gendered form of anti-Chinese rhetoric, effectively allegorizing the nation's economic and racial health on the bodies of Chinese Mexican brides.

Visually, Espinoza's work shows how cultural representations of Chinese-Mexican marriages developed into popular gendered critiques of economic nationalism throughout the twentieth century.[17] Still, the violence directed toward the Chinese was hardly only rhetorical, and Andrés shares portions of this material history during a conversational interplay between himself and Pancho, a representative figure of the Mexican Revolution's northern hero, the iconic Pancho Villa.

ANDRÉS: [T]hey [Mexican revolutionaries] take from me. Apple. From my puesto [store]. I take nothing. I came with nothing. Little bit I get, send home. Family in China. Many miles away. China many miles away now.

PANCHO: You carry yellow fever and syphilis, we must rid this country of you. Pests.

ANDRÉS: [I] go to Sonora. . . . I find marching band and bandits. Kill Chinese men on sight. They say a revolution. Mexican peasants fight revolution. I hide. . . . Talk to no one. . . . Swallow fear. Sonora. Desert. Home of Pancho Villa. Chinamen hang in trees. Chinamen shot in head. Villa steal [my] money. [I] go to Monterrey. In Monterrey they no kill Chinese, not like Sonora. I think Monterrey. I think not in city. For everyone to see. I think. . . .

PANCHO: If we do not run you out of our country, you will be the ruin of Mexico. You are the ones responsible for the misfortunes of this country.

ANDRÉS: In city they kill Chinamen. Just like Sonora. Kill them in plaza. I watch. . . . Rock in my hand. Rope round neck. Watch. Watch them hang. . . . Feet dangling. Body limp. You. You. You inherit the rock. The rope. The grief. The silence. They hang them in plaza downtown in middle of day. They kill men. You cannot find that story in your books. It has not been written but I see. Looking for Chinese temple during revolution, I find men with guns and ropes and rocks. (40–41)

Giving personal testimony of the murder of Chinese in Mexico, Andrés speaks in broken English, though one would presume his having learned Spanish during his many years in Mexico and considering his relationship with Maria. Without overlooking his curious orientalist diction or his bewildering inability to articulate fluently his immigrant experience in general, what emerges here is not so much the orientalist quality of Andrés's speech, but the racial and gendered violence that Hija has inherited as a Chicana woman of Asian heritage. Indeed, by 1916, more than a hundred Chinese had lost their lives in the border state of Sonora alone.[18] In Chihuahua, Piedras Negras, Mazatlán, and Mexico City, more than 550 Chinese were murdered between 1911 and 1919.[19] Robert Chao Romero notes that during this time, only one Chinese had been murdered in Monterrey, yet Andrés testifies otherwise, stating, "They [do] kill men [in Monterrey]. You cannot find that story in your books. It has not been written but I see."

What cannot be disputed, however, is that in 1911, Mexican revolutionaries massacred over three hundred Chinese and a few Japanese in Monterrey's neighboring city of Torreón, which lies only two hundred miles away. The murders came after revolutionaries took over the city from Federales and blamed Asians for exacerbating poverty in the area.[20] The law firm the Chinese hired to investigate the incident reported that civilian mobs joined revolutionary soldiers in pillaging businesses and homes while proceeding to carry out a series of gruesome murders. In one case, attackers severed the head of a Chinese resident and tossed it into the street. Other Chinese had their bodies cut to pieces with swords. In another instance, locals hitched a Chinese man to four horses and sent them in different directions, detaching his arms and legs from his body. And the young were not spared. One soldier is reported to have grabbed a boy by his ankles and swung his head into a lamppost, shattering his skull.[21]

Mexican violence against Asians and their Mexican brides serves as a cataclysmic, albeit silenced, history that casts doubt on the cultural futures of Chinese Mexican American children like Hija. At stake is the very historical memory of her Chinese relatives, which members of her own family have attempted to erase. On this point, Hija learns that when Andrés died, some members of her family "collected all of his belongings, his clothes, letters from his daughter in China, old photographs. They took them outside and burned them in a bonfire behind the house" (21). With the faint sounds of music from Andrés's old Chinese records playing

¡Ah infeliz!.... Creíste disfrutar de una vida barata al entregarte a un chino y eres una esclava y el fruto de tu error es un escupitajo de la naturaleza....

Fig. 8. "Oh unhappy woman! You thought you would enjoy an easy life together with a Chinese man, but you are a slave and the fruit of your mistake is a spit of nature." From *El ejemplo de Sonora* by José Ángel Espinoza, 1932.

in the background, Hija says chokingly, yet poetically, that as a result of this action, "mi espíritu [my spirit] left in gray ash [of] inquietude, [in] red embers of olvido [oblivion]" (23). The erasure of the racial and gendered violence against Chinese men and their Mexican brides—coupled with Hija's family having burned the relics of Andrés's life—constitutes the smoky historical terrain on which the play explores Hija's Chicana identity, and on which it inevitably attempts to recover her Asian past.

To stage this point, Grise blends shifting light, dance, and Chinese music to produce an opaque space accented by faint sounds of Chinese harmonics. This sepia-toned space of dim light inflected by Chinese music is the place that Hija and Andrés now co-inhabit, albeit during distinct temporal moments of their biographical histories. Hija shares with Esa that Andrés enjoyed dancing to his Chinese records, and that her mother and grandmother Maria likewise enjoyed music. When illumination shows Andrés dancing off to one end of the stage (25), Hija and Esa begin their own dance. The former tries to imagine how her mother and grandmother once moved to the music, saying, "I think [my grandmother] would have danced like Andrés" (26). During this transtemporal two-step between Hija and Esa (with Andrés still off to the side), lights illuminate "Maria dancing alone in her bedroom" (27). Soon the stage "lights up on Mother, Maria, & Andrés [at the same time]. They are having their own dance party" (28). Between lightness and darkness, visibility and obscurity, sound and silence, and proximity and distance, Hija, Esa, Andrés, Mother, and Maria now move in choreographic combination with one another—all on a stage that has become an interstitial and shadowy space for imaging their intersubjective union.

Visually and sonically, Hija's dance with Esa appropriates the darkness and dissonance of a history of racial violence, and of three cultural worlds colliding, to imagine a harmonious Chinocana lesbian identity for the future. Instead of sidestepping historical issues, her dance with Esa engages the gendered violence the women in her family have endured—and the racial discrimination these women and her Chinese ancestors have suffered—all in an attempt to find a rhythm of life moving forward. In this sense, the formal qualities of Grise's play produce nothing short of an image of a female subject caught between the discontinuous strands of national, cultural, and gendered differences across three national borders, and across history itself. Born from these clashes across time, Hija's transtemporal dance with her lesbian partner thus signals an attempt to make something coherent from the violence, "oblivion," and historical erasures that have left her "spirit in gray ash." Hija says at this instance of the play, "It's like the dance is the only place we [women] allow ourselves to completely take up space" (29). In other words, her ability as a woman to move and to inhabit the spaces between her Anglo, Mexican, and Chinese selves signals nothing less than an affirmation of her own presence and being. Dance in this instance actualizes for Hija her existence in an interstitial space bordered by three generations of women and triangulated between the United States, Mexico, and China. The result is a sense of selfhood that makes possible the potential to reconcile gendered and racial differences in the present and in the future. As such, Hija's transtemporal movements symbolize a conceptual coordination of the seemingly incommensurable racial, gendered, and national differences that constitute her very identity.

One family figure strikingly absent from this intergenerational dance party, however, is Hija's great-grandmother from China, a woman named "Wong." Shortly after the dance between Hija, Esa, Mother, Maria, and Andrés, "Wong appears [but only] in shadow" (49). Literally a specter in the gray space of the play's own ethereal production, great-grandmother Wong's presence is simultaneously affirmed and negated. Renamed "Concepción" by Mexican state officials upon her arrival from China, Wong never emerges clearly in full light on the stage. Speaking to this point of her obscurity, Hija says, "Concepción was her name. *Memorias de mi bisabuela que nunca conocí* [Memories of my great-grandmother I never met], whose pictures I never saw. Whose stories I never heard. Concepción. Wong. What was my great-grandmother's real name?" (49). Though self-directed, Hija's query finds a troubling response from her Mother. Grise writes:

> MOTHER: Your great grandmother never went to Mexico.... Chinese women didn't take that journey in those days.
> HIJA: But *she* did. I know she did.
> MOTHER: Your great grandfather was the first to come to the Americas. He's the one that traveled from Canton to Tampico.
> HIJA: I didn't just make up that story, mother. Where did I hear that story?
> MOTHER: I don't know.
> HIJA: You don't know?
> MOTHER: No.
> HIJA: What was her name, then? What's your grandmother's name, mother?
> MOTHER: I don't remember. (50)

Mother's denial of Wong's migration to Mexico reveals that what is at stake is more than the symbolic abstraction of the Immaculate Conception, despite her renaming as "Concepción" (and Hija's grandmother's name as "Maria"). Instead, Mother's refutation of Wong references not the sanctifying grace of a virtuous life free of original sin, but rather the very historical presence of Chinese women in Mexico.[22] Despite the negation, Hija remains adamant about Wong's presence and about her life in the Americas. She is convinced that she "didn't just make up that story" of her great-grandmother's transpacific migration, and of her lonely life far from her homeland. For this reason, when Wong reappears dimly lit in the shadows of the stage, she emerges not as a refined figure of absolute presence, but rather as a prefigurative image of Hija's own marginalized self within contemporary Chicana/o cultural communities. Positioned in the nearly invisible margins of the stage, Wong's erasure both on stage and by Mother symbolizes Hija's own figural absence in a culture that largely limits its rhetorical scope within the ideological borders of two nations, to the exclusion of its Asian past.

For this reason, Hija's *naming* of her great-grandmother—despite her Mother's refusal to do the same—is just as significant as, if not more significant than, her having a memory of her presence. "Concepción was her name. Memories of my great grandmother that I never met ... Concepción ... Wong." Américo Paredes notes that, "When we name things we give them a life of their own; we isolate them from the rest of our experience. By naming ourselves, we affirm our own identity."[23] Although largely focused on how derogatory references overdetermine the identity of the other, Paredes's insights help us to see how processes of naming are critical to identity formation, for they enable one to differentiate one's subjectivity in personal consciousness and in a social setting. In this instance, Hija and Mother's conversation about Wong stages the problem of naming as the governing problem of identity itself. With firm insistence on naming her Chinese great-grandmother, Hija reveals the complexity of subject formation marked by the "logos"—when the naming of the individual constitutes it as a subject.[24] Precociously, Hija senses how acknowledging Wong by her name repositions her in Chicana/o cultural and patriarchal discourses that have hitherto worked to delete her, thereby demonstrating an exemplary moment of what Louis Althusser calls in another context "interpellation": forms of ideological recognition, including those naming rituals that differentiate identity within an individual's (and culture community's) consciousness.[25]

However, the naming ritual here does more than conceptualize a sense of Wong's individuated self in Hija's consciousness; it also holds substantive consequences. In other words, Wong's naming positions her to assume a specific *material* existence in Chicana/o prehistory. Indeed, Wong's naming allows her to be recognized as a figure that gives shape to the Asian contours of the borderlands history that Hija has inherited. As such, Hija's insistence on her Chinese grandmother's presence does not indicate ethnic shame—about not wanting to be Mexican American. Rather, her firmness on the matter signals an attempt to make sense of the deletions in—and the discrepancies between—Mexican and Chicana/o social histories concerning Chinese immigrant women. For this reason, Hija's naming of Wong not only invokes the abstract process of subject formation, but it also holds substantive consequences that will delineate cultural and historical boundaries for Hija's membership in Chicana/o social communities. Put another way, Hija's naming of her great-grandmother signals an epistemic action with significant psychological and material effects: Hija senses her identity relative to her great-grandmother's erasure and to the forces of Mexican social ideologies, both of which script her day-to-day life as a Chicana coming to terms with Chinese history at the Texas-Mexico border.

Still, questions regarding the details surrounding Hija's Chinese great-grandmother persist. While Hija is certain of Wong's life in Mexico, she is largely uncertain about the particulars of her individuated experience as a Chinese immigrant woman. Furthermore, her family and community continue to participate in Wong's deletion, signaling a gap between the redemptive course of Chicana/o cultural history and the racial borders that delimit (and oftentimes delete) this community's Asian past. If anything, Hija's acknowledgment of her Chinese great-grandmother—despite national, cultural, and even familial attempts to forget the Chinese in Mexico generally—signals the difficulties of recuperating Wong's biographical life. In this sense, Hija's acknowledgment of her great-grandmother articulates how, for many contemporary Chicana/os who are ideologically divorced from important influences from beyond the Americas, their "Asian traits" may still be *remembered*, despite the difficulties of their absolute *knowing*.

This point is brought to bear as the play draws toward a conclusion, when Hija's queries regarding the details of her great-grandmother's life remain largely unanswered, and Wong remains a specter in the shadows of the play's dark diegetic production. Yet Hija refrains from romanticizing Wong's life; she refuses to insert her Chinese grandmother neatly into contemporary Chicana/o cultural frameworks. The young girl understands the impossibility of a stopgap attempt at understanding Chinese Mexicans by using long-standing cultural discourses about Chicana/o experiences. On the contrary, the formal arrangements of Grise's play force our attentions to the historical gaps that Wong symbolizes, and to the borders of the cultural historiographies that have constituted Chicana/o communities as we understand them today. Within a constructed space that actualizes historical gaps—ones produced from between lightness and darkness, absence and existence, sound and silence, and past and present—Grise's play communicates and then critiques the fissures Wong and China represent, both in Hija's life and in Chicana/o culture more generally.

Indeed, rather than fill these gaps with certainty and narrative resolution, *Rasgos* relies on ambiguity and openness, using an aesthetic strategy common to the borderlands regions. To be sure, Grise's work insists on "liminality," "interstiality," and "ambiguity" to describe Hija's cultural pluralities and to articulate her mixed-race life in the contemporary borderlands. This aesthetic arrangement, which uses intermittent light, faint echoes, and shifting temporalities, represents the constant flux of imagining one's own life in an undefined cultural, national, racial, and linguistic space that is the US-Mexico border. In other words, this play's formal designs make of the stage a space for articulating a host of discontinuities and convergences that have come to typify borderlands art, yet by way of a radically differentiated order that complicates a US-Mexico dyad.

Wong's parting words, which mark the end of the play proper, emphasize this point on discontinuity, convergence, and ambiguity. Standing before Hija, Mother, Esa, and Maria, the Chinese matriarch says cryptically: "xin zang, xin kong, you xin, xian, fei, xin zang, xin kong, you xin, xian, fei . . ." (55) (heart, sky of stars, deeply worried, existence, not to be, heart, sky of stars, deeply worried, existence, not to be . . .). Instead of resolution and closure, this final speech gives us fragmentation and ambiguity, all in Chinese, no less. Still, the unintelligibility is significant. Like Andrés's broken Chinese records, Wong repeats to the Mexican and Chicana/o women in her family a pattern of inaccessible speech that is syntactically unorganized, yet that affirms her presence nonetheless. Caught interminably between the past and the present, and between China and Mexico, Wong speaks one final time, but she fails at this critical juncture to qualify her familial and cultural existence in coherent terms. To be sure, her lack of lucidity (both in terms of being seen unclearly and of not being understood) reinforces her contemporary "nonbeing" (*fēi*; 非); while her very voice, fragmented and unintelligible as it is, simultaneously gestures to her "existence" (*xiàn*; 现), shadowy as it may be within an obfuscated historical past.

The repetition and unintelligibility of the play's coda leave both Hija and Wong having to navigate perpetually the interstitial spaces it has constructed, the gaps between the boundaries of the past and present, between absence and presence—and most importantly, between the seemingly concrete divides between Mexican, Texan, and Chinese cultures. As such, the play performs the critical work of denoting the confusion surrounding Asians in Chicana/o history and culture; yet it also works as a basis for recognizing and understanding an identity that has *always* existed in the shadows of Chicana/o communities. To be sure, Grise's play makes plain that this "Chinocana" identity, so to speak, transcends and exceeds the boundaries of nation-states, national histories, and even common ethnic categorizations of borderlands culture.

In many ways, then, the play's Mexican Chinese and Chinese Chicanas are left to negotiate states of being that have long defined borderlands life as they are described at the beginning of this chapter. Indeed, Grise's characters must continually navigate intersections and clashes of cultures, move incessantly across the liminal spaces of national and cultural borders, and constantly transgress "intersections of various historical trajectories."[26] As we may recall, Gloria Anzaldúa has eloquently theorized that the inhabitants of the US-Mexico borderlands "live in a constant state of transition" because they must perpetually "pass over, or go through the confines of the 'normal.'"[27] If this is the case, then Hija and her Chinese great-grandmother emerge as border-dwellers *par excellence*. Indeed, both experience indefinitely their historical lives in the interstitial spaces between not only gender and racial differences, but also between the national and linguistic divides that constitute the ambiguous cultural spaces between the United States, Mexico, and China. These transtemporal and circumpacific intersections, though seemingly atypical within traditional borderlands discourses, may very well be quintessential, for they symbolize the contradictions and discontinuities of this "nonsynchronous heteroglot zone" that has always been the US-Mexico border itself.[28]

Coda

Chicana/o Studies Then and Now: Paradigms of Past and Future Critique

In the fall of 1967, the first national journal of Chicana/o studies, *El Grito: A Journal of Contemporary Mexican-American Thought*, published its inaugural issue. *El Grito*'s editorial board recognized the significance of the moment for combating what had by this period become a veritable void in higher education regarding knowledge production from a Mexican American perspective. Editor Nick Vaca takes immediate issue with the state of institutional knowledge in the journal's opening pages, accusing the academy of constructing and repeating the notion that "Mexican-Americans are simple minded but lovable and colorful children who because of their rustic naïveté, limited mentality, and inferior, backward 'traditional culture,' choose poverty and isolation instead of assimilating into the American mainstream and accepting its material riches."[1] Seemingly alluding to the widely popular caricatures of the simple and impoverished paisanos of John Steinbeck's *Tortilla Flat*, and explicitly calling out "intellectual mercenaries" who formulate "[false] scientific rhetoric" of Mexican American essentialisms, Vaca damns the artistic and intellectual elite for constructing one-dimensional and ahistorical images of Mexican Americans.[2]

As a corrective, and in order to make plain the cultural and social realities of Mexican American life, Vaca insists that *El Grito* will deconstruct institutionalized structures of knowledge rooted in the tradition of the European Enlightenment. Further, he alerts readers that the journal will publish the pioneering work of Chicana/o artists so as to render the complexities of Chicana/o cultural ideas more accurately. In this way, the journal will demystify the essentialist logic of Mexican Americans and recuperate this community's social history. Combining artistic renditions of social life from a Chicana/o perspective with a healthy dose of skepticism regarding institutionalized knowledge production, Vaca and his colleagues assert a new means for speaking productively about Chicana/o communities. Indeed, this was the journal's avowed mission, and Vaca reiterates it with an ever-growing oppositional tone. It was to publish innovative art and insist on historical and sociological critiques as a corrective to the stereotype that had been "professionally certified and institutionally sanctified to the point where . . . it holds wide public acceptance. . . . [T]his great rhetorical structure [of Mexican American simplicity] is a grand hoax, a blatant lie—a lie that must be stripped of its esoteric and sanctified verbal garb and have its intellectually spurious and vicious character exposed to full view."[3] Having reached an impressive and inspiring tenor of resistance, Vaca concludes his opening editorial by emphasizing this vision of resistance, announcing, "*El Grito* has been founded for just this purpose—to provide a forum for Mexican-American self-definition and expression on [all] issues of relevance to Mexican-Americans."[4]

In revisiting these relatively lost pages of a monumental moment—one that in many ways marks the genesis of Chicana/o studies—one cannot but notice the journal's intense interest in exploring an ethnic epistemology that would help realize its commitments to self-definition and political action. To be sure, the identity politics of academic and aesthetic practices had as much to do with *El Grito*'s vision of scholarship as they did with articulating a distinct ethnic identity already experienced, yet not properly conceptualized or historicized.

Looking back on this moment, one cannot deny just how bold and necessary the vision of *El Grito* would become. Still, these opening pages of *El Grito*—which speak to a field on the verge of a cultural renaissance and which commit themselves to an activist surge wedded to matters of self-definition—evoke an important critical question: *Where was the journal to demarcate the geographical, gendered, classed, and racial boundaries that would bring into focus an accurate portrait of Mexican American cultural, political, and social life?*

Octavio Romano's lead article in *El Grito*, "Minorities, History, and the Cultural Mystique," offers a clue as to what the paradigms of a new social critique might look like for this emergent field and where it might establish its critical borders. According to Romano, this field "should begin with the premise that people and cultures do not evolve or exist as isolated or isolable entities, participating only in their own histories, independent of the world around them, and therefore responsible only to themselves. . . . [T]he history of the world is not that of independent historical traditions. Instead it is the existence of mutual histories."[5] In other words, if Chicana/o studies was to have future value, its methodologies must regard Mexican American identity and social realities globally, relationally, and relative to their intersections with other populations—both those with power and those without it.

Looking back at the five decades since the institutionalization of Chicana/o studies, the 1967 call in *El Grito* for global and interracial paradigms of Mexican American historical and cultural knowledge sounds surprisingly contemporary. Romano's words remind one immediately of the multicultural, hemispheric, and transnational shifts in the academy that have taken turns assuming critical vogue since the 1990s in American studies broadly. Despite the limitations and assumptions inherent in recent "hemispheric," "postnationalist," and "transnational" models of cultural critique—ones that scholars such as Ralph Bauer, John Carlos Rowe, Claire Fox, Vijay Prashad, José David Saldívar, Caroline Levander, and many others have noted—*El Grito* seems to anticipate by nearly three decades the need to assess ethnicity in ways that recognize that social formations are never a local process.[6]

From our contemporary vantage point, this may appear obvious, but it is not without concern. For example, José Limón's impassioned insistence that "critical regionalism" is a more productive paradigm of Chicana/o studies than José Saldívar's "critical globalization"—coupled with his more recent skepticism of Ramón Saldívar's work on Américo Paredes's "transnational imaginary"—reflects an intense intellectual suspicion of the field's hemispheric and transnational turns.[7] Skeptics of these critical shifts maintain that transnational methodologies of cultural analysis can run the risk of mystifying differences between distinct people and places.[8] Moreover, others suggest that such paradigms deemphasize nation-states, though their political borders have become more militarized and more oppressive than ever.[9] Pushing even further, some skeptics suggest that hemispheric and transnational methods depoliticize activist scholarship and deemphasize state-sanctioned forms of subjugation. For this reason, Sau-Ling Wong has asked us to reconsider denationalizing ethnic studies at the risk of easing off cultural nationalist concerns and compromising both the cohesiveness it has secured and the political gains within our respective communities it has achieved.[10]

Yet for the editors of *El Grito*, political gains and cultural advancements in the community were to be secured *not* by adhering to nationalist or regional methods, or by privileging ethnicity in ways that elide important global contours of Mexican American life. Romano puts this matter bluntly, stating that vast "social [and cultural] networks are more fundamental to historical processes of recuperation [and identity formation] than ethnicity [and] skin color."[11] In other words, Vaca, Romano, and their colleagues at *El Grito* believed that transnational and cross-racial methodologies for recuperating Mexican American identities would yield legitimate political and cultural value, for they would meet the historical and social needs of the people and demystify notions of their insularity, simplicity, and biological determinism. Recent transnational and interracial approaches in the field have illuminated this point as a major speculative concern at the heart of modern Chicana/o studies, one that scholars like the Saldívar brothers and others have boldly addressed: namely, the local's imbrication with the global, and the Chicana/o's historical relationship with other racial populations as both a national and transnational subject.

Given its opening theoretical pronouncements on the local and the global, it is hardly surprising that the inaugural issues of *El Grito* repeatedly assess the importance of the American War in Vietnam on Mexican American social consciousness. Early issues of the journal often take inventory of a range of minority matters in order to assess their impact on Mexican American communities. Yet it is the journal's consistent focus on Vietnam that illustrates most plainly the transnational and interracial ideas its editors conceptualize for articulating Mexican American identity, including its relationship to the state and its sociopolitical life beyond US borders. For example, in its third full issue, *El Grito* includes several pieces on Vietnam, all of which regard the war's significance for understanding Mexican American political thought. Robert Barron's piece "Viet Nam Veteran" is a conversation with a self-declared Chicano soldier who had been drafted into the war, where he witnessed the slaughter of nearly one hundred soldiers in his company, including "25 Negros," "some Puerto Riqueños," and "plenty" of Chicanos.[12] Complementing this conversation is Philip J. Jimenez's article entitled "Vietnam," which calls into question the legality of the war, including the burden of minority communities to wage it. This piece concludes as a cautionary tale that warns us that military intrusions in Vietnam set a dangerous precedent for unilateral interventions in foreign conflicts, thereby staging the possibility of minorities having to bear the burden of fighting another unnamed war in a third world country in the future.

This edition of *El Grito* also includes an art portfolio by Esteban Villa entitled ¡*Viet Nam!*, which consists of a series of abstract images in the style of Pablo Picasso's *Guernica* (1937). While Barron's piece focuses on the torment, grief, and injustice Chicano soldiers experienced before and after the war, Villa's emphasis on the mutilated bodies of Vietnamese peasants depicts how the conflict inflicts horrific pain and suffering on civilians (see figure 9). To be sure, the abstract shapes and disfigured postures of Villa's Vietnamese bodies express unmistakably his protest of the war, including the unfolding chaos that has wreaked havoc on representative art forms for depicting human anguish.

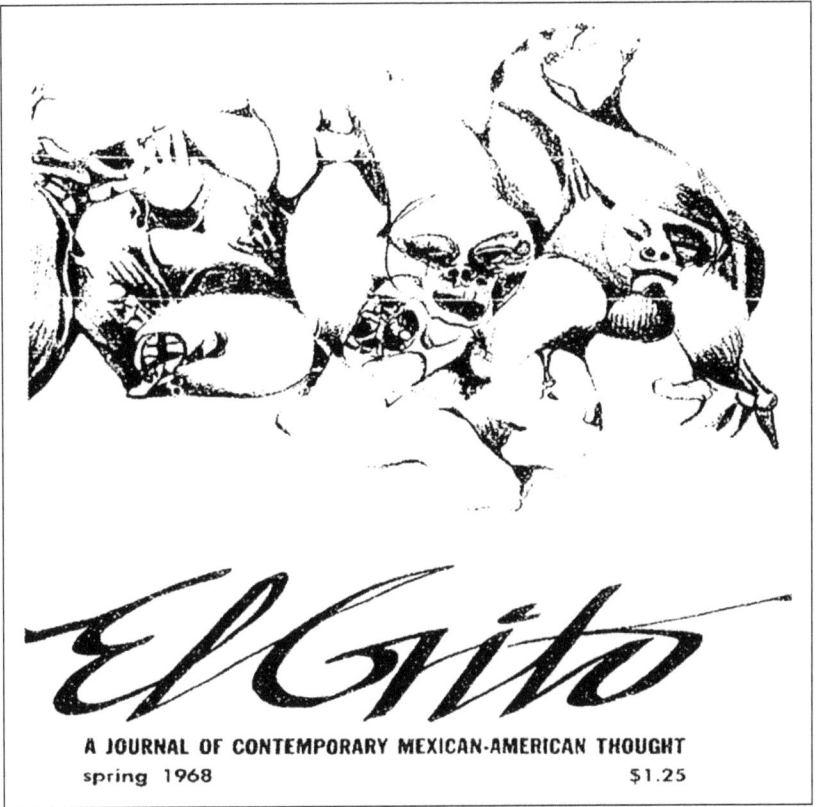

Fig. 9. Cover of *El Grito: A Journal of Contemporary Mexican-American Thought*, Spring 1968, featuring cover art entitled ¡*Viet Nam!* by Esteban Villa. Courtesy of the artist.

Collectively, Barron's, Jimenez's, and Villa's contributions to *El Grito* represent in unambiguous terms the significance of the American War in Vietnam for communicating the journal's titular emphasis on "Contemporary Mexican-American Thought." *El Grito*'s early critical approach to Chicana/o studies reveals the importance of regarding the transnational and cross-racial contours of Mexican American social attitudes, including their transpacific and interracial means for articulating forms of political and cultural self-definition. Indeed, the images of tormented Asian faces on the cover of a Mexican American journal emphasize and reiterate Romano's avowal to excavate how global intersections are fundamental to a project of Chicana/o social and historical recuperation.

In hindsight, *El Grito* seemed poised to assess the global and interracial contours of the Chicana/o texts I have examined in this book, and it is easy to imagine this journal hosting variants of the conversations I have hitherto entertained. At the very least, early issues of *El Grito* expose and anticipate by nearly three decades important transnational concerns that contemporary scholars have raised with respect to the global contexts of Chicana/o life. For example, Marissa López's recent hemispheric study on Chicana/o literature has reframed questions that scholars such as José and Ramón Saldívar have put forth, asking, "what happens to this story [of culture] when we shift perspective and see Chicana/o nationalism [and literature] developing in other times and other spaces. What happens when the space we want to identify as 'Chicana/o' . . . or 'Aztlán' emerges as transnational and multivalent, not newly so but historically and constitutively?"[13] Considering this query against the early issues of El Grito, it appears the field has come full circle, for the journal was short-lived, having published its final issue in 1975, when the critical focus of the field turned overwhelmingly toward narrow ethnocentric matters.

According to Michael Soldatenko, the early institutionalization of Chicana/o studies played a significant role in the field's scaling its critical attentions away from its transnational and interracial interests once it embedded itself firmly in the academy. He notes, "the resolution of the Third World strike in Berkeley and the development of an Ethnic Studies College [which resulted in the formation of Chicana/o studies proper] . . . led to a compromise [away from global politics and toward] academic self-preservation."[14] Where there were once transnational and third world approaches to political thinking and self-determination, individuated ethnic groups now competed against one another for limited campus resources. These groups had to work hard to distinguish themselves from other minority collaborators in order to justify the need for specific ethnic enclaves in the academy. As such, the institutional model of Chicana/o studies that emerged in the early 1970s emphasized a reexamination of institutional structures, as opposed to sharpening the transnational political rhetoric of the field's genesis. In this sense, Chicana/o studies was not detached from the Third World Liberation movement from which it was born—or the protests against the Vietnam War that inspired it—as much as it was committed to curricular matters and issues of campus inclusion. Put simply, Chicana/o studies had to establish intellectual and ethnic boundaries around its interests in order to validate its demands for an academic space controlled entirely by Chicana/o students and faculty, all to the exclusion of its interracial and transnational orientations.

Chicana/o studies' ethnic focus during its rapid inclusion on college campuses is mainly a result of its early academic management, which largely delimited the ideological differences of student activists, including the gendered, interracial, and global concerns of their protest. As a result, what began as a coalition of aggrieved minority students from across a spectrum of racial differences accumulated in related ethnic studies programs largely detached from each other and committed almost exclusively to local matters, including the formation of community-based academic curricula. This newfound institutional approach to Chicana/o studies, which had fought to carve out and then secure a niche in the academy, largely redirected transnational and interracial concerns toward classroom and street-level issues that drastically subsumed community and racial differences. These elisions included *intracultural* differences on class and gender; *interracial* differences with other US minority groups; and *global* differences with Asian freedom fighters in whose image Chicana/o artists often imagined their semblance.

As such, Chicana/o studies would have to wait nearly thirty years before the "hemispheric" and "transnational" turns in the academy would espouse working methodologies that regarded the local relative to global and cross-racial political matters. Although both the rise of Chicana/o studies across the world and the growing output of transnational scholarship on Chicana/o culture attest to how much has changed recently, it is fair to say that Chicana/o studies as a field has traditionally relied on binary paradigms of investigation in order to understand the political needs of the community; moreover, it has consistently deployed local interpretive frameworks to regard the symbolic and epistemological functions of its art. In this sense, the field has largely defined Chicana/o political culture institutionally in the absence of ethnic others, and almost exclusively at the US-Mexico border.

Having long recognized this trend, George Sánchez has suggested that Chicana/o studies' insistence on a binary model framed between "Mexico" and "Anglo America" stems from the political need to comment on racial and class oppression within Chicana/o communities in a manner that directly engages the social authority.[15] For Alvina Quintana, the problem of ethnic isolation reminds us of the contentious issues of university funding, for minority studies often continue to stress "racial autonomy" in order to compete for "institutional recognition and support."[16] Indeed, political competition and limited institutional resources often divided Chicana/os from other US minorities during the 1970s, leaving them to fight "their own battles."[17] If the relative dearth of critical studies on Chicana/o cultural relations with Asian Americans, African Americans, and Native Americans is any indication of our contemporary intellectual inclinations, it is safe to assume that political rivalries and limited academic assets continue to divide them today.

Still, in the face of persistent challenges and legitimate skepticism, interethnic analyses on political and cultural formations have gradually emerged in Chicana/o studies, as well as in American studies more broadly. Along the various trajectories of this paradigm shift in American studies, which

Shelley Fishkin has termed its "transnational turn," scholars have increasingly developed interethnic and global methods with which to investigate Chicana/o political histories and to critique this group's literary objects.[18] Furthermore, the growing global interest in Chicana/o culture in places like Spain, Germany, Turkey, Argentina, and Finland has further redirected the field's investigative trajectories outward, shifting the locus of cultural opposition from the subject within a nation-state to one that imagines its identity transnationally across many national boundaries beyond the US-Mexico border.[19] Nonetheless, only a handful of articles have emerged in the wake of this transnational shift to examine specifically Chicana/o literature's intersections with Asia, Asians, and Asian Americans. And while many important *historical* studies on these intersections do exist, very few book-length studies on Chicana/o writings have explored these points of transpacific contact at length.[20] Put concisely, studies of Chicana/o literature remain largely disconnected from Asia and Asian Americans, despite the incremental rise in output on interethnic and transnational studies on borderlands cultures.[21]

One reason for this disconnect is that the shift toward interethnic matters in Chicana/o studies has been marked mainly by an interest in the relationships between Chicana/os and other US Latino groups.[22] For this reason, transnational investigations have largely broadened the domains of Chicana/o political and cultural issues away from the US-Mexico border and into Latin America and the Caribbean.[23] With great reward, hemispheric models of critical analysis have allowed scholars to investigate broadly the transnational dynamics of Chicana/o social, cultural, and economic life across the Americas.[24] Yet despite this welcomed turn toward transnational and hemispheric matters in Chicana/o studies, this community's literary forms are rarely seen to intersect with Asia or Asian American social formations. Although the field has developed fresh perspectives that exceed national (and nationalist) paradigms, it is fair to say that it continues to neglect the real and imaginary relations between Chicana/os and Asians. This is so because the field continues to privilege hemispheric investigations on Chicana/o art to the exclusion of important transpacific axes of inquiry.[25] It is worth noting that historian Erika Lee makes a similar point about the dominant axes of analysis in Asian American studies, but with a twist. In a special issue of the *Journal of Asian American Studies*, Lee notes that transpacific perspectives (which are seldom seen in Chicana/o studies) have actually crowded out hemispheric evaluations in the field, undermining awareness of the messier histories of Asians that cut across the Americas.[26]

This book has attempted to address these critical voids, yet it does not pretend to exhaust the range of ethnic or Asian difference in the Chicana/o literary imagination, itself constituted by many regional and historical particularities. Undeniably, much remains to be done in order to examine how Chicana/o writers negotiate the particularities of US ethnicity and other global spaces in their cultural products. What I have shown, however, is that attending to interethnic contact and transpacific traffic in key Chicana/o texts yields an important understanding of how cultural and political transactions between Asians and Chicana/os inform the latter's self-perception, shape their aesthetic products, and anticipate by more than five decades the "inter-ethnic" and "transnational" turns in contemporary fiction written by people of color.[27] Indeed, Chicana/o narratives about wars in Asia, transpacific contact during US-Asian conflicts, and the Chinese diaspora at the US-Mexico borderlands all point to Chicana/o-Asian encounters as important elements in this community's cultural history. As such, this book justifies its particular focus on Chicana/o-Asian relations in Chicana/o literature by demonstrating how Chicana/o communities regularly configure self-perceptions outside the hemisphere and in relation to an Asian other, which it has encountered and imagined repeatedly throughout the twentieth century.

Yet just as important is the fact that this book's critical focus on the transpacific formations of Chicana/o literature challenges institutional structures that tend to compartmentalize culture inside exclusive areas of investigation. Stuart Hall rightfully argues that cultural politics in the United States have long been defined according to standing racial divisions and institutionalized ethnic hierarchies.[28] For this reason, we value writers such as Américo Paredes, Rudolfo Anaya, and Gloria Anzaldúa, for each has undeniably helped to open up exclusive cultural spaces such as the US literary canon, with the effect of challenging perceptions of Chicana/o cultural inferiority, or worse yet: cultural nothingness. Having inserted themselves firmly into popular discourses of US literary history, these Chicana/o writers and a handful of others have changed, no matter how slightly, the US landscape's "configurations of cultural power."[29]

Yet in the process of decentering Anglo narratives from dominant conceptions of US literary history, popular Chicana/o letters, like other key minority texts, tend to concretize inside ghettoized spaces of the US literary archive and institutional cultural instruction. Although Chicana/os can claim a few canonical texts, much remains to be done to defend these works from crystallizing into expressions of ethnic absolutism. To be sure, a few Chicana/o writers have emerged as stalwarts on syllabi at many colleges and universities serious about teaching ethnic American cultures. Yet these writers still run the risk of being safely regulated within the isolated disciplines that we call "Chicana/o studies" or "Mexican American studies." Stuart Hall is correct to recognize that cultural politics often stall when ethnic invisibility is replaced by a carefully policed and segregated form of visibility.[30]

For this reason, deliberating on how the Chicana/o literary imagination traverses racial and territorial categories positions it to resist its *barriozation*, so to speak, inside specific and manageable sectors of US cultural domains, including programs in Chicana/o and Mexican American studies. If, as David Palumbo-Liu argues, it is necessary to regard Asian America by considering how ideas about cultural difference, political history, and national belonging oscillate between Asia and the United States, then the writers I examined in this book instruct us that *Chicana/o literature* is a key repository in which scholars can study the movement of cultural ideas between these two spaces.[31] Consequently, I contend that Chicana/o literature is crucial for examining how the United States imagines Asian America broadly, for it identifies this transnational geography as a generative space for Asian American *and* Chicana/o cultural formations.

This does not suggest eliminating Chicana/o studies or Asian American studies; nor does it propose that all racialized populations are the same by virtue of a shared historical or cultural experience across the Pacific. Instead, I have shown here that historical contingencies regarding Asian and Asian Americans repeatedly activate Chicana/o literary politics in ways that cut across the seams of traditional paradigms of US ethnic studies, thereby opening up further questions about the significance of interracial associations in Chicana/o and other US minority cultures. In a related context, Vijay Prashad has revealed how minority art demonstrates ways that "people live culturally dynamic lives."[32] This reminds us, as Françoise Lionnet and Shu-mei Shih do, that "minority cultures as we know them are [always] the products of . . . multiple encounters."[33] Instead of flattening the cultural and historical differences of our dynamic lives, or disavowing interracial and cross-cultural engagements across the globe for purposes of political expediency, Prashad helpfully suggests that "we actively search for the grounds . . . into the cultural worlds that unite and divide us."[34] Indeed, Chicana/o literature teaches us that the rhetoric of authenticity and of ethnic nationalism that seemingly separates us is often conceptualized within interracial and global situations that ultimately bind us.

Undeniably, the interracial elements between Mexican Americans, Asians, and Asian Americans in Chicana/o literature reveal that these groups are not as divorced as early critiques of borderlands culture insist, or as removed as traditional paradigms of ethnic studies suggest. The constitution of a Chicana/o political identity in this community's literary culture has never been a local procedure. Instead, Chicana/o texts consistently communicate a transnational and cross-racial consciousness that is mindful of transpacific cultural traffic, attentive to Asian diasporas within the

US-Mexico borderlands, and forged by a critique of US military engagements across the Pacific. Asia, Asians, and Asian Americans repeatedly impact how Chicana/o texts articulate political attitudes, and they illustrate how the Chicana/o literary imagination develops between distinct yet related racial populations.

For these reasons, transnational and cross-racial dynamics in foundational and emergent Chicana/o texts force us to consider deeply this ethnic identity within a diverse field of affiliations and geopolitical spaces, generating important questions regarding the conceptual and analytical borders we apply to Chicana/o culture. As I have demonstrated here, interpretive frameworks that outline an exclusive ethnic boundary and totalize everything beyond it generically as "white America" or "European" cannot properly regard the social, cultural, and political concerns of Chicana/o art. Neither binary paradigms nor hemispheric frameworks can account for the racial diversity and the variegated transpacific geographies that consistently influence the literary formations of Chicana/o consciousness. Indeed, this culture's racial and spatial plurality shows that the term "Chicana/o" cannot be arrested to signify a singular identity that exhausts our senses of self relative to those with whom we align, rival, and persevere—on all corners of the globe.

NOTES

Introduction: Interracial Politics

1 Villarreal's *Pocho* (1959) was the first Chicana/o novel published by a mainstream American press. The novel was reprinted in 1970 and again in 1989. It was long regarded as the first Chicana/o novel until the Recovering US Hispanic Literary Heritage Project retrieved several nineteenth-century proto-Chicana/o texts in the 1990s. These works include two novels by María Amparo Ruiz de Burton: *Who Would Have Thought It?* (1872) and *The Squatter and the Don* (1885). John-Michael Rivera identifies de Burton's 1872 text as the first novel to be written in English by a Mexican living in the United States after annexation in 1848. See Rivera, *The Emergence of Mexican America*.
2 Saldívar, *The Dialectics of Our America*, 110.
3 Lipsitz, *The Possessive Investment in Whiteness*, 202.
4 Pulido, *Black, Brown, Yellow and Left*, 1.
5 Ibid., 3.
6 Mariscal, *Brown-Eyed Children of the Sun*, 69.
7 Ibid., 91.
8 Notable instances of Mexican American and Asian cooperation are found predominantly in each group's labor history. For example, Japanese and Mexican agricultural workers in Oxnard, California, formed the Japanese Mexican Labor Association (JMLA) in 1903 to organize a strike against owners, banks, and merchants vested in the sugar beet industry in that region. According to Tomás Almaguer, the JMLA was the first major agricultural workers' union in California to strike successfully against Anglo capital in the state. Of its charter members, approximately five hundred were Japanese and two hundred were Mexican. See Almaguer, *Racial Fault Lines*. The only significant and sustained instance of cross-racial labor cooperation between Asians and Mexican Americans during the 1960s took shape when Filipino members of the Agricultural Workers Organizing Committee joined César Chávez and the National Farm Workers Association to form the United Farm Workers Union (UFW) in 1965. The UFW staged a successful labor strike and boycott against grape growers in Delano, California, that same year. See Lien, *The Making of Asian America through Political Participation*; and Garcia, *From the Jaws of Victory*. Outside of these groups' labor histories, Wendy Cheng has demonstrated how Asian Americans and Mexican Americans have recently come together to deal with local political matters in a California suburb;

she addresses how interracial contact informed their political responses and influenced the racial consciousnesses of these groups. See Cheng, *The Changs Next Door to the Díazes*.

9 Alurista is the nom de plume of Alberto Baltazar Urista Heredia. Troubled by the threat of cultural and historical eradication, and providing poetic testimony to Chicana/o legal, economic, and educational discrimination, Alurista's experimental poetics in texts such as "History of Aztlán" (1969) and *Floricanto en Aztlán* (1971) romanticize a noble lineage between Chicana/os and Aztec Indians. In doing so, Alurista revitalized and popularized Amerindian myths in a contemporary context. To emphasize the influence of Alurista's cultural gestures and poetic sensibilities, Francisco Lomelí notes that *Floricanto en Aztlán* in particular stood as the standard by which Chicana/o poetry would be judged during the 1970s because of its thematic treatment of Chicana/o injustice and its emphasis on a neo-indigenist perspective. See Lomelí, "Contemporary Chicano Literature, 1959–1990." Unquestionably, Alurista emerged as a key figure for imagining and articulating Chicana/o ethno-cultural politics more generally, which, according to Philip Ortego, solidified a Chicana/o literary identity and precipitated a broad Chicana/o political and spiritual awakening ("Chicano Poetry: Roots and Writers").

10 The original title is "Ideología y estética en la significación poética chicana en la década 1965–1975." Seemingly wanting to come to terms with the extra-literary and transnational elements of Latin American nationalist poetics during the latter half of the twentieth century, Monique Lemaitre organized a high-profile panel of writers and critics at the 1983 annual meeting of the Latin American Studies Association in Mexico City. At the request of Tino Villanueva, himself a major Chicano poet of the era, Lemaitre invited Alurista to represent Chicana/o poets. Alurista presented his paper on September 26.

11 My emphasis and translation. The original reads: "La Guerra en Vietnam, paradigmático ejemplo del militarismo transnacional norteamericano establece las condiciones de la producción literaria Chicana en su sistemática significación poética."

12 This poem was written in 1969 but published in 1970. It enjoyed regular reprinting. Adding to its popularity, Nicolás Kanellos reminds us that it was also recorded on a 45 rpm vinyl record and distributed broadly by Luis Valdez ("José Montoya").

13 The impact of Montoya as cultural figure during and after the Chicana/o Movement cannot be overstated, nor can the importance of his most memorable poem, "El Louie." Montoya was a co-founder of the Royal Chicano Air Force (RCAF), a nationally renowned art collective that translated Chicana/o life into language and visual arts. Despite Montoya's lifetime of writing and painting, "El Louie" remains his most influential work. This elegiac piece appeared as one of the first to incorporate Montoya's innovative meter combining English, standard Spanish, non-standard Spanish, and unique Chicana/o dialectal features, often called "caló." This combination of languages and dialects opened up poetry to a generation of novice readers who recognized idiomatic and slang expressions local to their communities, and it has garnered intense critical attention from Chicana/o culture's most recognizable literary critics. For an outline of this poem's critical history, which includes overviews of readings by José David

Saldívar, Rafael Pérez-Torres, José Limón, and Renato Rosaldo, see Martínez, *Countering the Counterculture*.
14 The original Spanish reads: "Nuestra palabra, signo, metáfora, y glifo se niega a ... ser servil a otros. Somos Aztlán sin fronteras."
15 García, *Chicanismo*, 4.
16 See Forster, *Aspects of the Novel*, particularly chapter 3, titled "People."
17 The FBI tracked Acosta for several years during the 1970s. As a result, this incident appears in "United States Department of Justice, Federal Bureau of Investigation Report on Southern Christian Leadership Conference: Racial Matters, May 28, 1970, Los Angeles California." The two-page report was declassified in 1974.
18 Behnken, *Fighting Their Own Battles*, 9.
19 Mariscal, *Aztlán and Vietnam*, 4–5.
20 See Chávez, *"Mi Raza Primero!"*
21 See García, *Mexican Americans*; Sánchez, *Becoming Mexican American*; Gutiérrez, *Walls and Mirrors*; Oropeza, *¡Raza Sí! ¡Guerra No!*; and Griswold del Castillo, "Introduction."
22 There are a few notable exceptions. See Cutler, "Disappeared Men"; Sae-Saue, "Aztlán's Asians"; and Olguín, "Sangre mexicana/corazón americano," which includes analyses of Chicana/o political identities in literary works that concern nearly all major US wars.
23 Pérez-Torres, "Refiguring Aztlán," 15.
24 Ibid.
25 Bhabha, "Interrogating Identity: Frantz Fanon and the Postcolonial Prerogative," 59.
26 Mariscal, *Brown-Eyed Children of the Sun*, 13.
27 Said writes that part of his motivation for theorizing Orientalism as a colonial discourse was "to illustrate ... specifically for formerly colonized peoples, the dangers and temptations of employing this [discourse] upon themselves and others" (*Orientalism*, 25).
28 See Davies, *Voyagers to the New World*; and Williams, "GM Allotypes in Native Americans."
29 The original Spanish reads: "[E]l hombre americano es de origen asiático" (Paz, "Dos apostillas: Asia y América," 141).

Chapter 1 Racial Equivalence

1 See Rodríguez, "El florecimiento de la literatura chicana."
2 Aztlán emerges in the 1970s not simply as a catchword for resistance, but rather as an operational term for establishing Chicana/o identity and opposition to US Anglo America, writ large. Rudolfo Anaya and Francisco Lomelí note that the term not only signified "a rallying cry of the Chicano Movement ... [but also it] signaled a unifying point of cohesion through which [Chicana/os] could define the foundations for an identity. Aztlán brought together a culture ... allowing it, for the first time, a framework within which to understand itself" ("Introduction," ii).
3 Luis Valdez designated his stage work as *"actos"* in order to highlight the improvisational form of his theater. "Acto" works also to signify the "actions" of Valdez's

group to produce theater statements about farmworker concerns. In short, the term *acto* captures how a diverse group of nonprofessionals develop—through improvisational, comic, and poignant measures—a common political statement about farm labor and pressing issues in Mexican American communities. See Valdez, *Actos y El Teatro Campesino*; and Huerta, *Chicano Theater Themes and Forms*.
4. *Vietnam Campesino* was first performed in 1970 in Delano, California, and later reprinted in 1971, 1990, and 1994. Further references to this text are to the latest edition.
5. George Mariscal has noted how the oppositional values of the urban Chicana/o movement can be traced largely to rural protest (*Brown-Eyed Children of the Sun*, 70).
6. Wilson, "El Teatro Campesino Depicts Chicano Life, Struggle, Victories," *Utah Chronicle*, August 4, 1970.
7. Garcia, *From the Jaws of Victory*, 133.
8. Ibid.
9. Guzman, "Mexican American Casualties in Vietnam," 12–15.
10. Huerta, *Chicano Theater Themes and Forms*, 89.
11. Bhabha, *Nation and Narration*, 1.
12. For example, on October 14, 1972, the Old Town Plaza in Albuquerque, New Mexico, hosted an antiwar rally held by a coalition of La Raza and other minorities gathered to hear Vietnamese students speak against US forces in Southeast Asia. See "Anti-war Rally Held by Coalition of Raza."
13. Fredric Jameson argues that with the advent of navigation technologies, "cognitive mapping" came to refer to "the coordination of existential data (the empirical position of the subject) with the unlived abstract conceptions of the geographic totality" (*Postmodernism*, 52). Reformulated in cultural terms, Jameson asserts that "the aesthetic of cognitive mapping" works ideologically, for it "enable[s] a situational representation on the part of the individual subject to that vaster and properly unrepresentable totality which is the ensemble of society's structures as a whole" (*Postmodernism*, 51).
14. Ibid., 54.
15. According to Tomás Almaguer, the Japanese–Mexican Labor Association (JMLA) was the "first major agricultural workers' union in California" and the "first to strike successfully against white capital interests in the state" (*Racial Fault Lines*, 187). Of its charter members, approximately five hundred were Japanese and two hundred were Mexican. For more details on the success of this union, see Almaguer, *Racial Fault Lines*, 191–204.
16. García, *Mexican Americans: Leadership, Ideology, and Identity, 1930–1960*, 146.
17. Gómez-Quiñones, "Plan de San Diego Reviewed," 124.
18. Valdez, "The Plan de Delano," quoted in *The Words of César Chávez*, ed. Jensen and Hammerback, 17–18.
19. Brown, "Larry Itlong, Forgotten Filipino Labor Leader," *New York Times*, October 8, 2012.
20. For more on the tensions between Filipino and Mexican American labor during and after the Delano grape strike, see Garcia, *From the Jaws of Victory*, particularly 116–131.

21 Mariscal notes that international contexts often formed the basis for Chicana/o nationalist rhetoric, particularly in the context of a larger antiwar movement in Vietnam. His study also includes research into the transnational gestures of Chicana/o politics of this era more generally, especially across the Americas. See Mariscal, *Brown-Eyed Children of the Sun*, particularly pages 65–96.
22 For an overview of Chicana/o Movement poetry, see Lomelí, "Contemporary Chicano Literature, 1959–1990."
23 I borrow this term from Brian Fagan, who identifies "The Great Journey" of Asian migrants from the "Old World to the New World." This journey marked a migration pattern from northern Asia, to Alaska, to Canada, and then throughout North and South America. See Fagan, *The Great Journey*.
24 Lomelí, "Contemporary Chicano Literature, 1959–1990," 92.
25 Mariscal, *Aztlán and Vietnam*, 4–5.
26 Muñoz, *Youth, Identity, Power: The Chicano Movement*, 93.
27 Soldatenko, *Chicano Studies*, 137.
28 The original Spanish version of this poem is reprinted in Mariscal. It reads: "Vietnam, Vietnam, tu tragedia se extiende y escapa/Más allá de distancias y horas presentidas/ . . . En tu justa y heróica lucha/Se decide también el destino de mi lucha/Que es la lucha del hombre por ser/Y salvar el derecho a vivir/Para todo lo humano y hermoso/que encierra la vida" (de la Luz in Mariscal, *Aztlán and Vietnam*, 247).
29 Sánchez, *Becoming Mexican American*, 6–8.
30 Quintana, *Home Girls*, 19.
31 Sadowski-Smith, *Border Fictions*, 8–9.
32 Urista, "Oscar Z. Acosta: In Context," 73.
33 Armando Morales notes the testimonies of this protest gathering; he includes a very insightful social and psychological perspective based on popular media reports related to California and US law. See Morales, "Chicano-Police Riots."
34 It is worth noting that the commanding officer of the infantry unit responsible for the My Lai Massacre was a Mexican American, Ernest Medina of New Mexico. He was acquitted in a court-martial of war crimes charges in 1971. Although Chicana/o protestors became inflamed by the incident, their political institutions and cultural elite, including Acosta, have never acknowledged the role of Mexican American soldiers in this event. Lieutenant William Calley is the only soldier to have been convicted for his participation in the massacre. For more on Medina and Calley, including the cover-up of the massacre by US armed forces, see Belknap, *The Vietnam War on Trial*.
35 Delgado, *The Chicano Movement*, 14.
36 Fanon, *The Wretched of the Earth*, 209.
37 The original reads: "la Guerra en Vietnam, paradigmático ejemplo del militarismo transnacional norteamericano establece las condiciones de la producción literaria Chicana en su sistemática significación poética" (Alurista, "Ideología y estética en la significación poética chicana en la década 1965–1975," 8).
38 Fanon, *The Wretched of the Earth*, 209.

39 I use the term *overdetermined* to refer to what Louis Althusser calls "overdetermination": when a "vast accumulation of '[political] contradictions' come into play in the *same court*, some of which are radically heterogeneous—of different origins, different sense . . . but which nevertheless 'merge' into a ruptural and [revolutionary] unity . . ." ("Contradiction and Overdetermination," 100).

40 See Tomás Rivera's *Y no se lo tragó la tierra* for a similar narrative strategy in Chicana/o literature. Ramón Saldívar offers an important reading of the significance of Rivera's narrative form. See Saldívar, *Chicano Narrative*, 74–90. Other significant interpretations of Rivera's aesthetic are found in Testa, "Narrative Technique and Human Experience in Tomás Rivera"; and Sommers, "Interpreting Tomás Rivera."

41 Villalobos, "Border Real, Border Metaphor," 133.

42 Olstad, *"Peregrinos en Aztlán* (a review)," 120.

43 Bakhtin defines the chronotope to explain "the intrinsic connectedness of temporal and spatial relationships that are artistically expressed in literature. . . . In the literary artistic chronotope, spatial and temporal indicators are fused into one carefully thought-out, concrete whole. Time, as it were, thickens, takes on flesh, becomes artistically visible; likewise, space becomes charged and responsive to the movements of time, plot and history. This intersection of axes and fusion of indicators characterizes the artistic chronotope" (*The Dialogic Imagination*, 84).

44 Villalobos, "Border Real, Border Metaphor," 138.

45 The original Spanish reads: "Hasta hoy he escrito enfáticamente del dolor del hombre pequeño, del humillado que subsiste en la frontera (de ambos lados) y paradójicamente de la picaresca natural a estos lares" (Cárdenas and Alarcón, "Entrevista a Miguel Méndez M.," 155).

46 Olstad, *"Peregrinos en Aztlán* (a review)," 120.

47 Lionnet and Shih, "Introduction," 8.

Chapter 2 Transpacific Identities

1 Anderson, *Imagined Communities*, 7.

2 Noriega, "The Dissension of Other Things," 3.

3 Alarcón, "The Aztec Palimpsest," 35–36. For a discussion on the different deployments of Aztlán, including its varying conceptualizations in different historical and political contexts, see Pérez-Torres's "Refiguring Aztlán." Perhaps no other scholar of Chicana/o letters has examined the numerous political inflections Aztlán has assumed throughout the literary history of this community more thoroughly than Pérez-Torres. He notes that the various political deployments of Aztlán, for example, have signaled, throughout the course of Chicana/o cultural history, both inclusion and exclusion for the purposes of securing political unity, constructing a future sovereign state, and articulating borderlands spaces to allow for a historical identity that exceeds nationalist limits for expressing community experiences (15). In this sense, "Aztlán as a cultural/national symbol represents a paradox: it seeks to stand as common denominator among Chicana/o populations, yet it [also] divides rather than unifies; it maintains cultural traditions

while promoting assimilation into Anglo-American culture; it affirms indigenous ancestry while simultaneously erasing the very historical, cultural, and geographic specificity of that ancestry" (31).

4 Griswold del Castillo, "Introduction." It is worth noting that when the Japanese bombed Pearl Harbor, Mexico severed ties with Japan, Italy, and Germany. A year later, in 1942, Germany sank a Mexican tanker, after which Mexico declared war on the Axis powers. Mexican national sentiments in support of the Allied powers' war efforts impacted how many first-generation Mexican Americans viewed their relationship with their home nation (the United States) and the country of origin of their parents (Mexico). For many Mexican Americans, to align oneself politically on matters of war with an ancestral home, Mexico, was to align oneself with the national sentiments of the United States. To add to this political alignment, many Mexican Americans recognized that thousands of Mexican nationals were fighting in World War II on behalf of the US armed forces. Michael Gambone writes that as many as 250,000 Mexican nationals served in World War II, 14,000 of whom eventually saw combat (*The Greatest Generation Comes Home*, 128). In the most famous instance of this transnational soldiering, over three hundred Mexican nationals formed Escuadrón Aéreo de Pelea 201, nicknamed the "Aztec Eagles." These Mexican nationals were trained in the United States and were assigned to the US Air Force. They provided air defense in Japan and later served as ground support units against the Japanese Imperial Army.

5 Griswold del Castillo, "Introduction," 4.
6 Anderson, *Imagined Communities*, 7.
7 Acuña, *Occupied America*, 264.
8 This figure is an estimate taken from the jacket of *Mexican Americans and World War II*, edited by Maggie Rivas-Rodriguez. Rivas-Rodriguez does not specify the number of Mexican American servicemen and women in her introduction to this volume.
9 The precise number of Mexican Americans who served in World War II is unknown because, among all of the Latina/o populations living in the United States, the US Department of War kept exact records only on Puerto Rican servicemen and women.
10 García, *Mexican Americans*, 36.
11 Gambone, *The Greatest Generation Comes Home*, 128. At the start of the war, Mexican Americans' median annual income was $980, compared to $1,925 for their white counterparts (ibid., 128). Mario García documents some of the most severe cases of Mexican American labor discrimination in the US West and Southwest during the war era in *Mexican Americans*. See chapter 7 in particular.
12 Gambone, *The Greatest Generation Comes Home*, 131.
13 García, *Mexican Americans*, 62–83.
14 The League of United Latin American Citizens (LULAC) was formed in 1929. During the war era, LULAC emerged as a formidable and influential body for achieving full citizenship rights for Mexican Americans; at the same time, its elected officials took oaths to be loyal to the US government and to support the US Constitution. Through a commitment to working through legal means,

LULAC scored a significant number of legal victories for Mexican Americans during the first few decades of its inception while also encouraging its members to "teach [their] children to be good, loyal, and true American citizens" (García, *Mexican Americans*, 30). For more on LULAC, including its legal and social influence, see Gutiérrez, *Walls and Mirrors*, particularly 74–88.

15 Statement by Senator Diane Feinstein of California (*Congressional Record: Proceedings and Debates of the 106th Congress*, 1999: 25465).
16 Morin, *Among the Valiant*, 88.
17 Zaragosa, "Interview," 170.
18 Flores, "Interview," 295.
19 Suro, "Foreword," xi.
20 Servín, "Interview," 118.
21 Quoted in Takaki, *Double Victory*, 101.
22 Alcoser, "Interview," 111, my emphasis.
23 Bhabha, "Interrogating Identity," 59.
24 For more on war crimes, see Morrison, *History of United States Naval Operations in World War II*; and Knox, *Death March*.
25 For more on the significance of racial rhetoric during the war, see Thorne, *Allies of a Kind*; and Dower, *War without Mercy*.
26 Quoted in Luebke, *Bonds of Loyalty*, 174. Original quote spoken on June 14, 1916.
27 Forster, *Aspects of the Novel*, 108.
28 In his work on this story, Ramón Saldívar notes that the bases of "Ichiro Kikuchi" are the experiences of a young friend of Paredes's wife, Amelia ("Introduction," xxxix).
29 The only other story in the collection from the *Hammon and the Beans* that features an extended direct address to the reader is "The Gift," which, like "Ichiro Kikuchi," is set in Japan during World War II. This story also explores Chicano-Japanese relations. Neither of Paredes's novels, *George Washington Gómez* and *The Shadow*, features this style of narration. It is worth noting, however, that Paredes's poetry often makes use of narrative appeals that address the reader or the allegorical figure at the center of the poem.
30 See González, *Chicano Novels and the Politics of Form*, for an extended discussion on the relationship between racial associations, cultural forms, and elisions of Chicana/o identity.
31 Sánchez, "Ethnicity, Ideology, and Academia," 1985.
32 At the famous battle of the Alamo Mission near modern-day San Antonio, over a thousand Mexican soldiers under the command of General Antonio López de Santa Anna defeated and killed around two hundred soldiers of the Texan Army during the Texas Revolution. For more on this battle and the Texas Revolution, see Crisp, *Sleuthing the Alamo*; Hardin, *Texian Iliad*; and Barr, *Texans in Revolt*.
33 José Limón makes this point in his examination of this poem, adding that Anglo references to Mexican Americans as "Mexicans" were quite common in South Texas during this era (*Dancing with the Devil*, 6).
34 Arce, "Nation in Uniform," 111.
35 This is the title from Américo Paredes's landmark study on US ballads about Texas Mexican figures who resist in solitary and armed fashion the injustices of

Anglo encroachment at the US-Mexico border during the latter half of the nineteenth century. For more on Gregorio Cortez and the significance of the border ballad, see Paredes, *With His Pistol in His Hand*.

36 In his landmark poem "We Wear the Mask" (1896), Dunbar deploys this refrain to communicate how African American smiles make a statement of historical anguish, suffering, and double consciousness. For Houston Baker, this refrain (and the poem in general) articulates the complexities of double consciousness, and it demonstrates the mastery of the minstrel mask. See Baker, *Modernism and the Harlem Renaissance*, especially 39–42.

37 Saldívar, *Chicano Narrative*, 26.

38 Unlike Chicana/o literary critics, Chicana/o historians have consistently regarded World War II, the Korean War, and the American War in Vietnam as each representing a watershed moment in Chicana/o history. Mexican American participation in US wars in Asia has contributed significantly to this community's coming into political and cultural being, one marked by its involvement in labor movements, its commitment to social protest, its rise into the middle class through access to the US GI Bill, and its insertion into a class of professional artists. See García, *Mexican Americans*; Sánchez, *Becoming Mexican American*; Gutiérrez, *Walls and Mirrors*; Oropeza, *¡Raza Sí! ¡Guerra No!*; and Griswold del Castillo, "Introduction."

Chapter 3   Conquest and Desire

1 I have made this point briefly in my reading of Luis Valdez's *Vietnam Campesino*, highlighting how the imagined political solidarity between Chicana/os and Vietnamese peasants is predicated on the social, cultural, and historical erasure of the latter's particularity. My point here, however, is to show how the image of the female Asian in Cano's and Véa's novels undermines the oppositional sensibilities of a larger narrative by perpetuating the politics of dominance and conquest at the core of the American War in Vietnam.

2 I discuss this term, including its significance based on Homi Bhabha's theory of "jagged testimonies," in chapter 2.

3 Freud addresses the issue of war neurosis in several of his key texts, including in *Beyond the Pleasure Principle*, written just after World War I. In this text, Freud analyzes the relationship between "traumatic neurosis" of war and "hysteria" in the context of battle. He asserts that those who suffer from war neurosis, like victims of hysteria, suffer from the recollection of an external assault on consciousness given its inability to register the violence at the moment of its occurrence. In *Moses and Monotheism* (1939), Freud links collective war trauma to private experience most explicitly, noting that not all subjects respond to similar war traumas in the same way, for how one reacts depends on how the violence of war activates other psychic issues developed from previous experiences, including sexual ones. For a complete overview of Freud's work on trauma—including the relationship between war trauma and the psychic history of its victims, as well as a critical history of trauma studies generally, see Kaplan, *Trauma Culture*.

4 Kaplan, *Trauma Culture*, 32, 39.
5 Cheng, *The Melancholy of Race*, 17–18, my emphasis in first two instances.
6 Ibid., 19.
7 Ramón Saldívar's reading of Américo Paredes's *George Washington Gómez* offers an example of how a young proto-Chicano protagonist constructs masculinist values immediately following the violence of 1915 at the US-Mexico border. See Saldívar, *Borderlands of Culture*, 145–189.
8 Chris Garcia and Rudolph de la Garza outline the Chicana/o political experience according to various models of political understanding. One model, "internal colonialism," consists of four characteristics that make it reasonable to regard Chicana/os as a colonized population (177: 8–9). According to this model, Garcia and Garza note how "forced entry" [US conquest of Mexico], "cultural genocide" [destruction of native values], "external administration" [group management mainly coming from outside the community], and "racism" [the conquered group seen as inferior by nature] constitute the basis for recognizing how Chicana/os have been "internally colonized" in the United States. Regarding and deploying models of internal colonialism in order to consider Chicana/o cultural and political experiences was a prominent strategy of political critique during the 1970s and 1980s. See *The Chicano Political Experience: Three Perspectives*, especially chapter 1, "Models of the Political Process: Implications for Chicano Politics."
9 Said, *Orientalism*, 12, my emphasis.
10 Entry I.2a. "incorporate, v." *The Oxford English Dictionary*. Second Edition, vol. 7. Oxford: Oxford University Press, 823.
11 George Sánchez highlights the economic, social, and cultural conditions of Mexicans and Mexican Americans in Los Angeles in his benchmark study, *Becoming Mexican American*. Included in this piece is an analysis on the significance of World War II on this community, and the segregation and economic disparities that Cano's novel explores. Rudolfo Acuña offers an examination of Los Angeles similar to Sánchez's, yet in a contemporary context, in *Anything but Mexican*.
12 Citing the authority of psychologists Kenneth and Mamie Clark, Chief Justice Earl Warren's opinion in the landmark ruling that overturned *Plessy v. Ferguson* is just one example reminding us of the psychological impact of racial segregation on children, including their attitudes about racial difference, which they carry with them into adulthood: "To separate them [minority schoolchildren] from others of similar age and qualifications solely because of their race generates a feeling of inferiority as to their status in the community that may affect their hearts and minds in a way unlikely ever to be undone" (Chief Justice Earl Warren, quoted in Samuda, *Psychological Testing of American Minorities*, 347).
13 Cheng, *The Melancholy of Race*, 19.
14 Prashad, *Everybody Was Kung Fu Fighting*, 131.
15 Berger, "Who Is That Masked Woman? Or, the Role of Gender in Fanon's *Black Skin White Masks*," 80.
16 Gayle Rubin argues that women are "transacted" between men through both marriage and social unions, to the degree that one must characterize them as "commodities" that facilitate, affirm, and sustain homosocial bonds. Rubin writes,

"If it is women who are being transacted, then it is the men who give and take them that are linked, the woman being a conduit of a relationship rather than a partner to it" ("The Traffic in Women," 174). The commodification of Shiu in *Shifting Loyalties* literalizes the transaction of the female body, and it makes plain how her purchase facilitates the relationship and the rivalry between her fiancé and David.

17 Prashad, *Everybody Was Kung Fu Fighting*, 131.
18 Cheng, *The Melancholy of Race*, 19, 28.
19 Saldívar, *The Borderlands of Culture*, 359. Saldívar brings these issues to attention through the writings of Américo Paredes for the US Department of Defense periodical *Pacific Stars and Stripes* during the US occupation of Japan. For more on the issues of "comfort girls" and the "commodification of desire," see chapter 10, "The Postwar Borderlands and the Origin of the Transnational Imaginary," in *The Borderlands of Culture*.
20 Puntarigvivat, "A Thai Buddhist Perspective," 228.
21 Ibid., 229.
22 Ibid., 228.
23 Benjamin makes this point in relation to his discussions of Paris in "Mirrors" in *The Arcades Project*.
24 Puntarigvivat, "A Thai Buddhist Perspective," 72–73.
25 Fanon writes, "By loving me she [the white woman] proves that I am worthy of white love. I am loved like a white man. I am a white man. Her love takes me on the noble road that leads to total realization. I marry white culture, white beauty, white whiteness" (*Black Skin White Masks*, 63).
26 Hamilton, *Of Space and Mind*, 174.
27 Arce, "Nation in Uniform," 231.
28 Ibid., 229–232.
29 Cutler, "Disappeared Men," 595.
30 In a linguistics context, Jacques Derrida discusses a theory of "la différance," arguing that "the trace [of a sign] is not a presence but is rather the simulacrum of a presence that dislocates, displaces, and refers beyond itself" ("Difference," 156). I refer to Derrida in this instance to highlight how Carvajal's presence is perpetually "dislocated," and how it refers to an identity beyond how he cognitively registers his sense of self.
31 Pérez-Torres, *Mestizaje*, xiii.
32 Bhabha, "Interrogating Identity," 73.
33 Pérez-Torres, *Mestizaje*, xiii.
34 John Alba Cutler makes this point at one place in his reading of this scene, arguing "that Véa's novel . . . seems to represent the female body as the site of masculine identity formation, of sexual regeneration" ("Disappeared Men," 598).
35 It is worth noting how Carvajal's recovery—or what Cutler calls his "masculine regeneration" ("Disappeared Men," 597)—perpetuates a pattern of heterosexual reclamation in Chicana/o cultural politics. This point is highlighted powerfully by Lorna Dee Cervantes's memorable poem "Para un revolucionario" (1975), of which I speak briefly at the conclusion of this chapter. Addressing a Chicano radical committed to social justice, the Chicana female speaker acknowledges the

idyllic beauty of his vision, and yet she must share with him the realities of the gendered differences that divide them. The female speaker laments that the bond that links her to her revolutionary lover is exclusively sexual, and not ideological, for her body—and not the ideas of their oppositional politics—bridge the physical and ideological distance between them. See her poem in *Infinite Divisions*.

36 Corwall and Smith, *The Exhaustive Dictionary of Bible Names*, 185. Corwall and Smith identify the name of Tirza as "Tirzah." The most popular example of "Tirzah" in the tradition of English literature appears in William Blake's *Songs of Experience*, in a poem entitled "To Tirzah." S. Foster Damon argues that Blake's poem is a declaration of individuality, and hence of independence from the mother (*A Blake Dictionary*, 185). I mention this to suggest that Carvajal's sexing of Cassandra (imagined "as striking as Tirza") is similarly an act of identity formation, and of the actualization of the self.

37 Still, this moment of identity reformation not only untangles Carvajal's past, but it also disentangles the narrative's temporalities between contemporary San Francisco, Vietnam during the war era, and Chihuahua, Mexico, some decades earlier. In other words, the details of Carvajal's identity decode the narrative's complicated temporal and spatial arrangement, for they reveal that Carvajal is the only figure to have inhabited all three of the novel's conceptual spaces.

38 See Anzaldúa, *Borderlands/La Frontera*; Anzaldúa and Moraga, *This Bridge Called My Back*; and Lorna Dee Cervantes, "Para un revolucionario" for three classic examples of the relationship between Chicana/o culture, masculine ideologies, and oppositional feminist poetics.

39 Anzaldúa, *Borderlands/La Frontera*, 105–106.

40 Cervantes, "Para un revolucionario."

Chapter 4 Through Mexico and into Asia

1 This shift toward a reverence for Asia is marked by things that Latin American culture oftentimes had scapegoated Asians for: the decline of national economies in the region, and the demise of its national racial stocks. I examine this latter issue in great detail in chapter 5.

2 Camayd-Freixas, "Introduction," 8.

3 Ibid., 8.

4 Said, *Orientalism*, 1978.

5 Roberto Cantú reminds us that Paz "devoted many years of his life to the study of Asian civilizations. Although India remains the unequivocal cornerstone in Paz's work on Asian history and cultures, ancient China and Japan play a no less significant role. . . . Ancient China [in particular] turned into a constant source of literary allusion in Paz's critical essays, and an inspiration to translate poems and essays of Chinese masters between 1957 and 1996" ("Points of Convergence," 2).

6 Paz, "Dos apostillas," 142, my emphasis. This translation is mine. The original reads: "Las diferencias [entre las dos culturas] son menos turbadoras que las semejanzas: se diría que se trata de versiones distintas de una misma concepcíon. Estas analogías no significan forzosamente que haya habido influencia directa de

la civilización china en América. Las creencias chinas son anteriores a la reforma de Confucio, es decir, pertenecen a una época en la que el escaso adelanto del arte de la navegacíon prohíbe pensar en la posibilidad de relaciones marítimas entre ambos continentes. En consecuencia, es lícito inferir que son desarrollos independientes de una misma semilla."

7 This argument on the nearly complete cultural destruction of Amerindian culture, including the art of reading and writing Aztecan glyphs, has been emphasized by Octavio Paz's mentor, Pedro Henríquez Ureña. See Ureña, *La utopia de América*.

8 Camayd-Freixas, "Introduction," 15.

9 Raymond Williams writes that structures of feeling "are concerned with meanings and values as they are actively lived and felt . . . feeling as thought: practical consciousness of a present kind, in a living and inter-relating continuity" (*Marxism and Literature*, 132).

10 For an example of a critical analysis between Chinese and Mesoamerican values coded in the poetry of Octavio Paz, see Erik Camayd-Freixas, "The Tao of Mexican Poetry"; Roberto Cantú, "Points of Convergence"; and Jongsoo Lee, "Orientalist Universalism."

11 According to Derrida, the transcendental signified is the place in a chain of linguistic signifiers from which all signs begin and end. It marks the end of ambiguity, play, slippage, and difference between signs, giving way to absolute meaning. Derrida writes that the transcendental signified is that "which in and of itself, in its essence, would refer to no signifier, would exceed the chain of signs, and would no longer itself function as a signifier" ("Semiology and Grammatology," 242). Further, he adds that it is the place where the "signifier and the signified [must be] absolute and irreducible" (*Of Grammatology*, 20). According to Raymond Tallis, the transcendental signified is the "place where signs give way to absolute presence . . . [the place] of final meaning" ("The Linguistic Unconscious," 144).

12 Camayd-Freixas, "Introduction," 15.

13 Paz, "Dos apostillas," 147–149. This translation is mine. The original reads: "¿Cómo explicar entonces los parecidos? No lo sé. Por esto no digo que la teoría asiática es falsa: afirmo que sus hipótesis son frágiles y sus pruebas insuficientes. . . . La teoría asiática no me convence pero me impresiona. Si la reprueba mi razón, mi sensibilidad la acoge. Y el testimonio de los sentidos, para mí, no es menos decisivo que el juicio."

14 Paz, "Dos apostillas," 154. This translation is mine. The original Spanish reads: "el verdadero realismo es imaginario. . . . Más allá de verdad o error—la discusión sigue abierta—, la teoría asiática nos hace ver con otros ojos las obras de los antiguos americanos."

15 Saldívar, *Dialectics of Difference*, 104.

16 Quoted in Saldívar, ibid., 107.

17 Insisting on his Asian roots, Anaya's narrator highlights a complaint made by Paul Gilroy in an African American context. Gilroy writes that "modern black political culture has always been more interested in the relationship of identity to roots and rootedness than in seeing identity as a process of movement and mediation that is more appropriately approached via the homonym routes" (*The Black

Atlantic, 19). I include this point to show how Anaya's narrator insists on asserting his Asian roots, to the exclusion of the painful process of cultural formation that developed in relation to European colonialism.
18 Jussawalla, "Rudolfo Anaya," 133, my emphasis.
19 According to Enrique Florescano, Quetzalcoatl is one of the most recognizable and durable figures of the cosmogonic myths of the Mesoamerican peoples. For more, see Florescano, *The Myth of Quetzalcoatl*.
20 The modern-day name for the third largest pyramid of Teotihuacán is "Temple of the Feathered Serpent." On the side of this pyramid are some of the earliest representations of Quetzalcoatl, the feathered serpent god. Rebecca Storey writes that Teotihuacán is the earliest pre-Columbian city in Mexico, and one of the largest of its era (150 BC–AD 750). See Storey, *Life and Death in the Ancient City of Teotihuacan*.
21 Again, I mean here to refer to how Raymond Williams theorizes "structures of feeling." See Williams, *Marxism and Literature*.
22 Cass, "A White Man's Fantasies," 21.
23 Ibid., 20.
24 Said, *Orientalism*, 6.
25 This legend forms the basis of an important scene of Anaya's popular novel, *Bless Me Última* (1972). In this instance, the protagonist, Antonio, is told the story of the origins of the world. According to the story, the gods give man a fertile valley in which to live, so long as he does not fish the carp in the valley's river. The gods consider the carp a sacred fish. The people obey initially, yet are forced to eat the carp after the valley suffers a severe drought. In response, the angered gods prepare to destroy the people, "but one kind god argued against it, and the other gods were so moved by his love that they relented from killing the people. Instead, they turned the people into carp" (*Bless Me Última*, 74). Afterward, the kind god becomes a carp himself to be with the people he loves.
26 Cass, "A White Man's Fantasies," 21.
27 Huang, *Transpacific Displacement*, 3.
28 Anaya demonstrates his faith in uncovering a universal unconscious in an interview with Juan Bruce-Novoa, stating, "What we must not forget is that beneath the surface [of culture] we will find the archetypes and the values and the primal symbols which we share in common with all mankind" (*Chicano Authors*, 196).
29 For Wentworth, the two figurehead writers are inevitably linked as a result of their shared interest in alienation and spiritual reconciliation with the modern world. According to Wentworth, the alienation and spiritual reconciliation Paz describes in *Laberinto* informs the basis of Anaya's primary works. See Wentworth, "El laberinto de soledad de Octavio Paz y su aplicación temática en la novela chicana." I suggest both authors must be regarded in relation to each other as a result of their shared interest in Asia, and as a result of their use of common metaphors for addressing Asia's cultural influence on the Americas.
30 It is worth noting that Paz's integrations of ancient Asian poetry resemble what Rafael Pérez-Torres identifies in a related context as a formal "movement towards hybridization and crossbreeding on a cultural level that reflects the racial

mestizaje which has produced the Chicano [and Latin American] people" (*Movements in Chicano Poetry*, 8).
31 Paz, "Dos apostillas," 154.
32 For more on this, see Mariscal, *Brown-Eyed Children of the Sun*, particularly 65–96.
33 Lomelí, "Contemporary Chicano Literature," 92; Mariscal, *Aztlán and Vietnam*, 5.
34 Scholars have come to identify Africa as the "third root" of Latin America's racial and cultural heritage behind Indigenous and European influences. For example, Herman Bennett's *Africans in Colonial Mexico* highlights the significant presence of Africans across Mexico's territories. Although it does not deploy the term *third root*, Martha Menchaca's groundbreaking study *Recovering History, Constructing Race: The Indian, Black, and White Roots of Mexican Americans* explores the significance of African origins in Latin American and in both Mexican American and Chicana/o contexts.
35 See, for example, Hu-Dehart, "The Chinese Diaspora" and "Immigrants to a Developing Society"; Chao Romero, *The Chinese in Mexico, 1882–1940*; and Camacho, *Chinese Mexicans*.

Chapter 5   China-cana Feminisms

1 Saldívar, *Chicano Narrative*, 7.
2 In an early work that addresses this clash of cultures, Américo Paredes writes that "conflict—cultural, economic, and physical—has [always] been a way of life along the border between Mexico and the United States" ("The Problem of Identity in a Changing Culture," 68).
3 Pérez-Torres, "Refiguring Aztlán," 34.
4 Ibid., 35.
5 Ibid.
6 Canclini, *Hybrid Cultures*, 3.
7 Despite various performances, only excerpts of *Rasgos asiáticos* have been published formally—in *Frontiers: A Journal of Women Studies* (2003). The formal excerpts in *Women* mention earlier partial publication in *La Voz de Esperanza*, which I could not locate. Workshop productions of the play have been staged by Pregones Theatre, directed by Jorge Merced (2012), and the California Institute of the Arts, directed by Mira Kingsley (2008). The author notes in the opening pages to the excerpt published in *Frontiers* that she performed *Rasgos* prior to 2003 as a staged reading at the Esperanza Peace and Justice Center in San Antonio, Texas; the Mexican American Cultural Center (Red Salmon Arts) in Austin, Texas; and Project Reach, New York, New York. She also notes in this piece that *Rasgos* is a "forty-minute multi-media performance piece . . . an installation of different *altares* that include original photos, letters, papers, and a collection of Chinese records from the 1920s. I [the playwright] use the music, photos, and stories to weave a history of three generations of women—grandmother, mother, and daughter—as they explore shared stories of identity, violence, and love" ("*Rasgos asiáticos*," 132).

My reading of *Rasgos* is based on a 2011 written version made available by *Sweet Beans and Rice*, a cultural archive project spearheaded by Kenji Liu and

Vickie Vértiz in partnership with Intersection for the Arts. This version of *Rasgos* is linked to Vicky Vértiz, "*Rasgos asiáticos*: Theatre, Family, and Virginia Grise": http://sweetbeansnrice.files.wordpress.com/2011/08/rasgos-asiaticos1.pdf. The playwright has mentioned to the author that this piece will most likely be performed only as an "installation piece" in the future, as a result of the difficulties of its staging in the past.

8 Anzaldúa, *Borderlands/La Frontera*, 215.
9 Rosaldo, *Culture and Truth*, 149.
10 Hicks, *Border Writing*, xxiii.
11 Arteaga, "Beasts and Jagged Strokes of Color," 277.
12 Espinoza, *El ejemplo de Sonora*, 46.
13 Cruz, "Análisis demográfico de las corrrientes migratorias a México desde finales del siglo XIX," 41.
14 Hu-Dehart, "Racism and Anti-Chinese Persecution in Sonora, Mexico, 1876–1932," 1. Philip A. Dennis makes a similar point in "The Anti-Chinese Campaigns in Sonora, Mexico."
15 Chande, "La migración china hacia México a través del Registro Nacional de Extranjeros," 170.
16 See Chao Romero, "'El destierro de los chinos,'" and *Chinese in Mexico, 1882–1940*.
17 See Camacho, *Chinese Mexicans*; and Chao Romero, *Chinese in Mexico, 1882–1940*.
18 Hu-Dehart, "Immigrants to a Developing Society: The Chinese in Northern Mexico, 1875–1932," 290.
19 Chao Romero, *Chinese in Mexico, 1882–1940*, 147.
20 Ibid., 148; and Dennis, "The Anti-Chinese Campaigns in Sonora, Mexico," 67.
21 Chao Romero, *Chinese in Mexico, 1882–1940*, 152.
22 Although mostly men, Chinese immigrants to Mexico consisted of considerable numbers of women. Chande notes that the Fuente: Archivo General de la Nación, Registro Nacional de Extranjeros (AGNRNEM) lists 302 women as having immigrated to Mexico from China during the prerevolutionary era, compared to 13,911 men during the same period ("La migración china hacia México a través del Registro Nacional de Extranjeros," 171).
23 Paredes, "The Problem of Identity in a Changing Culture," 31.
24 Althusser, "Ideology and Ideological State Apparatuses (Notes Toward an Investigation)," 170.
25 Ibid., 171.
26 Pérez-Torres, "Refiguring Aztlán," 35.
27 Anzaldúa, *Borderlands/La Frontera*, 25.
28 Arteaga, "Beasts and Jagged Strokes of Color," 277.

Coda: Chicana/o Studies Then and Now

1 Vaca, "Editorial," 4.
2 Ibid.
3 Ibid.
4 Ibid.

5 Romano, "Minorities, History, and the Cultural Mystique," 9.
6 For more on this matter, see Bauer, "Hemispheric Studies"; Rowe, "Post-Nationalism, Globalism, and the New American Studies"; Fox, "Critical Perspectives and Emerging Models of Inter-American Studies"; Prashad, *Everybody Was Kung Fu Fighting*; Saldívar, *Border Matters*; and Levander, *Where Is American Literature?*
7 See Saldívar, "Asian Américo: Paredes in Asia and the Borderlands"; Limón, "Imagining the Imaginary"; and Limón, "Border Literary Histories, Globalization, and Critical Regionalism."
8 Bauer, "Hemispheric Studies."
9 Sadowski-Smith, "Introduction."
10 Wong, "Denationalization Reconsidered."
11 Romano, "Minorities, History, and the Cultural Mystique," 11.
12 Barron, "Viet Nam Veteran," 18–19.
13 López, *Chicano Nations*, 7.
14 Soldatenko, *Chicano Studies*, 40.
15 Sánchez, *Becoming Mexican American*, 6–8.
16 Quintana, *Home Girls*, 19.
17 This is the name of Behnken's book, *Fighting Their Own Battles*.
18 Fishkin, "Crossroads of Cultures," 17.
19 For an overview of global Chicana/o studies, see Leen and Thornton, *International Perspectives on Chicana/o Studies*.
20 Notable exceptions have been referenced and cited throughout this book, including George Mariscal's *Aztlán and Viet Nam* and Ramón Saldívar's *The Borderlands of Culture*. These works are among the few book-length studies to focus on the intersections between Chicana/os and Asia as they take shape in Chicana/o writings. They have been invaluable for this study. However, it is worth noting that the first limits itself to texts of the Vietnam War era, and the second focuses exclusively on the life and work of Américo Paredes.
21 On the flip side of this issue, inter-ethnic Asian American studies has tended to emphasize important Afro-Asian political and cultural relationships, while transnational analyses have largely connected Asians in the United States to their respective coethnics around the world. See, for example, Ho and Mullen, *Afro Asia*; Prashad, *Everybody Was Kung Fu Fighting*; Kim, *Writing Manhood in Black and Yellow*; Kim, *Bitter Fruit*; Ho-Jung, *Coolies and Cane*; Koshy, "Morphing Race into Ethnicity"; and Louie, "When You Are Related to the 'Other.'"
22 Sánchez, *Becoming Mexican American*, 9; Soldatenko, *Chicano Studies*, 183.
23 See, for example, Saldívar's *The Dialectics of Our America*, *Border Matters*, and *Trans-Americanity*. See also Gruesz, *Ambassadors of Culture*.
24 While many Chicana/o studies departments and programs have resisted the term "Latina/o studies" to characterize their hemispheric teaching and research, Michael Soldatenko suggests that this shift toward inter-American models of investigation links the field to Latin American studies and inevitably makes available its theoretical models to borderlands thinkers, particularly those developed by Enrique Dussel, Walter Mignolo, Maria Lugones, and Ramón Grosfoguel. See Soldatenko, *Chicano Studies*, 182–183.

25 Soldatenko, *Chicano Studies*, 182–183.
26 Lee, "Orientalisms in the Americas," 235–256.
27 According to Caroline Rody, contemporary plots of ethnic literature, and of Asian American literature in particular, have moved away from "binary face-offs" between an ethnic protagonist and a "monolithic America" and toward a self-inventive project expressed through interethnic relationships and cross-cultural articulations (*The Interethnic Imagination*, 19). Rody terms this shift away from binary paradigms in the ethnic literary imagination its "interethnic turn."
28 Hall, "What Is This 'Black' in Black Popular Culture?," 466.
29 Ibid., 468.
30 Ibid.
31 Palumbo-Liu, *Asian/American*, 1.
32 Prashad, *Everybody Was Kung Fu Fighting*, xii.
33 Lionnet and Shih, *Minor Transnationalism*, 10.
34 Prashad, *Everybody Was Kung Fu Fighting*, xii.

BIBLIOGRAPHY

Acosta, Oscar Z. *Revolt of the Cockroach People*. [1973.] New York: Vintage, 1989.
———. "Southern Christian Leadership Conference: Racial Matters." United States Department of Justice, Federal Bureau of Investigation report on *Southern Christian Leadership Conference: Racial Matters*, May 28, 1970, Los Angeles, California. Oscar Zeta Acosta papers, University of California, Santa Barbara, California Ethnic and Multicultural Archives (CEMA 1), box 7, folder 35.
Acuña, Rudolfo. *Anything but Mexican: Chicanos in Contemporary Los Angeles*. London and New York: Verso, 1995.
———. *Occupied America: A History of Chicanos*. [1981.] New York: Addison Wesley, 2003.
Alarcón, Daniel Cooper. "The Aztec Palimpsest: Toward a New Understanding of Aztlán, Cultural Identity and History." *Aztlán: A Journal of Chicano Studies* 19:2 (1992): 33–68.
Alarcón, Norma. "Chicana's Feminist Literature: A Re-vision through Malintzín/or Malintzín: Putting Flesh Back on the Object." In *This Bridge Called My Back: Writings by Radical Women of Color*, edited by Cherríe Moraga and Gloria Anzaldúa, 182–190. New York: Kitchen Table/Women of Color Press, 1983.
Alcoser, Joseph. "Joseph Alcoser," interview by René Zambrano, October 21, 2000. In *A Legacy Greater Than Words: Stories of the U.S. Latinos and Latinas of the World War II Generation*, edited by Maggie Rivas-Rodriguez, Julianna Torres, Melissa Dipiero-D'sa, and Lindsay Fitzpatrick, 111. Austin: U.S. Latino & Latina WWII Oral History Project, 2006.
Almaguer, Tomás. *Racial Fault Lines: The Historical Origins of White Supremacy in California*. Berkeley: University of California Press, 2009.
Althusser, Louis. "Contradiction and Overdetermination." In *For Marx*, translated by Ben Brewster, 87–128. New York: Verso, 2005.
———. "Ideology and Ideological State Apparatuses (Notes toward an Investigation)." In *Lenin and Philosophy and Other Essays*, translated by Ben Brewster, 127–186. New York and London: Monthly Review Press, 1971.
Alurista. *Floricanto en Aztlán*. Los Angeles: Chicano Cultural Center, University of California, 1971.
———. "The History of Aztlán." Alurista Papers, University of Texas, Austin. The Nettie Benson Latin American Collection, box 2, part 2, folder 3.
———. "Ideología y estética en la significación poética chicana en la década 1965–1975." Paper presented at the annual meeting of the Latin American Studies Association,

Mexico, DF, September 26, 1983. Alurista papers, University of California, Santa Barbara. California Ethnic and Multicultural Archives (CEMA 21), box 6, folder 4.

Anaya, Rudolfo. *Bless Me Última*. Berkeley: Quinto Sol, 1972.

———. *A Chicano in China*. Albuquerque: University of New Mexico Press, 1996.

———, and Francisco Lomelí. "Introduction." In *Aztlán: Essays on the Chicano Homeland*, edited by Rudolfo Anaya and Francisco Lomelí, ii–iv. Albuquerque: University of New Mexico Press, 1989.

Anderson, Benedict. *Imagined Communities: Reflections on the Origins and Spread of Nationalism*. London: Verso, 1991.

"Anti-war Rally Held by Coalition of Raza." *El Grito del Norte*, July–August 1973.

Anzaldúa, Gloria. *Borderlands/La Frontera: The New Mestiza*. San Francisco: Aunt Lute, 1987.

———, and Cherríe Moraga, eds. *This Bridge Called My Back: Writings by Radical Women of Color*. New York: Kitchen Table/Women of Color Press, 1982.

Arce, William. "Nation in Uniform: Chicano/Latino War Narratives and the Construction of the Nation in the Korean War and Vietnam War." PhD diss., University of Southern California, 2009.

Arteaga, Alfred. "Beasts and Jagged Strokes of Color: The Poetics of Hybridization on the US-Mexican Border." In *Bakhtin: Carnival, and Other Subjects*, edited by David Shepherd, 277–293. Amsterdam: Rodopi, 1993.

Baker, Houston. *Modernism and the Harlem Renaissance*. Chicago: University of Chicago Press, 1987.

Bakhtin, Mikhail. *The Dialogic Imagination*, edited by Michael Holquist, translated by Caryl Emerson. Austin: University of Texas Press, 1981.

Barr, Alawyn. *Texans in Revolt: The Battle for San Antonio, 1835*. Austin: University of Texas Press, 1990.

Barron, Robert. "Viet Nam Veteran." *El Grito* 1:3 (1968): 18–19.

Bauer, Ralph. "Hemispheric Studies." *PMLA* 124:1 (2009): 234–250.

Behnken, Brian D. *Fighting Their Own Battles: Mexican Americans, African Americans, and the Struggle for Civil Rights in Texas*. Chapel Hill: University of North Carolina Press, 2011.

Belknap, Michal R. *The Vietnam War on Trial: The My Lai Massacre and the Court-Martial of Lieutenant Calley*. Lawrence: University Press of Kansas, 2002.

Benitel, Tomas. "An Interview with Playwright Luis Valdez: Facing the Issues Beyond Zoot Suit." *Neworld* 4:4 (1978): 34–38.

Benjamin, Walter. "Mirrors." In *The Arcades Project*, translated by Howard Eiland and Kevin McLaughlin, 537–542. Cambridge, MA: Belknap Press of Harvard University Press, 1999.

Bennett, Herman. *Africans in Colonial Mexico: Absolutism, Christianity, and Afro-Creole Consciousness, 1570–1640*. Bloomington: Indiana University Press, 2003.

Berger, Gwen. "Who Is That Masked Woman? Or, the Role of Gender in Fanon's *Black Skin White Masks*." *PMLA* 110:1 (1995): 75–88.

Bhabha, Homi K. "Interrogating Identity: Frantz Fanon and the Postcolonial Prerogative." In *The Location of Culture*, 57–93. London and New York: Routledge, 1994.

———. *Nation and Narration*. New York: Routledge, 1990.

Brown, Patricia Leigh. "Larry Itlong, Forgotten Filipino Labor Leader." *New York Times*, October 8, 2012.
Bruce-Novoa, Juan. *Chicano Authors: Inquiry by Interview*. Austin: University of Texas Press, 1980.
Camacho, Julia María Schiavone. *Chinese Mexicans: Transpacific Migration and the Search for Homeland, 1910-1960*. Chapel Hill: University of North Carolina Press, 2012.
Camayd-Freixas, Erik. "Introduction: The Orientalist Controversy and the Origins of Amerindian Culture." In *Orientalism and Identity in Latin America: Fashioning Self and Other from the (Post) Colonial Margin*, edited by Erik Camayd-Freixas, 1–18. Tucson: University of Arizona Press, 2013.
———. "The Tao of Mexican Poetry: Tablada, Villaurrutia, Paz." In *Orientalism and Identity in Latin America: Fashioning Self and Other from the (Post)Colonial Margin*, edited by Erik Camayd-Freixas, 119–144. Tucson: University of Arizona Press, 2013.
Canclini, Néstor García. *Hybrid Cultures: Strategies for Entering and Leaving Modernity*. Minneapolis: University of Minnesota Press, 1995.
Cano, Daniel. *Shifting Loyalties*. Houston: Arte Público Press, 1995.
Cantú, Roberto. "Points of Convergence: Ancient China, Modernity, and Translation in the Poetry and Essays of Octavio Paz, 1956–1996." In *Alternative Orientalisms in Latin America and Beyond*, edited by Ignacio López-Calvo, 2–28. New Castle, DE: Cambridge Scholars, 2007.
Cárdenas, Lupe, and Justo Alarcón. "Entrevista a Miguel Méndez M." *Confluencia: Revista Hispánica de Cultura y Literatura* 4:1 (1988): 150–156.
Caruth, Cathy. *Unclaimed Experience: Trauma, Narrative, and History*. Baltimore: Johns Hopkins University Press, 1996.
Cass, Jeffrey. "A White Man's Fantasies: Orientalism in Rudolfo Anaya's *A Chicano in China*." In *Bloom's Modern Critical Views: Hispanic-American Writers—New Edition*, edited by Harold Bloom, 17–28. New York: Infobase, 2009.
Cervantes, Lorna Dee. "Para un revolucionario." [1975.] In *Infinite Divisions: An Anthology of Chicana Literature*, edited by Tey Diana Reybolledo and Eliana S. Rivero, 151–152. Tucson: University of Arizon Press, 1993.
Chande, Roberto Ham. "La migración china hacia México a través del Registro Nacional de Extranjeros." In *Destino México: Un estudio de las migraciones asiáticas a México, siglos XIX y XX*, edited by María Elena Ota Mishima, 167–188. México, DF: El Colegio de México, 1997.
Chao Romero, Robert. *The Chinese in Mexico, 1882–1940*. Tucson: University of Arizona Press, 2010.
———. "'El destierro de los chinos: Popular Perspectives on Chinese-Mexican Intermarriage in the Early Twentieth Century." *Aztlán: A Journal of Chicano Studies* 31:1 (2007): 113–144.
Chávez, Ernesto. *"Mi Raza Primero!" (My People First!): Nationalism, Identity, and Insurgency in the Chicano Movement in Los Angeles, 1966–1978*. Berkeley: University of California Press, 2002.
Cheng, Anne Anlin. *The Melancholy of Race: Psychoanalysis, Assimilation, and Hidden Grief*. Oxford: Oxford University Press, 2001.

Cheng, Wendy. *The Changs Next Door to the Díazes: Remapping Race in Suburban California*. Minneapolis: University of Minnesota Press, 2013.

Congressional Record: Proceedings and Debates of the 106th Congress. First Session, volume 145, part 18, 25311–26720.

Corwall, Judson, and Stelman Smith. *The Exhaustive Dictionary of Bible Names*. Alachua: Bridge-Logos, 1998.

Crisp, James. *Sleuthing the Alamo: Davy Crockett's Last Stand and Other Mysteries of the Texas Revolution*. Oxford: Oxford University Press, 2005.

Cruz, Sergio Camposortega. "Análisis demográfico de las corrientes migratorias a México desde finales del siglo XIX." In *Destino México: Un estudio de las migraciones asiáticas a México, siglos XIX y XX*, edited by María Elena Ota Mishima, 20–54. México, DF: El Colegio de México, 1997.

Cutler, John Alba. "Disappeared Men: Chicana/o Authenticity and the American War in Viet Nam." *American Literature: A Journal of Literary History, Criticism, and Biography* 81:3 (2009): 583–611.

Damon, S. Foster. *A Blake Dictionary: The Ideas and Symbols of William Blake*. Hanover, NH: Dartmouth College Press, 1965.

Davies, Nigel. *Voyagers to the New World*. New York: William Morrow, 1979.

de la Luz, Portilla. "La hora de todos." [1972.] Reprinted in George Mariscal, *Brown-Eyed Children of the Sun: Lessons from the Chicano Movement, 1965–1975*, 247. Albuquerque: University of New Mexico Press, 2005.

del Castillo, Adelaida R., ed. *Between Borders: Essays on Mexicana/Chicana History*. Encino, CA: Floricanto Press, 1988.

Delgado, Abelardo B. *The Chicano Movement*. Denver: Totinem Productions, 1971.

Delucchi, Mary Phelan. "El Teatro Campesino de Aztlán, Chicano Protest through Drama." *The Pacific Historian* 16:1 (1972): 15–27.

Dennis, Philip A. "The Anti-Chinese Campaigns in Sonora, Mexico." *Ethnohistory* 26:1 (1979): 65–80.

Derrida, Jacques. "Difference." [1968.] In *Speech and Phenomena and Other Essays on Husserl's Theory of Signs*, 129–160. Evanston, IL: Northwestern University Press, 1973.

———. *Of Grammatology*. [1967.] Translated by Gayatri Chakravorty Spivak. Baltimore: Johns Hopkins University Press, 1974.

———. "Semiology and Grammatology: Interview with Julia Kristeva (1968)." In *The Routledge Language and Cultural Theory Reader*, edited by Lucy Burke, Tony Crowley, and Alan Girvin, 241–248. London and New York: Routledge, 2000.

Dillon, Martin C. *Semiological Reductionism: A Critique of the Deconstructionist Movement in Postmodern Thought*. Albany: State University of New York Press, 1995.

Dower, John. *War without Mercy: Race and Power in the Pacific War*. New York: Pantheon, 1986.

"El plan espiritual de Aztlán." [1969.] In *Aztlán: Essays on the Chicano Homeland*, edited by Francisco Lomelí and Rudolfo Anaya, 1–5. Albuquerque: University of New Mexico Press, 1991.

Espinoza, José Angel. *El ejemplo de Sonora*. Mexico, DF: n.p., 1932.

———. *El problema chino en México*. Mexico, DF: n.p., 1931.

Fagan, Brian. *The Great Journey: The Peopling of Ancient America*. London: Thames and Hudson, 1987.
Fanon, Frantz. *Black Skin White Masks* [1967.] Translated by Charles Lam Markmann. New York: Grove Weidenfeld, 1998.
———. *The Wretched of the Earth*. [1961.] New York: Grove, 1963.
Feinstein, Diane. "Statements By." In U.S. Congress, *Congressional Record: Proceedings and Debates, 106th Cong*, 1999, 25465.
Fishkin, Shelley Fisher. "Crossroads of Cultures: The Transnational Turn in American Studies." Presidential Address to the American Studies Association, November 12, 2004. *American Quarterly* 57:1 (2005): 17–57.
Fitz, Earl. *Rediscovering the New World: Inter-American Literature in a Comparative Context*. Iowa City: University of Iowa Press, 1991.
Flores, Armando. "Armando Flores," interview by Bettina Luis, March 24, 2001. In *A Legacy Greater Than Words: Stories of the U.S. Latinos and Latinas of the World War II Generation*, edited by Maggie Rivas-Rodriguez, Julianna Torres, Melissa DiPiero-D'sa, and Lindsay Fitzpatrick, 295. Austin: U.S. Latino & Latina WII Oral History Project, 2006.
Florescano, Enrique. *The Myth of Quetzalcoatl*. Translated by Lysa Hochroth. Baltimore: Johns Hopkins University Press, 1999.
Forster, E. M. *Aspects of the Novel*. [1927.] London: Edward Arnold, 1958.
Fox, Claire. "Critical Perspectives and Emerging Models of Inter-American Studies." *Comparative American Studies* 3:4 (2005): 387–391.
Freud, Sigmund. *Beyond the Pleasure Principle*. [1920.] Translated by James Strachey. New York and London: W. W. Norton, 1961.
———. *Moses and Monotheism*. [1939.] New York: Vintage, 1955.
Gambone, Michael D. *The Greatest Generation Comes Home: The Veteran in American Society*. College Station: Texas A&M University Press, 2005.
Garcia, Chris F., and Rudolph O. de la Garza. *The Chicano Political Experience: Three Perspectives*. North Scituate, MA: Duxbury Press, 1977.
García, Ignacio M. *Chicanismo: The Forging of a Militant Ethos among Mexican Americans*. Tucson: University of Arizona Press, 1997.
García, Mario. *Mexican Americans: Leadership, Ideology, and Identity, 1930–1960*. New Haven: Yale University Press, 1989.
Garcia, Matt. *From the Jaws of Victory: The Triumph and Tragedy of Cesar Chavez and the Farm Worker Movement*. Berkeley: University of California Press, 2012.
Gilroy, Paul. *The Black Atlantic: Modernity and Double Consciousness*. Cambridge, MA: Harvard University Press, 1993.
Gómez-Quiñones, Juan. "Plan de San Diego Reviewed." In *Chicano: The Evolution of a People*, edited by Renato Rosaldo, Robert A. Calvert, and Gustav L. Seligmann, 123–127. Minneapolis: Winston Press, 1973.
González, Marcial. *Chicano Novels and the Politics of Form: Race, Class, and Reification*. Ann Arbor: University of Michigan Press, 2009.
Grise, Virginia. "*Rasgos asiaticos*." *Frontiers: A Journal of Women Studies* 24:2/3 (2003): 132–139.

———. *Rasgos asiaticos*. 2011 manuscript attached to Vicky Vértiz, "Theatre, Family, and Virgina Grise," at *Sweet Beans and Rice: Investigating a Chino-Latino Future*, edited by Kenji Liu and Vicky Vértiz, accessed March 2014, sweetbeansnrice.files.wordpress.com/2011/08/rasgos-asiaticos1.pdf.

Griswold del Castillo, Richard. "Introduction." In *World War II and Mexican American Civil Rights*, edited by Richard Griswold del Castillo, 1–6. Austin: University of Texas Press, 2008.

Gruesz, Kirsten Silvia. *Ambassadors of Culture: The Transamerican Origins of Latino Writing*. Princeton, NJ: Princeton University Press, 2002.

Gutiérrez, David. *Walls and Mirrors: Mexican Americans, Mexican Immigrants, and the Politics of Ethnicity*. Berkeley: University of California Press, 1995.

Guzman, Ralph. "Mexican American Casualties in Vietnam." *La Raza Magazine*, February 1970, 12–15.

Hall, Stuart. "What Is This 'Black' in Black Popular Culture?" In *Stuart Hall: Critical Dialogues in Cultural Studies*, edited by David Morley and Kuan-Hsing-Chen, 465–475. London: Routledge, 2005.

Hamilton, Patrick. *Of Space and Mind: Cognitive Mappings of Contemporary Chicano/a Fiction*. Austin: University of Texas Press, 2012.

Hardin, Stephen L. *Texian Iliad: A Military History of the Texas Revolution*. Austin: University of Texas Press, 1994.

Hicks, Emily. *Border Writing: The Multidimensional Text*. Minneapolis: University of Minnesota Press, 1991.

Hinojosa, Rolando. *Korean Love Songs from Klail City Death Trip*. Berkeley: Editorial Justa, 1978.

———. *Rites and Witnesses*. Houston: Arte Público Press, 1982.

Ho, Fred, and Bill Mullen, eds. *Afro Asia: Revolutionary Political and Cultural Connections between African Americans and Asian Americans*. Durham, NC: Duke University Press, 2008.

Ho-Jung, Moon. *Coolies and Cane: Race, Labor, and Sugar in the Age of Emancipation*. Baltimore: Johns Hopkins University Press, 2006.

Huang, Yunte. *Transpacific Displacement: Ethnography, Translation, and Intertextual Travel in Twentieth-Century American Literature*. Berkeley: University of California Press, 2002.

Hu-Dehart, Evelyn. "The Chinese Diaspora." In *The Asian Pacific American Heritage: A Companion to Literature and Arts*, edited by George J. Leonard, 299–310. New York: Garland Press, 1998.

———. "The Chinese in Baja California Norte, 1910–1934." *Proceedings of the Pacific Coast Council on Latin American Studies: Baja California and the North American Frontier* 12 (1985–1986): 9–28.

———. "Immigrants to a Developing Society: The Chinese in Northern Mexico, 1875–1932." *Journal of Arizona History* 21 (1980): 275–312.

———. "Racism and Anti-Chinese Persecution in Sonora, Mexico, 1876–1932." *Amerasia* 9 (1982): 1–27.

———, ed. *Across the Pacific: Asian Americans and Globalization*. Philadelphia: Temple University Press, 1999.

Huerta, Jorge, "Chicano Teatro: A Background." *Aztlán: Chicano Journal of the Social Sciences and the Arts* 2:2 (1971): 63–73.
———. *Chicano Theater: Themes and Forms*. Tempe, AZ: Bilingual Press/Editorial Bilingüe, 1982.
Hune, Shirley. "Reflections on Linking Global South and Asian American Studies." *Amerasia Journal* 35:5 (2009): 35–46.
Jameson, Fredric. *Postmodernism; or, The Cultural Logic of Late Capitalism*. Durham, NC: Duke University Press, 1991.
Jimenez, Philip J. "Vietnam." *El Grito* 1:3 (1968): 31–33.
Jussawalla, Feroza. "Rudolfo Anaya." In *Conversations with Rudolfo Anaya*, edited by Bruce Dick and Silvio Sirias, 131–141. Jackson, MI: University of Mississippi Press, 1998.
Kanellos, Nicolás. "Chicano Theatre to Date." *Tejidos: A Bilingual Journal for the Stimulation of Chicano Creativity and Criticism* 2:8 (1975): 40–46.
———. "José Montoya." In *Hispanic Literatures of the United States: A Comprehensive Reference*, 125–126. Westport, CT: Greenwood, 2003.
———. "Luis Valdez." In *Hispanic Literatures of the United States: A Comprehensive Reference*. 125. Westport, CT: Greenwood, 2003.
Kaplan, E. Ann. *Trauma Culture: The Politics of Terror and Loss in Media and Literature*. New Brunswick, NJ: Rutgers University Press, 2005.
Kim, Claire Jean. *Bitter Fruit: The Politics of Black-Korean Conflict in New York City*. New Haven: Yale University Press, 2000.
Kim, Daniel Y. *Writing Manhood in Black and Yellow: Ralph Ellison, Frank Chin, and the Literary Politics of Identity*. Stanford, CA: Stanford University Press, 2005.
Kim, Jodi. *Ends of Empire: Asian American Critique and the Cold War*. Minneapolis: University of Minnesota Press, 2010.
Knox, Donald. *Death March: The Survivors of Bataan*. New York: Harcourt, 1981.
Koshy, Susan. "Morphing Race into Ethnicity: Asian Americans and Critical Transformations of Whiteness." *Boundary 2* 28:1 (2001): 153–194.
Leal, Luis. "In Search of Aztlán." *Denver Quarterly* 16:3 (1981): 16–22.
Lee, Erika. "Orientalisms in the Americas: A Hemispheric Approach to Asian American History." *Journal of Asian American Studies* 8:3 (2005): 235–256.
Lee, Jongsoo. "Orientalist Universalism: Aztec Time and History in Octavio Paz's 'Piedra del sol.'" In *Alternative Orientalisms in Latin America and Beyond*, edited by Ignacio López-Calvo, 29–45. New Castle, DE: Cambridge Scholars Publishing, 2007.
Lee, Rachel. *The Americas of Asian American Literature: Gendered Fictions of Nation and Transnation*. Princeton, NJ: Princeton University Press, 1999.
Leen, Catherine, and Niamh Thornton, eds. *International Perspectives on Chicana/o Studies: "This World Is My Place."* New York: Routledge, 2014.
Levander, Caroline. *Where Is American Literature?* Malden, MA: Wiley-Blackwell, 2013.
Lien, Pei-Te. *The Making of Asian America through Political Participation*. Philadelphia: Temple University Press, 2001.
Limón, José. "Border Literary Histories, Globalization, and Critical Regionalism." *American Literary History* 20:1–2 (2008): 160–182.

———. *Dancing with the Devil: Society and Cultural Poetics in Mexican-American South Texas*. Madison: University of Wisconsin Press, 1994.

———. "Imagining the Imaginary: A Reply to Ramon Saldívar." *American Literary History* 21:3 (2009): 595–603.

———. *Mexican Ballads, Chicano Poems: History and Influence in Mexican-American Social Poetry*. Berkeley: University of California Press, 1992.

Lionnet, Françoise, and Shu-mei Shih. "Introduction: Thinking through the Minor Transnationally." In *Minor Transnationalism*, edited by Françoise Lionnet and Shu-mei Shih, 1–23. Durham, NC: Duke University Press, 2006.

Lipsitz, George. *The Possessive Investment in Whiteness: How White People Benefit from Identity Politics*. Philadelphia: Temple University Press, 1998.

Lomelí, Francisco. "Contemporary Chicano Literature, 1959–1990: From Oblivion to Affirmation to the Forefront." In *Handbook of Hispanic Cultures in the United States: Literature and Art*, edited by Nicolás Kanellos and Claudio Esteva-Fabregat, 86–108. Houston: Arte Público Press, 1993.

López, Marissa K. *Chicano Nations: The Hemispheric Origins of Mexican American Literature*. New York: New York University Press, 2011.

Louie, Andrea. "When You Are Related to the 'Other': (Re)locating the Chinese Homeland in Asian American Politics through Cultural Tourism." *positions: east asia cultures critique* 11:3 (2003): 735–763.

Luebke, Frederick C. *Bonds of Loyalty: German Americans and World War I*. DeKalb, IL: Northern Illinois University Press, 1974.

LULAC NEWS, Washington, DC, July 1945.

Mariscal, George. *Aztlán and Viet Nam: Chicano and Chicana Experiences of the War*. Berkeley: University of California Press, 1999.

———. *Brown-Eyed Children of the Sun: Lessons from the Chicano Movement, 1965–1975*. Albuquerque: University of New Mexico Press, 2005.

Martínez, Manuel Luis. *Countering the Counterculture: Rereading Postwar American Dissent from Jack Kerouac to Tomás Rivera*. Madison: University of Wisconsin Press, 2003.

McClennen, Sophia. "Inter-American Studies or Imperial American Studies?" *Comparative American Studies* 3:4 (2005): 393–413.

Mencha, Martha. *Recovering History, Constructing Race: The Indian, Black, and White Roots of Mexican Americans*. Austin: University of Texas Press, 2001.

Méndez, Miguel. *Pilgrims in Aztlán*. [1974.] Tempe, AZ: Bilingual Press/Editorial Bilingüe, 1992.

Mignolo, Walter. *The Idea of Latin America*. Oxford: Blackwell, 2005.

———. *Local Histories/Global Designs*. Princeton, NJ: Princeton University Press, 2000.

Montoya, José. "Chicanos en Korea." In *Information: 20 Years of Joda*, 250–251. San Jose, CA: Chusma House, 1992.

———. "El Louie." [1969.] In *Information: 20 Years of Joda*, 16–18. San Jose, CA: Chusma House, 1992.

Moraga, Cherríe. *Loving in the War Years: Lo que nunca pasó por sus labios*. Cambridge, MA: South End Press, 1983.

Morales, Armando. "Chicano-Police Riots." In *Chicanos: Social and Psychological Perspectives*, edited by Nathaniel N. Wagner and Marsha Haug, 184–202. St. Louis: C. V. Mosby, 1971.

Morin, Raul. *Among the Valiant: Mexican Americans in World War II and Korea*. Alhambra, CA: Borden Publishing, 1963.

Morrison, Samuel Eliot. *History of United States Naval Operations in World War II*. Boston: Little, Brown, 1951.

Muñoz, Carlos Jr. *Youth, Identity, Power: The Chicano Movement*. London: Verso, 2009.

Newmark, Kevin. "Traumatic Poetry: Charles Baudelaire and the Shock of Laughter." In *Trauma: Explorations in Memory*, edited by Cathy Caruth, 236–255. Baltimore: Johns Hopkins University Press, 1995.

Ngai, Mae. *Impossible Subjects: Illegal Aliens and the Making of Modern America*. Princeton, NJ: Princeton University Press, 2004.

Noriega, Chon A. "The Dissension of Other Things." In *The Chicano Studies Reader: An Anthology of Aztlán, 1970–2010*, edited by Eric Avila, Karen Mary Davalos, Chela Sandoval, Rafael Pérez-Torres, and Chon A. Noriega, 1–6. Los Angeles: UCLA Chicano Studies Research Center Press, 2010.

Olguín, Ben V. "Sangre mexicana/corazón americano: Identity, Ambiguity, and Critique in Mexican-American War Narratives." *American Literary History* 14:1 (2002): 83–114.

Olstad, Charles. *"Peregrinos en Aztlán* (a review)." *Journal of Spanish Studies: Twentieth Century* 2:2 (1974): 119–121.

Oropeza, Lorena. *¡Raza Sí! ¡Guerra No! Chicano Protest and Patriotism during the Viet Nam War Era*. Berkeley: University of California Press, 2005.

Ortego, Philip. "Chicano Poetry: Roots and Writers." *Southwestern American Literature* 2:1 (1972): 8–24.

Palumbo-Liu, David. *Asian/American: Historical Crossings of a Racial Frontier*. Stanford, CA: Stanford University Press, 1999.

Paredes, Américo. "Ichiro Kikuchi." In *The Hammon and the Beans and Other Stories*, 151–159. Houston: Arte Público Press, 1994.

———. "The Problem of Identity in a Changing Culture." [1978.] In *Folklore and Culture on the Texas-Mexican Border*, edited by Richard Bauman, 19–47. Austin: Center for Mexican American Studies, University of Texas at Austin, 1993.

———. *With His Pistol in His Hand: A Border Ballad and Its Hero*. Austin: University of Texas Press, 1958.

Paz, Octavio. "Dos apostillas: Asia y América." [1966.] In *Puertas al campo*, 133–154. Barcelona: Seix Barral, 1972.

Pérez-Torres, Rafael. *Mestizaje: Critical Uses of Race in Chicano Culture*. Minneapolis: University of Minnesota Press, 2006.

———. *Movements in Chicano Poetry: Against Myths, Against Margins*. Cambridge: Cambridge University Press, 1995.

———. "Refiguring Aztlán." *Aztlán: A Journal of Chicano Studies* 22:2 (1997): 15–41.

Porter, Carolyn. "What We Know That We Don't Know: Remapping American Literary Studies." *American Literary History* 6:3 (1994): 467–526.

Prashad, Vijay. *Everybody Was Kung Fu Fighting: Afro-Asian Connections and the Myth of Cultural Purity*. Boston: Beacon, 2001.

Pulido, Laura. *Black, Brown, Yellow and Left: Radical Activism in Los Angeles*. Berkeley: University of California Press, 2006.

Puntarigvivat, Tavivat. "A Thai Buddhist Perspective." In *What Men Owe to Women: Men's Voices from World Religions*, edited by John C. Raines and Daniel C. Maguire, 211–238. New York: State University of New York Press, 2001.

Quintana, Alvina E. *Home Girls: Chicana Literary Voices*. Philadelphia: Temple University Press, 1996.

Rasmussen, Morten, Sarah L. Anzick, Michael R. Waters, Pontus Skoglund, Michael DiGiorgio, Thomas W. Stafford, Simon Rasmussen, et al. "The Genome of a Late Pleistocene Human from a Clovis Burial Site in Western Montana." *Nature* 506 (2014): 225–229.

Rees, Richard W. *Shades of Difference: A History of Ethnicity in America*. Lanham, MD: Rowman & Littlefield, 2007.

Renan, Ernest. "What Is a Nation?" [1882.] In *Nation and Narration*, edited by Homi K. Bhabha, translated by Martin Thom, 8–22. New York: Routledge, 1990.

Rivas-Rodriguez, Maggie, ed. *Mexican Americans and World War II*. Austin: University of Texas Press, 2005.

Rivera, John-Michael. *The Emergence of Mexican America: Recovering Stories of Mexican Peoplehood in U.S. Culture*. New York: New York University Press, 2006.

Rivera, Tomás. *Y no se lo tragó la tierra/And the Earth Did Not Devour Him*. [1971.] Houston: Arte Público Press, 1992.

Rodríguez, Juan. "El florecimiento de la literatura chicana." In *La otra cara de México: El pueblo chicano*, edited by David R. Maciel, 348–369. Mexico City: El Caballito, 1977.

Rody, Caroline. *The Interethnic Imagination: Roots and Passages in Contemporary Asian American Fiction*. Oxford: Oxford University Press, 2009.

Romano, Octavio Ignacio. "Minorities, History, and the Cultural Mystique." *El Grito* 1:1 (1967): 5–11.

Rosaldo, Renato. *Culture and Truth: The Remaking of Social Analysis*. Boston: Beacon, 1989.

Rowe, John Carlos. "Post-Nationalism, Globalism, and the New American Studies." *Cultural Critique* 40 (1998): 11–28.

———. *Post-nationalist American Studies*. Berkeley: University of California Press, 2000.

Rubin, Gayle. "The Traffic in Women: Notes on the 'Political Economy' of Sex." In *Toward an Anthropology of Women*, edited by Rayna Reiter, 157–210. New York: Monthly Review Press, 1975.

Rustomji-Kearns, Roshni. "Introduction." In *Encounters: People of Asian Descent in the Americas*, edited by Roshni Rustomji-Kearns, 2–9. Boulder, CO: Rowman & Littlefield, 1999.

Sadowski-Smith, Claudia. *Border Fictions: Globalization, Empire, and Writing at the Boundaries of the United States*. Charlottesville: University of Virginia Press, 2008.

———. "Introduction: Comparative Border Studies." *Comparative American Studies: An International Journal* 9:4 (2011): 273–287.

Sae-Saue, Jayson Gonzales. "Aztlán's Asians: Forging and Forgetting Crossracial Relations in the Chicana/o Literary Imagination." *American Literature* 85:3 (2013): 562–589.

———. "The Inter-ethnic Return: Cultural and Racial Multiplicity in Foundational Asian American and Chicana/o Literatures." *Comparative American Studies: An International Journal* 8:4 (2010): 267–282.

Said, Edward. *Orientalism*. New York: Vintage, 1978.

Saldívar, José David. *Border Matters: Remapping American Cultural Studies*. Berkeley: University of California Press, 1997.

———. *The Dialectics of Our America: Genealogy, Cultural Critique, and Literary History*. Durham, NC: Duke University Press, 1991.

———. *Trans-Americanity: Subaltern Modernities, Global Coloniality, and the Cultures of Greater Mexico*. Durham, NC: Duke University Press, 2012.

Saldívar, Ramón. "Asian Américo: Paredes in Asia and the Borderlands: A Response to José Limón." *American Literary History* 21:3 (2009): 584–594.

———. *The Borderlands of Culture: Américo Paredes and the Transnational Imaginary*. Durham, NC: Duke University Press, 2006.

———. *Chicano Narrative: The Dialectics of Difference*. Madison: University of Wisconsin Press, 1990.

———. "Introduction." In *The Hammon and the Beans and Other Stories*, vii–li. Houston: Arte Público Press, 1994.

Saldívar-Hull, Sonia. *Feminism on the Border: Chicana Gender Politics and Literature*. Berkeley: University of California Press, 2000.

Samuda, Ronald J. *The Psychological Testing of American Minorities: Issues and Consequences*. Thousand Oaks, CA: SAGE, 1998.

Sánchez, George. *Becoming Mexican American: Ethnicity, Culture, and Identity in Chicano Los Angeles, 1900–1945*. Oxford: Oxford University Press, 1993.

Sánchez, Rosaura. "Ethnicity, Ideology, and Academia." *The Americas Review* 15:1 (1987): 80–88.

———. "From Heterogeneity to Contradiction: Hinojosa's Novel." In *The Rolando Hinojosa Reader: Essays Historical and Critical*, edited by José David Saldívar, 76–100. Houston: Arte Público Press, 1985.

Sánchez, Rosaura, and Rosa Martinez Cruz, eds. *Essays on la mujer*. Los Angeles: Chicano Studies Center Publications, University of California, Los Angeles, 1977.

Servín, Ignacio. "Ignacio Servín," interview by Brenda Sendejo, June 29, 2004. In *A Legacy Greater Than Words: Stories of U.S. Latinos and Latinas of the World War II Generation*, edited by Maggie Rivas-Rodriguez, Julianna Torres, Melissa DiPiero-D'sa, and Lindsay Fitzpatrick, 118. Austin: U.S. Latino & Latina WWII Oral History Project Group, 2006.

Soldatenko, Michael. *Chicano Studies: The Genesis of a Discipline*. Tucson: University of Arizona Press, 2009.

Sommer, Doris. *Proceed with Caution, When Engaged by Minority Writings in the Americas*. Cambridge, MA: Harvard University Press, 1999.

Sommers, Joseph. "Interpreting Tomás Rivera." In *Modern Chicano Writers: A Collection of Critical Essays*, edited by Joseph Sommers and Tomás Ybarrra-Fausto, 94–107. Englewood, NJ: Prentice Hall, 1979.

Storey, Rebecca. *Life and Death in the Ancient City of Teotihuacan.* Tuscaloosa: University of Alabama Press, 1992.
Suro, Roberto. "Foreword." In *A Legacy Greater Than Words: Stories of U.S. Latinos and Latinas of the World War II Generation*, edited by Maggie Rivas-Rodriguez, Juliana Torres, Melissa Dipiero-D'sa, and Linsay Fitzpatrick, xi–xii. Austin: U.S. Latino & Latina WWII Oral History Project, 2006.
Takaki, Ronald. *Double Victory: A Multicultural History of America in WWII.* New York: Back Bay Books, 2001.
Tallis, Raymond. "The Linguistic Unconscious: Saussure and the Post-Saussurians." In *Theory's Empire: An Anthology of Dissent*, edited by Daphne Patai and Will H. Corral, 125–146. New York: Columbia University Press, 2005.
Tenayuca, Emma, and Homer Brooks. "The Mexican Question in the Southwest." *Communist* 18:3 (1939): 257–268.
Testa, Daniel P. "Narrative Technique and Human Experience in Tomás Rivera." In *Modern Chicano Writers: A Collection of Critical Essays*, edited by Joseph Sommers and Tomás Ybarra-Fausto, 86–93. Englewood Cliffs, NJ: Prentice Hall, 1979.
Thorne, Christopher. *Allies of a Kind: The United States, Britain, and the War against Japan, 1941–1945.* Oxford: Oxford University Press, 1978.
Trujillo, Charlie. *Soldados: Chicanos in Viet Nam.* San Jose, CA: Chusma House, 1990.
Ureña, Pedro Henríquez. *La utopia de América.* [1937.] Edited by Ángel Rama and Rafael Gutiérrez Giradot. Caracas: Ayacucho, 1978.
Urista, Alberto H. "Oscar Z. Acosta: In Context." PhD diss., University of California San Diego, 1983.
U.S. Congress. *Congressional Record: Proceedings and Debates, 106th Cong.,* 1999: 25465.
Vaca, Nick. "Editorial." *El Grito* 1:1 (1967): 4.
Valdez, Luis. *Actos y El Teatro Campesino.* San Juan Bautista, CA: Menayah Productions, 1971.
———. "The Plan de Delano." [1966.] In *The Words of César Chávez*, edited by Richard Jensen and John C. Hammarback, 16–21. College Station: Texas A&M University Press, 2002.
———. "Soldado Razo." [1971.] In *Luis Valdez—Early Works: Actos, Bernabé, and Pensamiento Serpintino*, 121–133. Houston: Arte Público Press, 1994.
———. "Tale of La Raza." [1971.] In *Chicano: The Evolution of a People*, edited by Robert A. Calvert, Gustave L. Seligmann, and Renato Rosaldo, 293–296. Minneapolis: Winston Press, 1973.
———. *Vietnam Campesino.* [1970.] In *Luis Valdez—Early Works: Actos, Bernabé, and Pensamiento Serpintino*, 98–120. Houston: Arte Público Press, 1994.
Vasconcelos, José. *La raza cósmica.* [1925.] Translated by Didier T. Jaen. Baltimore: Johns Hopkins University Press, 1997.
Vásquez, Mary S. "The Representation of the Southwest in Selected Fiction of Miguel Méndez and Ramón Sender." *Confluencia* 17:2 (2002): 104–110.
Véa, Alfredo. *Gods Go Begging.* New York: Plume, 1999.
———. "An Interview with Alfredo Véa," by Daniel D. Zarazua, March 2000. Saginaw, MI.
Villa, Esteban. "¡Viet Nam!" *El Grito* 1:3 (1968): 22–30.

Villalobos, José Pablo. "Border Real, Border Metaphor: Altering Boundaries in Miguel Méndez and Alejandro Morales." *Arizona Journal of Hispanic Cultural Studies* 4:1 (2000): 131–140.
Villarreal, José Antonio. *Pocho*. [1959.] New York: Anchor, 1989.
Wentworth, Theordore Oscar. "El laberinto de soledad de Octavio Paz y su aplicación temática en la novela chicana." PhD diss., University of Florida, 1995.
Williams, Raymond. *Marxism and Literature*. Oxford: Oxford University Press, 1977.
Williams, R. C. "GM Allotypes in Native Americans: Evidence for Three Distinct Migrations across the Bering Land Bridge." *American Journal of Physical Anthropology* 66:1 (1985): 1–19.
Wilson, Bill. "El Teatro Campesino Depicts Chicano Life, Struggle, Victories." *Utah Chronicle*, August 4, 1970.
Woloch, Alex. *The One vs. the Many: Minor Characters and the Space of the Protagonist in the Novel*. Princeton, NJ: Princeton University Press, 2003.
Wong, Sau-Ling. "Denationalization Reconsidered." *Amerasia Journal* 21:1–2 (1995): 29–60.
Zaragosa, José R. "José R. Zaragosa," interview by Anica Butler, March 23, 2002. In *A Legacy Greater Than Words: Stories of U.S. Latinos and Latinas of the World War II Generation*, edited by Maggie Rivas-Rodriguez, Julianna Torres, Melissa DiPiero-D'sa, and Lindsay Fitzpatrick, 170. Austin: U.S. Latino & Latina WWII Oral History Project, 2006.
Zilles, Klaus. *Rolando Hinojosa: A Reader's Guide*. Albuquerque: University of New Mexico Press, 1991.

INDEX

Acosta, Oscar, 1, 7, 11, 18, 33, 35–36, 43, 81, 95, 109; *Autobiography of a Brown Buffalo*, 7; FBI files on, 11–12. *See also The Revolt of the Cockroach People*
Acuña, Rudolfo, 48, 148n11
African Americans, 147n36; black nationalism, 8; *The Bluest Eye* (Morrison), 67; and Chicana/o studies, 133; culture, 151–152n17. *See also* Davis, Angela; Jackson, Jesse; Morrison, Toni; race
Alamo, 45, 58, 146n32; historical pain of, 45; Mexican Army at, 58. *See also* Texas
Alarcón, Daniel, 46, 144n3
Alcoser, Joeseph, 51
Almaguer, Tomás, 139n8, 142n15
Althusser, Louis, 124, 144n39
Alurista (Alberto Baltazar Urista Heredia), 5–6, 18, 35, 140nn9–11, 143n37; and Amerindian myths, 140n9; *Floricanto en Aztlán*, 140n9; and ethno-cultural poetics, 140n10; "Ideology and Aesthetics in the Meaning of Chicana/o Poetics, 1965–1975," 5–6; on Vietnam and Chicana/o culture, 5–6, 143n37
American studies, 133; and its "transnational turn," 134
American War in Vietnam, 5, 10, 17, 23–26, 32, 34, 36, 40–41, 43, 46, 52, 66, 68, 70, 78–81, 85, 130–131, 143n37, 150n37. *See also* military
Amerindians, 93, 106; Aztec Indians (*see* Aztec Indians); culture, and Asia, 150–151n6; myths of, 140; Nahuatl, 113–114; Pueblo Indians, 100; Quetzalcoatl, 98, 152n19; Teotihuacán, 98, 152n20; Yaqui Indians, 40. *See also* Asia: Asia-Aztec theory; Paz, Octavio
Anaya, Rudolfo, 20–21, 91, 95, 97, 135, 152n28; on Aztlán, 141n2; *Bless Me Última*, 95, 152n25. *See also A Chicano in China*

Anderson, Benedict, 45, 48, 50
Anglo Americans: Anglo Saxonism, 56; hegemony, 101; wages relative to Mexican Americans, 48; white desire, 67–68, 71, 76; white ideal, 67–68, 71–73, 77–78, 87; white privilege, 71–72. *See also* Lipsitz, George; race
Anzaldúa, Gloria, 89–90, 111–114, 126, 135, 150n38; *Borderlands/La Frontera*, 111–113, 150n38; *This Bridge Called My Back* (with Moraga), 150n38
Arce, William, 60, 79
area studies, 21
Arteaga, Alfred, 117
artwork: *La victoire* (Magritte, painting), 107–108, 108*fig*; ¡*Viet Nam!* (Villa, art piece), 130–131, 131*fig*; *Viet Nam Aztlán* (Montoya, art piece), 13–15, 15*fig*
Asia: and Amerindian culture, 92, 150–151nn5–6; as analytic paradigm, 35; Asia-Aztec theory, 91–94; as conceptual geography, 35, diaspora, 136–137; as imaginary topography, 35; immigrants in the Americas, 20, 31, 92, 101, 110; Philippines, 53; prostitution during American War in Vietnam, 77; racial codes in, 77; racial inequalities in, 62; sex industry of, 76; sex market in, 71, 74, 76; Southwest, 79; Thailand, 68, 70, 73. *See also* China; Japan; Korean War; Paz, Octavio; transpacific; Vietnam
Asian Americans, 3, 4, 134, 136; Asian American studies, 134, 136, 155n21; marginality in Chicana/o literature, 3–4. *See also* Asia; race
Aztec Indians, 15, 35, 86, 105, 114; glyphs, 93
Aztlán, 5–6, 12–13, 16, 18–19, 28–29, 36, 45, 114, 141n2; cultural discourses of, 45–46;

171

Aztlán (*continued*)
Floricanto en Aztlán (Alurista), 140n9; as homeland, 29; national formation of, 45; nationalist ideas of, 24; as nation-state, 35; as precolonial metaphor, 36

Baker, Houston, 147
Bakhtin, Mikhail, 38, 144n43
Barron, Robert, 130–131
Bauer, Ralph, 129
Behnken, Brian, 12, 141n18
Benjamin, Walter, 77
Bennett, Herman, 153n34; *Africans in Colonial Mexico*, 153n34
Berger, Gwen, 75–76
Bhabha, Homi, 19, 27, 86, 141n25; "horizon of ideology," 27; theory of "jagged testimony," 51
Blacks. *See* African Americans
Blake, William, 150n36; "To Tirzah," 150n36
Bond, James (fictional character), 74; as colonial allegory, 75
borderlands: as analytic space, 112–113; Lower Rio Grande Valley, 61–62; Mexican American life in, 60; modernity at, 68; "New World Man," 97, 99; between North and South Korea, 58, 61; pachucos in, 38; recovering history of, 68; regions of, 37–38; theories of, 117; US-Mexico, Asians in, 110. *See also* Anaya, Rudolfo; Anzaldúa, Gloria
Brooks, Homer, 29; (with Tenayuca) "The Mexican Question in the Southwest," 29
Bruce-Novoa, Juan, 152n28

California: Chicano Moratorium, 32; Delano strike, 25, 30, 139n8; grape boycott, 25, 139; labor conditions, 25; police oppression, 34; Oxnard strike, 29; Third World strike at UC Berkeley, 132; US Defense Department intrusion in, 25. *See also* Chávez, César; labor
Calley, William, 143n34
caló, 140n13
Camayd-Freixas, Erik, 91, 93, 151n10
Cano, Daniel, 17, 20, 65–66, 147n1. *See also Shifting Loyalties*
Cantú, Roberto, 151n10
Casal, Julián del, 91
Cass, Jeffrey, 99, 103

Cervantes, Lorna Dee, 89–90, 149–150n35; "Para un revolucionario," 89, 149–150n35
Chám (Vietnamese ethnicity), 81–82, 86
Chao Romero, Robert, 110, 120
character: as chronotope, 38; distribution, 56; "flat," 9, 56; space, 24, 65
Chávez, César, 30, 139n8. *See also* California; labor
Chávez, Ernesto, 16
Cheng, Anne, 66–67
Cheng, Wendy, 140
Chicana/o: and Amerindian values, 31; Asian roots, 21, 92–95; authenticity, 87, 97, 103; "Chinocano," 97; deaths in Vietnam, 25, 34; fantasies about heritage, 21, 31; historians, 18, 147n38; identity, Amerindian, 96; and internal colonialism, 68, 148n8; and internationalist politics, 4; memory, cultural and historical forgetting, 43–46, 124–125; Moratorium, 33; national homelands, 109; nationalism, cultural, 4, 31, 46, 52; *neo-indigenismo*, 16; pachucos, 38; social experience, as reproduction of political domination, 76. *See also* gender; inter-ethnic relations
Chicana/o culture: Aztec identity, romanticization of, 16; denial of Asian identity, 62; exclusions from and inclusions in, 111; fantasies about heritage, 105; feminist discourse, 31; global interest in, 134; hemispheric studies of, 132; institutionalized critiques of, 32; nationalist qualities of, 111; patriarchal tendencies in, 111; political agency, development of, 53; political geographies of, 35, 54; political possibilities of, 54; postnationalist literature, 46
Chicana/o Movement, 7, 12, 15–16, 31, 57; poetry of, 31, 140n9
Chicana/o studies, 21, 31–32, 127–137, 155n24; and Asian American studies, 134; and the Caribbean, 134; hemispheric turn in, 133; institutionalization of, 132–133; "inter-ethnic" turns in, 135; international perspectives on, 155nn19,24; and Latin America, 134; relations with Asian Americans, African Americans, and Native Americans, 133; transnational turn in, 133. *See also* ethnic studies; Mexican American studies

A Chicano in China (Anaya), 20, 91, 95–110; biological essentialisms in, 100; cultural determinism in, 106; cultural relativism in, 100; false positivism in, 96; romanticization of Chinese in, 99–100. *See also* Anaya, Rudolfo
China: Beijing, 97; Chinese-Mexican marriages, 119; "Chinocana/o" identity, 100, 126; dragon symbol in, 98–99, 101–103, 106; immigration to Mexico, 21, 114, 116–118, 123; population and people, 99–100, 104. *See also A Chicano in China*
Clark, Kenneth, 148n12
Clark, Mamie, 148n12
colonialism: European aggressions in Vietnam, 41; homosocial colonial situations, 76; internal, 68, 148n8; James Bond as allegory of, 75. *See also* Bhabha, Homi; Said, Edward
El Congreso del Pueblo de Habla, 29
The Communist (magazine), 29
Connery, Sean, 74
consumerism: commercialization of desire, 74, 76; and global capitalism, 29; and patriarchal economies, 76; race as capital, 74
Cortez, Gregorio, 63
"critical globalization," 129. *See also* Saldívar, José David
critical regionalism, 129. *See also* Limón, José
culture: African American, 151–152n17; cultural nationalism, 31, 109; cultural syncretism, 86; Native American, 106; pre-Cortesian, 105; transpacific, 106. *See also* Chicana/o culture
Cutler, John Alba, 81, 141, 149n34

Darío, Rubén, 91
Davis, Angela, 7–9
Declaration of Independence, 11
Delgado, Abelardo, 6, 35–37
Derrida, Jacques, 85, 94, 149n30, 151n11
desire: racial formations of, 77; white, 67–68, 71, 76. *See also* Cheng, Anne
Dunbar, Paul Laurence, 63, 147n36; "We Wear the Mask," 147n36

Elizondo, Sergio, 6
Eres, Narciso "Smokey," 49*fig*

Espinoza, José Ángel, 118–119, 121; *El ejemplo de Sonora*, 118, 121*fig*; *El problema chino en México*, 118
ethnicity. *See* African Americans; Amerindians; Anglo Americans; Asian Americans; Chám (Vietnamese ethnicity); Chicana/o; race
ethnic studies, 21, 31, 129, 132, 136

Fanon, Frantz, 35, 65, 78; *Black Skin White Masks*, 65; on white love, 149n25
Feinstein, Diane, 48–49
Fishkin, Shelley Fisher, 134
el florecimiento, 23
Flores, Armando, 50
Florescano, Enrique, 152n19
Forster, E. M., 9, 56, 141n16, 146n27; *Aspects of the Novel*, 141n16
Fox, Claire, 129
Freud, Sigmund, 66; *Beyond the Pleasure Principle*, 147n3; *Moses and Monotheism*, 147n3

Gambone, Michael, 48, 145n11
Garcia, Chris, 148n8
García, Ignacio, 7
García, Mario, 18, 29, 48
García, Matt, 25, 139n8
García Canclini, Néstor, 113
Garza, Rudolph de la, 148
gender: Chicana feminism, 21, 89, 112, 148–149n15, 150–151n35; Chicano masculinity, 68, 72, 89; Chicano obfuscations of, 31; Chicano patriarchy, 73, 89, 112; patriarchal economies, 76; regeneration of patriarchy, 149–150n35; reproduction of patriarchy, 89; and race, 73, 75, 90. *See also Gods Go Begging*; sexuality; *Shifting Loyalties*
Gilroy, Paul, 151–152n17
Gods Go Begging (Véa), 20, 66–67, 78–90; caesura in, 85; narrative and temporal structure of, 79; narrative effacement in, 85; as protest to American War in Vietnam, 78. *See also* Véa, Alfredo
Gómez Carrillo, Enrique, 92
Gómez-Quiñones, Juan, 30
Gonzáles, Marcial, 146n30
Gonzales, Rodolfo "Corky," 6–7, 9–10

Gonzales, Samuel G., 47*fig*
Grise, Virginia, 21, 110–111. *See also Rasgos asiáticos*
Griswold del Castillo, Richard, 18, 47, 145n4
El Grito: A Journal of Contemporary Mexican-American Thoughts, 127–131
Gutiérrez, David, 18
Guzman, Ralph, 25

Hall, Stuart, 135
Ham Chande, Robert, 119
Hama, Mie, 74
Hamilton, Patrick, 78
hemispheric studies, 129, 155n6; turn in American studies, 129
Herrera y Reissig, Julio, 91
Hicks, Emily, 117
Hinojosa, Rolando, 17, 19, 51–52, 109; paratactic prose of, 60. *See also* Klail City Death Trip series; *Korean Love Songs*
Ho Chi Minh, 13
Huang, Yunte, 106
Hu-Dehart, Evelyn, 110, 119. *See also* Asia: diaspora; Asia: immigrants in the Americas; Mexico: Chinese immigrants to
Huerta, Jorge, 26, 142n10

"Ichiro Kikuchi" (Paredes), 19, 51–58, 64, 74, 109; autodiagetic narrator in, 57; character system of, 56; deconstruction of identity in, 54; deconstruction of ideologies in, 56; denial of Asian identity in, 55, 57; inspiration for, 56; textual marginalization in, 55–56. *See also* Paredes, Américo
identity: absolute/100 percent Anglo Americanism, 57–58, 61; Anglo Saxonism, 56; Asian, denial of, 55, 57, 62; Chicana/o Asian, 62–63; Chinocana/o, 100, 126; cultural forgetting of, 45, 56; cultural social boundaries of, 46, 128; deconstruction of, 54; and fantasies about heritage, 97; and gender politics, 89; historical memory of, 46; historical pain of, 45; imagined communities, 46, 48; Latin American, "fourth root" of, 109; and masculine regeneration, 149–150n35; "New World Man," 97, 99; pachuco, 38; pre-Cortesian, 109; queer, 114; "roots vs. routes," 151–152n17; stopgap politics in, 105; "transversalism," 44. *See also* Anaya, Rudolfo; Anderson, Benedict; Chicana/o inter-ethnic relations, Chicana/o: Asian images as political double, 13–15; claims of solidarity with Vietnamese, 12–13; with other US Latino groups, 134; subordination of inter-ethnic appeals, 12

Jackson, Reverend Jesse, 11
Jameson, Fredric, 29, 142n13
Japan: attack on Pearl Harbor, 51; Japanese internment in western US, 2–3, 8, 56; Japanese Mexican Labor Association (JMLA), 29–30, 139n8, 142n15; positive impact of internment of on Mexican labor, 3; US occupation of, 17, 76
Jimenez, Philip J., 130–131; "Viet Nam Veteran" (article), 130
Journal of Asian American Studies, 134
Jussawalla, Feroza, 97

Kanellos, Nicolás, 140n12
Kaplan, Ann E., 66, 147n3
Klail City Death Trip series (Hinojosa), 58; fragmented plot lines of, 60; *Rites and Witnesses*, 60. *See also* Hinojosa, Rolando
Korean Love Songs (Hinojosa), 19, 51, 58–64, 74, 83, 109; Chicana/o Asian identity in, 62–63; denial of Asian identity in, 62; "The Eighth Army at the Chongchon," 58; "Nagoya Station," 60–62; oppressed oppressor in, 63; paratactic architecture of, 59; as political critique, 59. *See also* Hinojosa, Rolando
Korean War, 6, 17, 51, 58–60. *See also* Hinojosa, Rolando; Montoya, José

labor: Agricultural Workers Organizing Committee (AWOC), 139; California, conditions, 25; Delano strike, 25, 30, 139n8; exploitation, Chicana/o, 24–25; Chicana/o history forgetting of, 30; Filipino, 30, 139n8; grape boycott, 25, 139; Japanese Mexican Labor Association (JMLA), 29–30, 139n8, 142n15; Mexican, positive impact of Japanese internment on, 3; Oxnard strike, 29; United Farm Workers (UFW), 30, 139n8. *See also* Chávez, César; Vietnam: farmworkers
language: *caló*, 140; Nahuatl, 113–114

Latin America: Asian heritage of, 153n34; nationalist poetics of, 140n10; Orientalism in, 92; poetics of, 91–92, 150n5; and its "third root," 153n34. *See also* Mesoamerica; Mexico

Latin American Studies Association, 5, 140n10

Lattin, Vernon, 95

Lee, Erika, 110, 134

Lee, Jongsoo, 151n10

Lemaitre, Monique, 140n10

Levander, Caroline, 129

Lévi-Strauss, Claude, 94

Lien, Pei-Te, 139n8

Limón, José, 129, 140–141n13, 146n33

Lionnet, Françoise, 44, 136

Lipsitz, George, 3, 139n3; *The Possessive Investment in Whiteness*, 139n3

literature: American ethnic, "interethnic turn" of, 156n27; Chicana/o, and cultural forgetting, 44; Chicana/o renaissance, 18, 23, 57; and gender, 20; hybridism of, 113; postnational trends of, 57, 111; themes of, 37, 65; US literary canon, 135

Lomelí, Francisco, 31, 109, 140n9; on Aztlán, 141n2

López, Marissa, 132

Luz, Portilla de la, 32; "La hora de todos," 32

Mabalon, Dawn Bohulano, 30

Magritte, René, 107–109; *La victoire* (painting), 107–108, 108*fig*

Mariscal, George, 4, 15, 31, 109, 139n6, 141nn19,26, 142n5n, 143n21

Los Más Cabrones (magazine), 13–14, 14*fig*

memory: cultural forgetting, 31; political forgetting, 30

Menchaca, Martha, 153n34

Méndez, Miguel, 18, 37, 95, 144n45. *See also Pilgrims in Aztlán*

Mesoamerica: and dragon symbol, 98; myths of, 152nn19–20; symbols of, 98; worldview, 93, 107

Mexican Americans, 47; commitments to war, 47; envisioned as "oppressed oppressor," 52; and ethnic shedding, 72; as hyphenated identity, 55; income during World War II, 145n11; national belonging, 51; poverty among, 47–48; as second-class citizens, 48; segregation of, 47; soldiering in Asia, 109; upward mobility among, 47, 72; wages relative to whites, 48. *See also* Chicana/o; Chicana/o culture; Chicana/o Movement

Mexican American studies, 135–136. *See also* Chicana/o studies; ethnic studies

Mexico, 40, 43, 86; African heritage of, 153n34; Chinese immigrants to, 154n22; Chinese population in, 119; European conquest of, 93; gendered and nationalist ideologies, 118; Mexican Revolution, 37–41, 43, 119; *movimiento anti-chino* in, 118–120; racial discrimination against Chinese in, 118; Teotihuacán, 98, 152n20; Torreón, Chinese massacre at, 120; and World War II, 145n4. *See also* Villa, Pancho

migration: from Asia to America, 31, 92–95; Chinese to Mexico, 118–121; "The Great Journey," 143n23; pre-Colombian, 92

military: "Aztec Eagles" (Escuadrón Aéreo de Pelea), 145n4; Latina/o participation in US, 48; League of United Latin American Citizens (LULAC), 48, 145–146n14; Mexican Americans, commitments to war, 47; Puerto Rican servicemen in World War II, 145n9; Royal Chicano Air Force, 140n13; Screaming Eagles, 72; soldiering in Asia, 109. *See also* American War in Vietnam; Korean War; World War II

"Mi Raza Primero," 16*fig*

Montoya, José, 6, 140–141n13; "El Louie," 6, 140–141n13

Montoya, Malaquías, 13–15; *Viet Nam Aztlán* (art piece), 13–15, 15*fig*

Moraga, Cherríe, 45, 89–90; *Loving in the War Years*, 45; *This Bridge Called My Back* (with Anzaldúa), 150n38

Morales, Armando, 143n33

Morales, Victoria, 51

Moreno, Luisa, 29

Morin, Raul, 49–50

Morrison, Toni, 67; *The Bluest Eye*, 67

music, *corridos*, 63

Nahuatl, 113–114

nationalism: and Aztlán, 23–24; black, 8; Chicana/o, 16, 23–24, 31–32, 35–36;

nationalism (continued)
cultural, 31, 109; ethno-nationalism, 31; imagined communities, 46, 48; Mexican, 118; postnationalist studies, 129; third world movements, 36. *See also* Anderson, Benedict
Native Americans. *See* Amerindians
Nixon, Richard, 25
Noriega, Chon, 45

Olguín, Ben, 141
Olstad, Charles, 40
oppressed oppressor, 45, 52, 63, 66; Mexican Americans as, 52
Orientalism, 70–71, 100, 141n27. *See also* Said, Edward
Oropreza, Lorena, 18
Ortego, Philip, 140n9
Ota Mishima, María Elena, 110
Our Lady of Guadalupe, and religion, 53–54

Palumbo-Liu, David, 136
Paredes, Américo, 17, 19, 51–53, 58, 81, 109, 123, 129, 135, 146nn28–29, 146–147n35, 153n2; *George Washington Gómez*, 146n29; inspiration for "Ichiro Kikuchi," 56; *The Shadow*, 146n29; *With His Pistol in His Hand*, 63, 146–147n35; writings for US Department of Defense, 149n19. *See also* "Ichiro Kikuchi"
Paz, Octavio, 20, 91–94, 107–109, 141n29, 150n5, 150–151n6, 151nn7,10,13–14; aesthetic theory of, 107; on Asian immigration, 92–93; on Asian poetry, 152; countercolonial poetics of, 20, 93; *Puertas al campo*, 107–108, 108*fig*; surrealist poetics of, 93
Pearl Harbor, 47, 50–51, 145n4; Japanese attack at, 48
Peregrinos en Aztlán. *See Pilgrims in Aztlán*
Perez-Torres, Rafael, 86, 113, 140–141n13, 141n23; on Aztlán, 144–145n3, 152–153n30
Philippines. *See under* Asia
Pilgrims in Aztlán (Méndez), 18, 23, 37–44, 58, 64, 74; analepsis in, 38; chronotope in, 38; intergenerational pain in, 41; narrative doubling in, 41; narrative loops in, 41; palimpsest in, 40; political topography in, 43. *See also* Méndez, Miguel

poetry: Asian, 152nn29–30; of the Chicana/o Movement, 31; "The Eighth Army at the Chongchon" (Hinojosa), 58; "La hora de todos" (Luz), 32; Latin American, 91–94, 107; "El Louie" (Montoya), 6, 140–141n13; "Nagoya Station" (Hinojosa), 60–62; "Para un revolucionario" (Cervantes), 89, 149–150n35; surrealist poetics, 106–107, 109; "To Tirzah" (Blake), 150n36; "We Wear the Mask" (Dunbar), 147n36. *See also* Alurista; Cervantes, Lorna Dee; *Korean Love Songs*; Paz, Octavio
politics: internationalist, 4; international leftist, 29; *neo-indigenismo*, 16; New Left, 30; political cohesion, 109; political domination and social experience, 76; political forgetting, 30; political topography, 43; Third World Left, 4. *See also* Nixon, Richard; Reagan, Ronald; Roosevelt, Theodore; Villa, Pancho
Prashad, Vijay, 74, 76, 129, 136
pre-Cortesian: culture, 105; values, 68. *See also* Amerindians
Pulido, Laura, 4, 139n4
Puntarigvivat, Tavivat, 76–77

Quintana, Alvina, 32, 133

race: as capital, 74; and gender, 73, 90, and masculinity, 75; *mestizaje*, 83, 86–87, 152–153n30; pedagogy of, 67; psychology of, 148n12; racial absolutism, 56; racial codes in Asia, 77; racial conflation, 13–15, 18–19, 21, 23, 26–29, 33–36, 60–62, 82–83, 109; racial discrimination, against Chinese in Mexico, 118; racial flattening, 18–19, 21; racial inequalities in Thailand, 62; racial injury, 66–67; racial melancholy, 67; and segregation, 72, *Plessy v. Ferguson*, 148n12; as social and psychological affliction, 74; social education on, 73, 90; trauma of racial difference, 77; and US imperialism, 68–78; white desire, 67–68, 71, 76; white ideal, 67–68, 71–73, 77–78, 87; white privilege, 71–72. *See also* Cheng, Anne; Mexico, *movimiento anti-chino*; trauma
Ramparts (magazine), 30
Rasgos asiáticos (Grise), 21, 110–111, 113–126, 153–154n7. *See also* Grise, Virginia

Reagan, Governor Ronald, 7–8
Recovering US Hispanic Literary Heritage Project, 139
Renan, Ernest, 45
representation: "absolute knowledge," 103; chronotope, 38, 144n43; cognitive mapping, 29, 142n13; *différance*, 149n30; double consciousness, 147; "jagged testimonies," 19, 58, 64; "overdetermination," 124, 144n39; of Southwest Asia, as conceptual and imaginary geography, 35; "trace," 85; transcendental signified, 94, 151n11; transnational imaginary, 129. *See also* Althusser, Louis; Derrida, Jacques; Saldívar, Ramón
The Revolt of the Cockroach People (Acosta), 1, 7–10, 18, 23, 33, 44, 58, 64, 74, 83; aesthetic arrangement of, 11; and Aztlán, 24; narrative space in, 9; narrative weight in, 11, 36. *See also* Acosta, Oscar Zeta
Rivas Rodriguez, Maggie, 48, 50
Rivera, John-Michael, 139n1
Rivera, Tomás, 37, 144n40; *Y no se lo tragó la tierra*, 37, 144n40
Rodríguez, Juan, 23
Rody, Caroline, 156
Romano, Octavio, 128–129
Roosevelt, Theodore, 55, 61; and ideology of 100 percent Americanism, 56
Rosaldo, Renato, 140–141n13
Rowe, John Carlos, 129
Rubin, Gayle, 76, 148–149n16; "The Traffic in Women," 148–149n16
Ruiz de Burton, María Amparo, 139n1; *The Squatter and the Don*, 139n1; *Who Would Have Thought It?*, 139n1

Sae-Saue, Jayson Gonzales, 141n22
Said, Edward, 20, 70, 90, 100, 141n27
Salazar, Antonio, 16
Saldívar, Jose David, 129–130, 132, 139n2, 141n13; *The Dialectics of Our America*, 139n2
Saldívar, Ramón, 63, 76, 112, 130, 132, 144n40, 146n28, 148n7; *Chicano Narrative*, 144n40
Sánchez, George, 18, 32, 133, 148n11
Santa Anna, General Antonio López, 146n32
Schiavone Camacho, Julia, 110

scopophilic gaze, 87
Second World War. *See* World War II
Servín, Ignacio, 50–51
sexuality: affirmation of Chicano masculinity on female bodies, 89; interracial sex, 70; queer identity, 114; sex industry in Asia, 76; Thailand, prostitution in during American War in Vietnam, 77, Thailand, sex market in, 71, 74, 76. *See also* gender
Shifting Loyalties (Cano), 20, 66, 82, 87, 89; antiwar ethics of, 67–78; interracial sex in, 70. *See also* Cano, Daniel
Shih, Shu-mei, 44, 136
Sinatra, Nancy, 74
Soldatenko, Michael, 132, 155n24
Southern Christian Leadership Conference Community Coalition, 11
Steinbeck, John, 127; *Tortilla Flat*, 127
Storey, Rebecca, 152n20
structures of feeling, 151n9, 152n21; transhistoric, 98
Suro, Robert, 50
Sweet Beans and Rice (cultural archive), 153–154n7

Takaki, Ronald, 51
Tallis, Raymond, 151n11
Teatro Campesino. *See* Valdez, Luis
Tenayuca, Emma, 29; (with Brooks) "The Mexican Question in the Southwest," 29
Texas, 48; segregation in, 45; University of Texas, 50; US annexation of 45; War of Independence, 59, 146n32. *See also* Alamo
Thailand. *See under* Asia
theater: "actos," 24, 27, 141–142n3, 142nn4,6. *See also* Valdez, Luis
third world: Left, 4; Liberation, 132; nationalist movements, 36; strike at UC Berkeley, 132
transnational: imaginary, 129; studies, 129; "transgeographic," 37; "transversalism," 44; turn in American studies, 129
transpacific: culture, 106; cultural geography, 109; displacement, 106; structures of feeling, 98; structures of knowledge, 93. *See also* Huang, Yunte
trauma, 68, 85, 90, 147n3; as narrative structure, 79; of racial difference, 77; theory, 66; as type of knowledge, 80

unions. *See* labor
United States: hegemony, 66, 70; imperialism, racial dynamics of, 68–78; Kent State, 9–10; literary canon, 135; occupation of Japan, 17, 76. *See also* Alamo; American War in Vietnam; California; *Declaration of Independence*; Korean War; Nixon, Richard; Pearl Harbor; Reagan, Ronald; Roosevelt, Theodore; Texas
Ureña, Pedro Henriquez, 151n7
Urista Heredia, Alberto Baltazar. *See* Alurista

Vaca, Nick, 127, 129
Valdez, Luis, 18, 24, 26–27, 30, 35–36, 43, 81, 95, 109, 141–142n3, 142n18, 147n1; "El Plan de San Diego," 30, 142n18; "The Tale of La Raza," 30. *See also Vietnam Campesino*
Valencia, Guillermo, 92
Vasconcelos, José, 111; *La raza cósmica*, 111
Vásquez, Mary, 38
Véa, Alfredo, 17, 20, 66, 78, 147n1. *See also Gods Go Begging*
Vértiz, Vicky, 154
Veteran's Memorial Wall at Las Cruces, New Mexico, 49, 49*fig*
Vietnam: Chám (ethnicity), 81–82, 86; European colonial aggressions in, 41; farmworkers, 26–27, 147n1; My Lai, 34, 143; South Vietnamese government, 25; Viet Cong, 13, 34, 69. *See also* Ho Chi Minh

Vietnam Campesino (Valdez), 18, 22–24, 31, 34, 36, 44, 58, 64, 74, 83, 147n1; and Aztlán, 24; parabasis in, 28, 28*fig*; and *Soldado Razo*, 27, 31. *See also* Valdez, Luis
Vietnam War. *See* American War in Vietnam
Villa, Esteban, 131; ¡*Viet Nam!* (art piece), 130–131, 131*fig*
Villa, Pancho, 119
Villalobos, José Pablo, 37–38
Villanueva, Tino, 140n10
Villarreal, José Antonio, 1; *Pocho*, 1–4, 6, 8–9, 31, 36, 58, 64, 139n1
VOCES oral history project, 50

Warren, Chief Justice Earl, 148n12
Wentworth, Theodore, 152n29
whites. *See* Anglo Americans
Williams, Raymond, 151n9, 152n21
Wood, Natalie, 76
World War II, 17, 47–49, 51, 56, 72; distinction in field of battle in, 49; Puerto Rican servicemen in, 145n9; US and Japanese war crimes during, 53. *See also* military
World War II, Mexican Americans in, 48–49; conscription of, 48; lack of schooling during, 48; median income compared to whites during, 48; testimonies of, 50–51; volunteers in, 48–49

You Only Live Twice (movie), 74

Zaragoza, José R., 50

ABOUT THE AUTHOR

JAYSON GONZALES SAE-SAUE is an assistant professor of English literature at Southern Methodist University.

Available titles in the Latinidad: Transnational Cultures in the United States series:

María Acosta Cruz, *Dream Nation: Puerto Rican Culture and the Fictions of Independence*
Rodolfo F. Acuña, *The Making of Chicana/o Studies: In the Trenches of Academe*
Xóchitl Bada, *Mexican Hometown Associations in Chicagoacán: From Local to Transnational Civic Engagement*
Adriana Cruz-Manjarrez, *Zapotecs on the Move: Cultural, Social, and Political Processes in Transnational Perspective*
Marivel T. Danielson, *Homecoming Queers: Desire and Difference in Chicana Latina Cultural Production*
Rudy P. Guevarra Jr., *Becoming Mexipino: Multiethnic Identities and Communities in San Diego*
Colin Gunckel, *Mexico on Main Street: Transnational Film Culture in Los Angeles before World War II*
Marie-Theresa Hernández, *The Virgin of Guadalupe and the Conversos: Uncovering Hidden Influences from Spain to Mexico*
Lisa Jarvinen, *The Rise of Spanish-Language Filmmaking: Out from Hollywood's Shadow, 1929–1939*
Regina M. Marchi, *Day of the Dead in the USA: The Migration and Transformation of a Cultural Phenomenon*
Desirée A. Martín, *Borderlands Saints: Secular Sanctity in Chicano/a and Mexican Culture*
Marci R. McMahon, *Domestic Negotiations: Gender, Nation, and Self-Fashioning in US Mexicana and Chicana Literature and Art*
A. Gabriel Meléndez, *Hidden Chicano Cinema: Film Dramas in the Borderlands*
Priscilla Peña Ovalle, *Dance and the Hollywood Latina: Race, Sex, and Stardom*
Amalia Pallares, *Family Activism: Immigrant Struggles and the Politics of Noncitizenship*
Luis F. B. Plascencia, *Disenchanting Citizenship: Mexican Migrants and the Boundaries of Belonging*

Cecilia M. Rivas, *Salvadoran Imaginaries: Mediated Identities and Cultures of Consumption*

Jayson Gonzales Sae-Saue, *Southwest Asia: The Transpacific Geographies of Chicana/o Literature*

Mario Jimenez Sifuentez, *Of Forest and Fields: Mexican Labor in the Pacific Northwest*

Maya Socolovsky, *Troubling Nationhood in U.S. Latina Literature: Explorations of Place and Belonging*

www.ingramcontent.com/pod-product-compliance
Ingram Content Group UK Ltd.
Pitfield, Milton Keynes, MK11 3LW, UK
UKHW021326180426
11947UKWH00017B/1475